D1609757

A Contract Officer in the Oman

A Contract Officer in the Oman

Alan J Hoskins

Costello

British Library Cataloguing in Publication Data
Hoskins, Alan J
  A Contract Officer in the Oman
  1. Omani Military Forces
  I. Title
  355'.00953'53

ISBN 0-7104-3041-8

First Published 1988
© Alan J Hoskins, 1988

Typeset by RHM Computing, Essex
Printed and bound in Great Britain by
Page Brothers, Norfolk

List of the Most Common Abreviations Used

ACDS	-	Assistant Chief of Defence Staff
BAF	-	Bait al Falaj
CJS	-	Commander of the Joint Staff
(ACJS	-	Assistant Chief of the Joint Staff)
(DACJS	-	Deputy Assistant Chief of the Joint Staff)
CDS	-	Chief of Defence Staff
D of P	-	Director of Purchasing
HE the US	-	His Excellency the Under Secretary
HRM	-	Head of Resource Management
MA	-	Military Advisor
MAM	-	Muaskar al Murtafa'a
MoD	-	Ministry of Defence
MoDED	-	Ministry of Defence Engineering Division
MoDUK	-	Ministry of Defence (UK)
NCO	-	Non-commissioned officer
ROP	-	Royal Oman Police
RGR	-	Royal Guards Regiment
(CRGR	-	Commander of RGR)
SAF	-	Sultan's Armed Forces
SNCO	-	Senior non-commissioned officer
SOAF	-	Sultan of Oman's Air Force
SOLF	-	Sultan of Oman's Land Forces
SON	-	Sultan of Oman's Navy
(CSOAF	-	Commander of SOAF)
(CSOLF	-	Commander of SOLF)
(CSON	-	Commander of SON)
UAE	-	United Arab Emirates

Preface

In 1984 a British civilian named Robin Walsh, who was a contract staff officer in the MoD (Oman), died in a very unpleasant manner in Rumais Prison. The UK media got hold of the story, and it became a major scandal. Articles then appeared which made it look as if most of the contract officers out there were idle layabouts whose lives revolved around: 'drink, sex, and fraud'. The truth, however, lay somewhere in the middle.

There are thousands of young men with military training who can earn big money in the developing countries, as mercenaries, or contract officers as they prefer to be called. Not so numerous however are the grey-haired ones who have done their fighting and have gone on to learn how to organise and administer a military force.

A Contract Officer is mainly about them.

Not so many tales of derring-do perhaps, but rather an account of four years spent as a staff officer with the MoD (Oman). It was a country where, just ten years before, there was only one car - a Rolls Royce - owned by the Ruler who used his slaves to push it (and him) to the mosque.

So far, all of the books that have been written about the Sultan of Oman's Armed Forces (SOAF) have been laudatory. My book is dedicated with affection to Omani, Indian and Pakistani friends and colleagues in the MoD (Oman) and to those British contract officers who have my respect for their honest and unremitting efforts in administering and improving the efficiency and operational capability of the Sultan's Armed Forces. However, the 'Easy Riders' know who they are and will hardly be surprised if I exclude them from this dedication.

Apologia

Written at the end of my contract was an undertaking 'not to publish, or cause to be published, any account or history concerning the past, present or future plans of the Sultan's Armed Forces without obtaining the written approval of the Ministry of Defence in Oman'. This embargo is supposed to extend for five years beyond the completion of my service in Oman. It is now over three years since I left the Oman and settled in Australia and, since then, three factors have made me look at such undertakings in a new light.

The first is that the Australian press have a more uninhibited and inquiring approach to government activities; the second is that I recently read Harold Evans' *Good Times, Bad Times* and learnt the uses to which such restrictions have been and can be put; the third is the unpleasant death of Robin Walsh in Rumais Prison. The appallingly bad publicity which followed that event makes a nonsense of any such undertaking.

Is the foregoing an excuse? I don't know. I do know however that while this book may bruise a few egos, it will not harm the security of the Sultanate of Oman, a country whose ruler and people I greatly admire.

Many of the people in this book appear as christian names only for this was how I knew them and spoke to them. In some cases, to avoid possible embarassment, I have changed their names.

Author's note on The Oman

Oman has not yet been opened to tourism, and one cannot enter the country without an Omani sponsor. Because of this isolation, most people know little or nothing about the Sultanate, and so the following has been written with this in mind.

Oman lies on the south-eastern corner of the Arabian Peninsular and occupies an area of over 300,000 square kilometres. A jagged mountain range some 2-3,000 metres high called the Hajar, runs from Mussandam in the far north, and parallels the coast along its initially gentle easterly curve of 500 kilometres, until it reaches Cape Ras al Hadd. Here, the seaboard takes a sharp swing to the south-west and travels for a further 1000 kilometres to the Sultanate's western border with the People's Democratic Republic of the Yemen. Throughout its length, the coastine successively overlooks the Arabian Gulf, the Straits of Hormuz, the Gulf of Oman, and the Arabian Sea.

In the north of the country a relatively fertile, cultivated plain, some twenty kilometres wide, lies between the Hajar range and the coast, whilst inland of the mountains gravel plains and sand dunes extend to the borders with the United Arab Emirates (UAE) and Saudi Arabia. South of Cape Ras al Hadd, 300 kilometres of the Wahiba sands, and 500 kilometres of stony steppes have to be crossed before the Dhofar uplands are reached: a hostile environment.

The climate of the country varies considerably, ranging from hot and humid on the northern coast for most of the year (the capital, Muscat, sometimes recording temperatures of 120°F and humidity of 90%) through the hot and dry interior, to the temperate climate of the mountain ranges. Rainfall is minimal throughout the country, although the Dhofar region, being monsoonal, receives slightly more than the north. During the cooler months (December to April) extremely violent thunderstorms can occur, sometimes with disastrous results, as I shall recount in a later chapter.

Of an estimated population of one and a quarter million, the majority follow the Ibadi rites of Islam, the remainder, about 25%, being Sunni Muslim.

The national costume of the Omani male consists of a long white gown called a dishdash and a wrapped turban known as a masar or shimaag, and for the majority this is everyday wear. On formal or ceremonial occasions a cloak (bisht) and a silver, sometimes gold, decorated dagger (khanja) completes the dress. A recent trend towards more exotic colours for the dishdash has been frowned upon by the Sultan who is anxious that his rapidly emerging country does not lose its identity or traditions.

His Majesty Sultan Qaboos bin Said is the scion of a dynasty spanning more than 200 years, but it was not until his accession in 1970 that the turbulent relationship between the regions known as Muscat and Oman quietened and they became the unified country known as The

Sultanate of Oman. It was also in 1970 that the Omanis entered the twentieth century.

Sultan Qaboos's father, Said bin Taimur, had denied his countrymen the more positive advantages of the modern world, such as medicine and education, and, during his latter years, became increasingly reactionary and eccentric. He confined his British educated and militarily trained son to his rooms, ordering him to study the Qu'ran, and two examples of his obsessive determination to maintain his country's medieval lifestyle, were his banning of sunglasses and electric torches. The British sponsored *coup d'etat* which ousted him in 1970 was inevitable. Details of the remarkable progress which has been made since then under the guidance of Sultan Qaboos can best be obtained by reading *The Omanis - Sentinels of the Gulf* (see Selected Bibliography).

Currently the Sultanate is an absolute monarchy with Sultan Qaboos as Head of State and Prime Minister. As a step towards the ultimate goal of an elected democracy however, he is now supported by a Council of Ministers whose members, entitled Deputy Prime Ministers, are responsible to him for major aspects of the country's activities, such as defence, foreign affairs, finance, and so on.

The country is divided into districts (wilayats), administered by governors (walis). The judicial system is based on the Shariya Law of Islam, a pragmatic form of justice whose courts, like their counterparts throughout the world, have their lighter moments.

Chapter One

If you were recruited in the United Kingdom, and most staff officers were, your contract would entitle you to three weeks leave every three months. Usually this started with a few light-hearted drinks in the Bamboo Bar of the Officers' Mess at Bait al Falaj, followed by an overnight flight from Muscat to London. This time however, my trip to Seeb airport was being made with very mixed emotions, for this was my final departure from the Sultanate of Oman.

Looking back over the past four years, I recalled that I had been endlessly frustrated and totally unsuccessful in my particular field of expertise: the complementing of military manpower. All that I had gained, apart from some good friends, was the knowledge that some military minds are dangerous because they honestly believe that the higher the rank, the greater the wisdom. Certainly, I needed no confirmation of the fact that the military must always be subject to civilian government audit and control.

I was a mite depressed. The Omanis were a gentle and courteous people and eminently likeable, but it was particularly aggravating to leave knowing that of the three British Commanders of the services, two were as egocentric and deeply entrenched as ever and apparently still not answerable to anyone with the knowledge and authority to curtail their extravagance and wastefulness. This was the situation three years after a four-star general had arrived from England tasked with unifying the three military arms and controlling their spending. Leaving at this moment, I felt that the British had no reason to feel proud of their attempts at running the Sultan's Armed Forces (SAF).

God knows, the Brits were not as worthless and wicked as the UK media had been suggesting since Robin's death, but there were far too many 'Easy Riders' and potential and practising alcoholics among the 'White Faces'.

A post as administrative staff officer at the Joint Staff Headquarters of the Sultan of Oman's Armed Forces was my remedy for the potential boredom of early retirement. Up to this point, though, my life had hardly been inactive.

During the war I had served as a flight navigator in the Far East. When the atom bomb ended war with Japan, we started flying skeletal prisoners of war out of Saigon and Bangkok, then moved south to Singapore to repeat the exercise.

Although the physical condition of our new passengers was heartrendingly similar to the survivors of the 'Death Railway', the Dutch internees from Java and Sumatra far outnumbered the Australian, British and Dutch prisoners of war. It was here I met the girl I later married, living with her sister and mother and 10,000 other Dutch women and children in Tjideng Camp in Batavia.

On being demobbed in 1946, I obtained my Civil Aircraft Navigator's licence, and started work with the doomed charter company, London Aero Motor Services (LAMS), based at Stanstead Airfield in Essex. Having survived my slice of war, my brush with death came as a result of the crash and destruction of our Halton G-AHZJ [1] at Bergamo in northern Italy. I began to have doubts about continuing with this remunerative, but possibly very short-term career. However in the event the decision was made for me, for LAMS collapsed into bankruptcy. Any possibility of the company being resuscitated vanished completely when most of the senior management were arrested and put on trial for selling government surplus radio and radar equipment which still belonged to the government.

Stanstead had been a Flying Fortress (B17) base during the war, indeed, just short of the runways ends, were large signs reading: 'If you have wounded on board, turn off here', and I had occasionally wondered what was in the many large hangars scattered around the airfield. Now I knew what used to be in them. Clearly, aviation possessed hazards I had not even dreamed of! I began to look around for other ways of supporting a growing family.

A year passed, during which time I tried a number of vocations, but in these post-war years uncertainty hovered over most commercial activities as the British met their bills for the recent hostilities. Eventually an opportunity arrived to enter government service, and I took it - a settled career and a regular income.

It was hardly surprising that my first appointment should be to the Air Ministry (as it was then known) and, after Bergamo, it was highly appropriate that my first few years should be devoted to trying to improve flying safety. Not an easy job in those days with piston engine aircraft making way for jets with all their new (and unknown) idiosyncrasies. For example, it took a long time to reduce one of our most common accidents: the tendency of jet engines to suck in spanners, screwdrivers, stones and even passing airmen!

So I joined the Civil Service, where my changes of job were frequent and functionally diverse. The idea was that you gained a wide knowledge of the many activities of the ministry, so that as you attained more senior and specialised positions, you possessed the information on which to make good decisions.

In my case, postings (home and abroad) in flying safety, finance, costings, contracts, audit and secretarial duties all proved invaluable as I specialised more and more in the administration and complementing of uniformed and civilian personnel overseas.

At this point, I should perhaps explain the word 'complementing' in some detail so that you may enjoy to the full my unsuccessful assaults on the military mind later on in this book. However, I shall keep the sermon as short as possible. One important fact to grasp though, is that for most countries over half their defence costs are spent on the person-

---

[1] Four-engined Halifax bombers converted to a peacetime cargo carrying role by the removal of machine guns, turrets, etc, and the addition of a large pannier below the bomb bay.

nel of the armed forces - a staggering thought in this age of ultra high-cost weaponry.

In essence, a complement (or establishment) is a document which lists the number of personnel (and sometimes weapons and transport) needed to operate a military unit, be it a ship, squadron of aircraft, infantry battalion, headquarters, hospital etc. All of the personnel are shown, uniformed and civilian, with details of their numbers, ranks (grades) and specialities; for example, Pilot, Padre, Doctor, Road Sweeper Operator, Radar Technician, or Labourer Unskilled. There are very few jobs in military life that do not appear somewhere on a military establishment. By itself it is an essential document and, in aggregate, vital for planning everything from accommodation to assessing next year's money requirements.

Fixing these numbers, ranks and specialities on an establishment is basically a matter of agreement between the military (who, for obvious reasons, want as many personnel as possible), and the finance divisions (who, for equally obvious reasons, want the minimum number of bodies necessary), and it is in this area of disagreement that the establisher operates.

Agreement between the two sides is never easily obtained. Every re-equipment of a unit or change in its role requires another on-site establishment review and it is a well-known fact (which I know from experience to be neither well-known nor a fact) that, to the military man, all establishment officers are disenchanted, cynical and parsimonious morons who know nothing about military matters; whereas to the establisher, all military personnel are moronic spendthrifts who suffer from delusions of grandeur, tunnel vision, and whose solution to every problem is more men. [2]

An on-site establishment review is a hard game, but at the Army Camp, Naval Dockyard or RAF Station in the real world of the UK Forces, the rules are known, followed and obeyed. In the romantic world of the Sultan of Oman's Armed Forces however, the game was not known; let alone the rules.

But I am ahead of myself, for my attempts to contain the manpower explosion in the SAF did not start until a couple of years after my arrival in the Sultanate of Oman.

By the 1970's, financial necessity forced ruthless cuts on the British Defence Votes, and my life seemed to consist of imposing ten percent personnel reductions instead of assessing what military units really needed. It became increasingly difficult to answer such comments as: 'What is the point of having an on-site establishment review, if you come along six months later and take away ten percent of the people you gave us?'

What was the point indeed? In company with many of my colleagues, I was becoming distinctly disenchanted with this externally imposed and clumsy negation of the past twelve years' work. It was this and a cer-

---

[2] It is perhaps appropriate to note here that the Establishment Committee which carries out the on-site review, consists of a senior military officer (chairman), a senior civilian officer (finance member), a uniformed SNCO secretary and such military specialist advisers as may be necessary.

tain amount of middle-aged *ennui* that made many of us welcome the call by the Ministry of Defence to volunteer to become part of the civilian ten percent cut. Rumour had it that in my grade, response was over ninety percent, and management had to resort to drawing lots. True or not, the redundancy terms were good, and I counted myself fortunate enough to be selected. I soon realised however, that over twenty years of living or travelling abroad did not condition you to early retirement to a Bournemouth bungalow. I began to look for something to do, and called on the Officers' Association.

As always, I met with a courteous and helpful reception, and they gave me a number of interesting vacancies that might prove suitable. They were not to know that I have always regarded people who blast birds out of the sky for sport as possessing as much sensitivity as a football hooligan, and I did not apply for the secretary's post within a fun-loving co-operative rearing pheasants as future targets.

Having spent a fortune over the years on ridiculously cheap video and music cassettes in Bahrain, Singapore and Hong Kong, I also hesitated about working for an organisation devoted to stamping out these pirate practices. One job did interest me however, and that was as administrative officer at the Joint Staff Headquarters of the Sultan of Oman's Armed Forces. It sounded rewarding, both financially and in content, and the leave conditions were excellent. I applied.

It was ten years since my last visit to the country in 1970. Then, it had been to the RAF airfield on the island of Masirah. A more God-forsaken and barren spot would have been hard to imagine and, used only as a staging post by the RAF on their way to and from the Far East, the airport was no bustling hive of activity either. It had always remained happily in my memory however, because of the small wooden fenced enclosure in the sandy waste of the airfield which had a sign at its entrance: 'The Lazy M Corral'.

The island's only signs of vegetation consisted of two palm trees and a sparse collection of camel thorn bushes. I used to wonder what the few Arabs, camels and donkeys lived on. It was hardly surprising that there was no security fence around the base, because any mischief maker would have to travel hundreds of miles of desert or sea to get to the airfield. This created one small problem though, in that stray camels and donkeys would wander on to the runway in search of food. Airfield activity however, was so infrequent, that it was no problem to send out a couple of airmen in a Land Rover shortly before any aircraft arrived to round up the wandering ruminants and put them in the corral out of harm's way.

Sometimes, however, the animal would remain in the corral for a week or more, and the RAF would find themselves with the problem of feeding the strays. Whoever it was who discovered that the cardboard used in large cartons contained very palatable vegetable fibre was a genius. I will always remember my first visit to the 'Lazy M', and the spectacle of a camel and a donkey chewing away at opposite ends of a Surf carton.

Inevitably, it took little time for the locals to discover that their scrawny brutes returned from confinement looking much sleeker and healthier. The ongoing problem then, was to dissuade the islanders from driving their beasts onto the airfield so that they might enjoy a visit to the 'Lazy M' health farm.

In those days, Sultan Said bin Taimur ruled Muscat and Oman (as it was then known) and he was notorious for his medieval views on his country and his people. Millions of dollars had been accumulated from Oman's oil, and this, converted into bullion bars, rested in the vaults beneath his palace at Salalah in the south of the country. He was convinced however (and the Western mind boggles at such thought processes), that it was better for his people to live without electric power, music, medicine and education, to name a few of the least harmful benefits to human civilisation.

Life was indeed harsh and primitive in 1970, but Masirah was not Muscat the capital and, I reminded myself, Sultan Qaboos had been in power since then, and the country had taken enormous strides forward. Thus I reassured myself, and obtained - and read - whatever books about Oman I could lay my hands on.

Not that there were many of them I discovered, and most of those that existed had been written by British soldiers after approval by the British MoD. It was fascinating to read about the Dhofar War, but that official blessing worried me. No soldier was going to be totally honest and confess, for example, that he made an absolute cock-up of the attack on Sheikh Hassan's fort, and, even if he wanted to, the Ministry of Defence UK, (MoDUK), were certainly not going to allow him to broadcast the fact. It seems that all British military men are jolly good chaps who undergo appalling hardships, but still win at the end of the day because they played a straight bat. An exaggeration? I read the books avidly, and put them down wondering what it was really like. Later I was to find out from some of those who had been through it. Not quite the official version, but still something to be proud of.

A large and bulky pack arrived from Airwork Ltd, who were the recruiting agents for the Sultan's Armed Forces, and I waded through and filled in the pages of questions. Questions I had answered scores of times during my time with MoDUK: 'When was your grandfather (on your father's side) born?', 'Where was he born?', 'Was he British?' etc, etc. 'Had you (the applicant) ever belonged to a Communist or Fascist organisation?' I often wondered about that one. If you had ever been a member of the CP or the British Fascist League, and devoted to destroying democracy, would you be likely to answer 'Yes'? Asinine or not, the questions were answered - apparently satisfactorily - because I was sent for the usual comprehensive medical examination. However the joining instructions came and I started packing.

The Gulf Air Tristar flight to Muscat was an overnight one and, in spite of the high standard of cabin service, a tedious journey for we seemed to stop at most of the major cities in the Gulf before we finally took off for the last leg south-eastwards into Oman. It was eleven o'clock, therefore, on a June morning when we finally landed at Seeb airport. This time of day enabled me to appreciate the steam-bath atmosphere of the Capital Area to the full. I was not uplifted by recalling from somewhere in my recent reading that because Muscat is surrounded by the mountains and spurs of the Hajar range, they store the daytime heat and radiate it back at night - the capital gaining little nocturnal relief from the heat and humidity.

I mopped my face as I made my way with the other dozen or so passengers into the air-conditioned cool of the terminal. Glancing around, the airfield gave the impression of smooth efficiency. Similarly, inside the security area there were impeccably dressed armed policemen in khaki drill and peaked caps with chequered bands. However, after our hand-baggage had been checked and we had moved into the immigration hall, the scene changed dramatically. There was chaos and bedlam. A hoard of shouting Indians and Pakistanis, all waving their passports were pleading for priority treatment from the white-gowned, white-turbanned Omani officials behind the counters. Later, I learned the proper name for their garb, but at the time, all I could do was recall unhappily that there had been an Air India 747 just outside the terminal - and wonder how long it would take me to work my way up to one of the officials. There was no queuing here, and no chance of escape if I waited patiently for my turn.

I had started to push when I heard my name called. Looking round I saw an army officer fighting his way towards me. 'Mike Lloyd,' he introduced himself. 'I've come to meet you. Lets get out of this shambles,' and, grabbing my passport, he pushed his way to the nearest counter, calling cheerfully, 'Come on chaps, make way for an officer.'

The mob looked over its shoulder, grinned and parted before him. Then, after a few words of Arabic, the official thumped my passport with enthusiasm. We collected our luggage, a cursory glance from customs, and were out into the steam-bath again. When the doors opened and we walked outside, the noise rose to a crescendo again. As I looked around, I realised that for every excited passenger in the immigration hall, there was an equally excited friend or relative waiting outside to greet him. It was a considerable relief, both mentally and physically, to climb into the cool quiet of Mike's staff car and be driven down the dual highway towards the capital.

Mike was a very pleasant man. A Lieutenant-Colonel in the Sultan of Oman's Land Forces (SOLF), he came originally from what was sometimes referred to in the UK as one of the better cavalry regiments and, from what an earthy Royal Engineer friend of mine referred to as the 'Brown Boots and Horseshit Brigade'. During the half hour journey I looked around with interest at the undulating brown plain and the jagged mountains converging on our right, whilst Mike briefed me on the place I was going to and the office I was going to work in.

Bait al Falaj it was called - the House of Water - a reference to the Falaj system. [3] deep beneath the camp. It was an appropriate name, I came to realise for among the isolated apartment blocks and in the rudimentary streets and barren landscape of Ruwi, BAF (as I came to call it) was a splendid oasis of trees and shrubs. Mike explained that Ruwi was due to become the business centre of the capital area, with high-rise buildings and wide avenues. Difficult to believe as the car bumped

[3] The underground irrigation system built by the Persians nearly a thousand years before.

through rubbish, ruts, and pot-holes to enter the camp. 'I'll drop you off at the mess so that you can have a shower; pick you up later and take you over to the office to meet the others.' He summoned the mess manager, Harvey, and departed.

'Let me show you to your room,' said Harvey, and led me round the back of the mess to one of the white painted bungalows scattered about behind. I was to learn the reason for this apparent lack of uniformity at a later date. We trailed along a dark verandah until he threw open a door and proudly announced, 'This used to be one of the store-rooms for the old mess. Been converted. Brigadier Thwaites asked me to make sure it was nicely furnished for you. The Brigadier's ex-Guards. So am I,' he announced proudly. Clearly, theirs was a very exclusive club.

He looked anxiously at me as I glanced around the room thinking to myself, 'Dear God! He made a special effort to acheive *this* ?' One stained, threadbare carpet; one stained sagging armchair; one chest of drawers, battled-scarred from many cigarettes; one bed; a bedside table that had lost most of its varnish; an enormous green metal cupboard; and a small, ancient refrigerator. In the corner, an equally ancient air-conditioner banged and rattled, and a second glance at the refrigerator confirmed that its lead could not possibly reach the one wall socket at shoulder height. The room had to have some good points. There were two small, wooden-framed windows opening straight outside, instead of onto a dark verandah, so the room would get a reasonable amount of daylight; the walls were a least two feet thick so the room would be cool; the floors were quarry-tiled, and the ceiling was a natural one of branches supporting rush matting. I should be able to do something with this I thought - that is, as soon as I can replace the junk.

Harvey was becoming anxious about my continued silence, so I smiled at him. 'It'll do,' I said, and dumped my suitcase on the bed. It sagged even more.

'Come across and have a coffee when you've had a shower. I'll tell Colonel Lloyd you'll be in the ante-room.'

I thanked him for the offer and started to unpack.

Over coffee, I received a run-down on Harvey's career. An ex-Guards' senior NCO, he had worked in one of the BAF offices, in charge of printing and duplicating. 'Boring, a job for a trained monkey,' as he put it, and he saw a chance of promotion - and more interesting work - when the post of mess manager became vacant. 'Last bloke took to his room, and wouldn't come and talk to anybody,' he confided, 'so they had to get rid of him.' He paused, and leaned forward, 'Mind you, everybody gets at you in this job - but I ignore them,' he added triumphantly.

I thought of mess managers I had known socially and professionally in the RAF. They had all undergone years of training and numerous trade tests before they attained their positions. I wondered whether enthusiasm was a substitute for professional training and experience. Fortunately, Mike's arrival saved me from further comment.

The drive from the officers' mess to the Joint Staff Headquarters was a short one, which was a relief for I was beginning to flag. It was fortunate too, that the six-hour working day finished at 1.30pm, so there was little time to do more than shake hands and try to remember names. Inevitably, after my years as an establishment officer, I possessed an inbuilt sensor which reacted to the atmosphere of an office, and although the staff officers themselves could not have been more pleasant, I gained the distinct impression that little was going on - and that they were aware of it. The Brigadier was away for some reason, as was the one Omani officer, a Muqaddam (lieutenant colonel) Hassan Ehsan Naseeb; the remainder consisted of Dominic, a towering lieutenant colonel, on loan from the Scots Guards; Ned, a charming and nervously-mannered contract lieutenant commander, who was ex-Royal Navy, and Denis, a short and pedantic wing commander, ex-RAF. Their ages were compatible with their ranks, except for Ned - one of those fortunate people who remain forty forever. Finally there was Mike, whom I had already met.

Whilst the other three were ostensibly the representatives of SOLF, SON and SOAF (I was later to discover that nothing was further from the truth), Mike was 'Secretary to the Joint Staff', and his purpose in life was to see that the office and its operations ran smoothly. Hardly a suitable job for a member of the 'Brown Boots Brigade', I thought, and yet this, I was to learn, was the main reason for my arrival. Given that the office was rather like a small, placid pond, it looked as if my task might not be too demanding.

The building which housed the Joint Staff was a simple modern bungalow on the raised bank of the large wadi which ran through Bait al Falaj camp. It was a good indication of how often the rains came to flood this dried river bed when one saw that it was crossed by a number of graded roads, delineated by white-painted boulders, that led to some aged married-quarter bungalows on the far side. In the middle of the wadi the scattered scrub had been cleared away from a circle and outlined like the roads. An ancient and rusty fire-extinguisher stood at its side suggesting, correctly, that this was the helicopter landing pad.

With these numerous impressions fresh in my mind, I thanked Mike for the lift back to my room and collapsed onto my bed. Lunch did not interest me. Perhaps I would sample dinner later on. For now, I closed my eyes, and tried to ignore the enthusiastic rattling of the air-conditioner above me. At least, while the noise continued, the room remained cool. You cannot have everything, was my last conscious thought. It was a philosophy I was to use a lot during the next few years.

Later I awoke and thought of various coarse phrases for the condition of my mouth. I had forgotten the effects of sleeping in an air-conditioned room. Having showered (in tepid water), I prepared myself for what I thought would be a quiet evening in the mess.

The mess block was two-storeyed and easy to locate among the bungalows. As I entered, I glanced through the glass doors at the dining room on the left with its polished tables, subdued lighting, candles and white-garbed stewards. On the right were the toilets. From idle curiosity, I pushed open the door and noted one badly-stained wash basin; one Asian toilet (basically, a hole in the floor over which you squat); and one European toilet, which, from the myriad markings, I guessed had also been used as an Asian toilet. I shut the door quickly and went up the stairs. I continued up until I saw a door on my left marked 'Bamboo Bar'. On the right, a glass door gave access to a large ante-room.

From the Bamboo Bar came cacophony, not quite as shrill as the mob at the immigration hall, but certainly as loud. Shouts, guffaws of laughter, and a loud crash as something like a stool fell over. I retreated smartly into the ante-room, to be greeted by total silence, disturbed occasionally by the rustle of a newspaper. The noise from across the landing was muted as the door closed behind me, but it was still evident. In the ante-room, there were only a handful of officers present, all were white, and none lowered their papers to see who had entered. I walked quietly to the bar, ordered a Scotch and soda, and sank into one of the deep armchairs to sip my drink and glance around. Uninspired was the word for the decor, but then, I never had entered an officers' mess that had shown originality or flair in its furnishings. Armchairs arranged geometrically around large, low tables, carpets in line abreast and two dark, ornately carved tables bearing magazines and newspapers. In the adjacent room was the bar, separated from us only by a row of pillars, in which there was an identical arrangement of furniture, with the addition of a television set. I walked across to the magazines, and, as expected, found a two-month old *Field* , a ten-day old *Financial Times* , and a *Sunday Times* supplement printed in January. I stopped looking, drained my glass, and headed for the door. A quarter past seven - dinner must have started by now!

Only three officers were seated at one of the tables when I entered the dining room, and, uncertain of protocol, I took my place at an empty table. The menu was presented and my mouth fell open. I could have had a good guess at a sweet called 'APRICOAT PLAN', but 'CHICKEN CHOPSY FRY NOODLE (CHINESS)' left me in some doubt. I settled for 'BRASED STEAK': at least I knew what that should look and taste like. I wondered if that menu - and what it signified - was one of the reasons why there were so few people in the mess.

I was chewing on the braised steak, when a tall, balding man with a greying moustache sat down opposite me. I replied to his 'Good evening', and, after resting his folded arms on the table and regarding me for a moment, he spoke again. 'You're Alan Hoskins, aren't you?' I admitted it, and he half rose and extended a hand across the table. 'I'm Maurice O'Brien. Camp Commandant. Major. Used to be in the Guards. Brigadier Thwaites asked me to look after you and I'll be showing you around the camp tomorrow. He used to be Guards, you know.'

I knew this, but thought I'd better keep the conversation going. 'Who, Brigadier Thwaites?'

'Yes. There's an awful lot of us ex-Guards chaps around.'

I didn't have the heart to tell him I had already begun to suspect this, and remarked that Brigadier Thwaites was very kind to make sure that I was met and looked after. If I had wondered which regiment Maurice had come from, his next statement would have made it clear.

'He's a darlin' man, is the Brigadier. You're going to enjoy working for him. Did you meet him this morning?'

'No, he was away somewhere.'

'Oh,' said Maurice, 'he was probably at MAM.'

He saw the puzzled look on my face and explained. 'Muaskar al Murtafa'a. We call it MAM. It's the big garrison about twenty miles north of Muscat. Near Seeb airport. It's where all the Headquarters are - SOLF, SOAF and SON. He's often out there.'

It crossed my mind to wonder why, if the three Headquarters were at MAM, the Joint Staff was down at Muscat. I was to find out as the weeks went by.

Maurice continued. 'I expect you're feeling pretty bushed if you came in on last night's flight.' I admitted I was, and stole a glance at him. He seemed a friendly soul, so I decided to chance it.

'Weird scene upstairs,' I ventured.

'What do you mean?'

'Well, when I got to the top of the stairs, all hell seemed to have broken loose in the...um...what do you call it? 'Bamboo Bar'. On the other side of the landing though, the ante-room was like a morgue. Is that the only alternative out here in the evenings?'

Maurice had a puzzled look. 'Not with you.'

'Well, you get to the top of the stairs, and it looks as if you turn left into the Bamboo Bar and get smashed out of your mind, or you turn right into the ante-room and get bored to death. I mean, the magazines are as old as the hills, and no-one seems very chatty.'

'See what you mean,' replied Maurice. He paused, collecting his thoughts. 'You'll find most people out here pretty weird, one way or another.' He grinned. 'Even me, although I'm more normal than most. I hope. You see, a lot of them prefer their own company and you won't see much of them except in their offices. Some wouldn't get through the day without their bottle or two, and some just can't stand mess cooking.

'Me,' he tapped his chest, 'a spot of dinner over here, then a nice, smooth malt and coffee in the ante-room afterwards. That's my highspot of the day. Sometimes, I even have a game of chess. Do you play chess?'

I shook my head. 'Sorry.'

'Pity, I could do with some competition.' He relapsed into silence as the steward removed his plate. 'Anyway, come and join me in a nightcap.'

The coffee was vile, but the malt was very smooth, and I listened in interest as Maurice talked about Bait al Falaj and its personalities. At one point, a distant roar erupted from the Bamboo Bar, and he paused and commented, 'Sounds as if they're having a good time, but don't call on any of them in their offices tomorrow. Not before ten o'clock anyway.'

I slept well and in the morning took the opportunity to stand outside my room and study the surroundings while I waited for Maurice. I was on a gentle slope and, straight ahead, I looked across the camp to the west and some of the dramatically jagged mountain spurs that permeated the capital area. After a few months I was to realise that all of the open roads followed the labyrinthine valley floors and you could easily drive two miles in order to achieve two hundred yards towards your destination. To my left in the immediate foreground was the mess, while similar bungalows to the one behind me stretched from the mess to the main road which ran through the camp. Beyond that road, now busy with arriving buses and cars, were other white-washed blocks, one of which, sprouting a tall aerial mast, was clearly the camp's signal centre. To its right, and farther away, the great, white cube of the fort rose above a clump of trees. Surmounting one of the corner towers was a pole, on which the red, white and green Omani flag hung limply in the still warm air of morning. Further to the right, more mountains and the distant port of Mina Qaboos, while the foreground contained a walled enclosure. I didn't need the lurid Indian film posters to tell me that it was the camp cinema, for I remembered waking the night before to some distant eerie wailing, and telling myself that it was too early for the muezzin. Next to the cinema were numerous humps of earth and scattered slabs of rock. Could be a Muslim cemetery, I decided, for they did not bother with engraved and carved headstones; but it was a strange place to find one.

A shining white Toyota arrived, and Maurice climbed out. The usual salutations, then: 'I think we'll meet the Brigadier first, then do the ususal round. You know, pay accounts, sick quarters, barrack stores, and so on. If there's time afterwards, I'll give you the grand tour of the camp and Ruwi.' He grinned. 'That should take about ten minutes. You doing anything this afternoon?'
'Not so far as I know.'
'Good. I'll take you down to the Aqua Club. Bit of a swim and so on. OK?'
'Yes. Thanks very much.'
The morning was even busier than the previous one. As I entered his office, Peter Thwaites stood up and shook my hand. A charming man of good height and build, he was bespectacled and softly spoken - except, as I discovered later, on those rare occasions when he was very angry. I liked him immediately and had little doubt that I could work hard and happily for him. Mike and Dominic, who shared one office, were discussing a party they had both attended the previous evening and down the corridor Ned and Denis, who similarly shared an office, were both chattering away about something equally inconsequential.
Near the end of my interview with the Brigadier, he asked, 'Have you met Colonel Hassan?'
'No, Sir.'
'You must. He's my deputy.' He pressed a button on his intercom. 'Hassan, Would you come in for a minute please.' A moment later, the door opened, and in walked Muqaddam Hassan Ehsan Naseeb.
Until that moment I had not truly appreciated the fact that up until 1861, Zanzibar had been part of the Oman Empire and that slavery had been its major industry. Hassan Ehsan's African ancestry was very evident, as it was, I later discovered, with many Omanis. His father had been a palace slave who had nearly lost his life saving the old Sultan from an assassination attempt. Personal loyalty was highly regarded by the Omanis, and because of this, Hassan's father and his offspring would always be highly favoured by the Royal Family. As I later learnt,

Hassan was a good and brave soldier in his own right, who had earnt gallantry awards in the Dhofar War. I warmed to him immediately.

Twenty minutes later, Maurice and I were just leaving the Joint Staff offices to start our tour, when the main door opened and a soldier rushed in. He was a tubby little man whose uniform hung around him in myriad folds and wrinkles, and he stopped his headlong dash when he saw us standing in the doorway.

'Good morning, Sir,' came his greeting at the same time as his salute and melon-slice grin.

Maurice returned the salute.

'Why are you rushing around Imam Bux?'

'Sir, there is a helicopter landing, and I have to tell the sahibs in case their windows are open.'

'Carry on,' said Maurice, and stood aside. He turned to me. 'We might as well have a coffee while we're waiting,' and we walked into an office where he introduced me to George Kutty, the Chief Clerk.

'Doe coffee minfadlak. Mafee sugar,' said Maurice in an entertaining mixture of Urdu and Arabic, whilst George put his head outside to bellow for an orderly.

We were waiting for the coffee, and I was wondering why the arrival of a helicopter should generate such alarm, when the distant tok-tok of its blades became an increasing roar. Suddenly the windows rattled in their frames, and as I glanced at them the shrubs and distant hills diappeared in a thick brown fog.

'Jesus!' I exclaimed, and Maurice grinned.

'Be ten minutes before we can go out now,' was his comment. 'And I'll have to get that bloody car washed again.'

I thought about this as I sipped my coffee. It was ridiculous that every time a helicopter arrived the camp was covered in sand and dust - it was no great problem to overcome. I decided not to comment: I'd chanced my arm enough last night.

Maurice was right about his car, and we had to wipe the heavy brown dust off the windshield before we could continue. I took the opportunity to ask him about the haphazard arrangement of bungalows around the officers' mess.

'Grown up like that over the years,' came the reply. 'The bungalow you're in was the first officers' mess way, way back. Then they built the Muscateer.' He saw my look and explained.

'That's the building just behind the mess. It's a sort of club now, but it was in use as a mess in the Dhofar War I understand, when the MoD was in the fort.' He pointed at the great, white cube coming into view as we turned the corner. I had noticed it the previous day and had promised myself a closer look when time permitted. With a few low, white-washed buildings behind it, it rose fifty feet or more above a flat, sandy area which had to be a parade ground. An old British armoured car stood below the tower at the near corner, and an equally aged naval gun was nearby. Its muzzle pointed down, and it presented a strangely forlorn picture.

'Bloody people,' muttered Maurice as he stopped the car. 'Won't be a minute.' He walked over to the gun, stopped, and picked up a large boulder which he placed carefully on the gun's breech. Slowly, the muzzle rose, and the gun assumed a more dignified and menacing stance. Maurice climbed back into the car.

'If I've told the bloody labourers once, I've told them fifty times: when they've cleaned the gun, put the bloody stone back.' We drove off. 'I hear they're planning to turn the fort into a museum,' he continued, 'I hope so. Be a shame if it is allowed to carry on decaying like it is now.'

Our next stop was at the camp tailors. Maurice exlained: 'You're issued with a light-weight DJ for formal occasions.'

'Are there many of them?' I queried.

'No. Usually, only two a year. One is in November at the palace - His Majesty gives a dinner every year for the officers of his armed forces. The other occasion is for Christmas dinner in the mess. If you're here, of course. Most people bugger off back to the UK for Christmas.'

As we walked out of the tailors, he glanced at his wristwatch.

'Finish off the rounds, and we might have time before lunch to see His Highness.' Later, as we drove past the Joint Staff, he explained, 'His Highness Said Faher is the Sultan's uncle. 'Deputy Prime Minister for Security and Defence' is his title. The big man, in every way. He's a charming bloke though. His office is at the end of the road here.'

He parked the car and we climbed the steps to the old bungalow, enclosed by trees and flowering shrubs. 'Better see Mac first,' said Maurice, 'he's the number one personal assistant to HH. Been out here for God knows how long. He's getting on a bit, and he's a bit deaf.' He uttered these words as he saluted the guards who sprang to attention at the entrance. As we strode down the corridor Indian clerks and white-robed Omani orderlies scurried past us.

It was a gloomy office, and with its haphazard arrangement of tin trunks and old furniture, I gained the impression of an unsuccessful antique shop. Some reasonably modern electronic equipment belied this however. Behind the large and ornate desk an elderly gentleman peered at us across the top of his spectacles.

'Good morning, Maurice,' he smiled. 'And who's this you've here?'

Maurice was at rigid attention. 'Alan Hoskins, Sir. He's just joined us and he's going to work for Brigadier Thwaites.'

'Hallo Alan. How are you?' said Mac and stood up, extending his hand. 'Glad to have you with us.'

Uncertain of his rank, but certain he could give me a few years, I played it safe. 'I'm fine, thank you Sir.' Mindful of Maurice's words, I also increased my decibel output.

Mac flinched a little and, a mite irritably, stated 'Not so loud, I'm not deaf lad.'

'Sorry, Sir.'

'When did you get here?'

Conscious of his reproof I dropped my voice. 'I arrived yesterday, Sir.'

His face darkened. 'For God's sake speak up. What the hell are you whispering for?' I glanced helplessly at Maurice.

Fortunately Mac looked at his watch at that moment. It transpired that the British Ambassador was due to arrive in about five minutes, so we abandoned the idea of paying my respects to His Highness. 'I'll try to fit you in during the next day or two,' were Mac's farewell words, 'But pop along some time and we'll have a nice chat.' After the recent skirmish, I had some reservations about the 'nice chat'.

The afternoon's visit to the SAF Aqua Club proved to be much more entertaining than I had anticipated, for evidence of the country's rapid development was everywhere. It seemed that no matter where you looked, office blocks, apartment buildings and shopping centres were crawling skywards. Often however, there was no road or other sign of access to the growing structure. Later of course the government were to insist on the services being provided before building started.

Outside the camp entrance stood a handsome red and white building. This was the Ruwi post office; but beyond it, for a mile or so in front of our windscreen, nothing rose from the rocky brown plain. Maurice nodded towards the scene. 'The airfield used to be there,' and as I gazed at the narrowing galley floor and the jagged peaks surrounding it, I could easily believe his next comment. 'Our pilots used to reckon it was bloody awful - even worse than Hong Kong.'

It was early afternoon, and watching the heatwaves shimmering above the ground, I was grateful for the car's air-conditioner. We seemed to be the only vehicle on the road, and I remarked upon this.

'Wait until we come back,' was Maurice's reply.

The road was a dual carriageway with large roundabouts at the junctions. There was something unfinished about it though. It puzzled me at first, until I realised that although shops and houses and the inevitable rocky mounts bordered the avenue, there were no lamp-posts - street lighting was still to come.

Soon, we swung off Qaboos Street and, after a short climb to the north, descended to the coast. Ahead was a large bay, and along its shore spread the shining steel chimneys, pipes and tanks of an oil refinery. 'Mina al Fahal,' explained Maurice. 'They refine their own petrol. I want to show you something else,' he added as we made a sharp detour into a small valley. It was as dun and arid as the surrounding hills, and contained rows of headstones. We looked at the names - British and Indian. 'God! He was a good lad,' Maurice said as he pointed at a nearby gravestone. 'Bloody sad.'

I looked around and shivered inwardly. Anything further removed from the green of England was hard to imagine. 'Bloody sad for anybody to end up in this place,' was my inevitable comment. Maurice studied the hills as if with fresh eyes. 'See what you mean.'

The atmosphere at the Aqua Club was very different. We left the car on the flat headland which served as the car-park and descended a flight of steps. At the top, a rather grubby, ancient cannon pointed towards the distant houses of the oil company staff, while at the bottom, in a small bay, lay a straggling collection of sheds, huts, portacabins, and one permanent building - the clubhouse. Scattered around, in similar disarray, were numerous speedboats, sailing dinghies and catamarans. Symptomatic of Oman, the place presented an unfinished look. No comments I reminded myself and shook the hand of the jovial, red-faced uniformed officer I was introduced to.

'Captain John,' said Maurice, 'he runs the place.'

'Have a drink,' said my new acquaintance, more as a statement than a question, and his staff beamed at me from behind the bar. Clearly, there were all accustomed to this ritual and not only prefered to let me pay for a round, but served tots that would have brought giddy spells to a British publican. Normally, I enjoy my Scotch and soda, but at that time of the day and in that suffocating heat I flagged very quickly and was glad to escape to the water. Not that the sea brought much physical relief; the bay was obviously a heat trap and the water warm. It was marvellously buoyant though - and a vivid blue that hurt your eyes. Sailing had been a major sport of mine for many years, and floating there, I gazed at the distant tankers off-shore, and decided that the Aqua Club would have to be the favourite place for relaxation at the weekend.

Later, as we inched forward on the five mile drive back to Bait al Falaj, I recalled Maurice's earlier comment. It had taken us about ten minutes to reach the Aqua Club, but now, it was going to be at least an hour before we arrived back at camp. I looked into the cars around us. Plainly, the re-opening of the shops for evening trade was the cause of the problem. Not only were the shop and office staff going back to work, but those employees who had finished for the day were driving their wives, sisters, mothers, aunts, and grandmothers into Ruwi so that they could enjoy their shopping in the cool of the evening. I realised that some of the less attractive aspects of modern city living were already with us. I wondered if the Sultan and his advisers had envisaged that the Omanis would adopt civilisation so enthusiastically?

I looked to the left. A white-haired ancient in traditional garb was driving a taxi occupied by a number of plump Indian women. Dear God! He must have been in his sixties when he first saw a motor-car, let alone learnt to drive one!

I thought that during my visit to Beirut some years ago I had seen Arab driving at its most dangerous. Since my arrival in Oman, I had begun to wonder. Is an Arab who learns to drive at twenty with his faith in Insh'allah and the arrogance of youth, any more dangerous than the sixty year old that may have little Insh'allah, less arrogance and absolutely no skill? I was to find out later.

On our return I decided that I couldn't really be bothered to get dressed up and go across to the mess. Jet-lag and the Aqua Club hospitality had caught up with me, and I suspected that I would not be missing any culinary masterpieces in the dining room. I crawled onto my bed and slept easily until half past four, when the faithful of Ruwi were summoned out of their beds to acknowledge that there was only one Allah.

The next few weeks were occupied with learning: my job, the organisation, names, addresses, Senior staff (of which there were far too many) and - oh my God! - that bloody filing system. The first file I opened generated a large question mark which grew in size as I turned each enclosure. What possible connection could there be between the loss of some fodder from the Dhofar Donkey Company, and an accident to a Jundi (private) on a Salalah rifle range? I puzzled over this for some time, but finally acknowledged defeat. I called for George. The explanation was blindingly simple but as I listened to it, my heart sank. One letter was headed 'Loss of Donkey Fodder', and the other 'Loss of Finger - Jundi Mahomet Aziz'. I suspected from this meagre evidence, that the filing clerk read no further than the first few words on each letter. I looked at the title of the file:

'SOMAN BRIGADE'.

I plunged in. 'George', I asked. 'Does everything that happens in Soman go into this file?'

'Oh no Sir. Only if there is a military enquiry.'

I thought about that and tried another tack. 'George. Where would you put a letter which said that the Commander of Soman Brigade was posted to MoD (Oman)?'

George thought for a moment, then his face cleared. 'That would be under DEPLOYMENTS Sir.'

I goggled. 'Suppose the Muscat regiment was moved down to Salalah. Where would you put that?'

George smiled triumphantly. 'That would certainly go under SOMAN BRIGADE Sir.' Clearly, some satisfactory circle had been completed. I groaned inwardly.

There was some wierd, tenuous train of logic present, but there was no chance that an average staff officer would follow it. Now I understood Mike's recent comment that 'we always seem to have trouble tracing recent correspondence'. 'Trouble' was an understatement. I assessed it as a miracle that any letter that went into our present system was ever located again.

George smiled bravely, hiding his obvious concern. 'Is there a problem, Sir?'

I smiled equally bravely. 'No George. I shall have to think about the files, though.' He rose to go. 'George,' I added, 'would you get me a cup of coffee please?' I fought against the desire to add 'and a couple of aspirins, too.'

Once I had mastered my responsibilities, I found it possible to look out over wider fields although, occasionally, some mini-crisis in the office would drag me back to my *raison d'etre* .

Beside the entrance to the Brigadier's office was another door which led, so I was told, into the office of His Excellency Saleem Al Ghazali, Under Secretary of the Ministry of Defence. As he had direct access to Peter Thwaites through an interconnecting door however, we rarely saw him in our office suite. On this occasion the door opened and a tall, slim, bespectacled Omani clad in the traditional white gown and headdress, with a handsomely decorated silver khanja at his waist entered. He spoke abruptly and wanted to get in touch with CJS immediately. Where was he? I told him how to contact the Brigadier and he returned to his office. So, this was the Saleem Al Ghazali whose name was so often mentioned in the mess. I could see why.

Unlike those of his countrymen I had met so far, he had a quick and decisive manner and speech. Not for him the interminable formal greetings and even after our few words I was left with the impression of a highly intelligent and incisive person. Later dealings with him gave me no reason to change my opinion and what I learnt about his background went a long way towards explaining his character. It seemed that as a youth he had been one of the fortunate few who had received an overseas education during the reign of the old Sultan. The gossip was that he had graduated from Peking University. Later, determined to remove Said Bin Taimur whose medieval rule kept his countrymen in such misery, he gathered around him a number of like-minded Omanis and the nucleus of an armed force. The story goes that it was a close run thing with the *coup d'etat* in Salalah occurring only days before he was due to march into Muscat and Oman, as the country was then known.

It had already been suggested in some newspaper and magazine articles - and I now began to find it easier to believe - that the British had been involved in the overthrow of the old Sultan. I had been on a visit to the RAF airfield on Masirah island when it occurred, and recalled the praiseworthy speed with which the old boy had been flown to Bahrain for treatment to his wounds. I also remembered a SOLF officer who had recently told me that his only memory of that day was his instructions to see that no aircraft flew to the south; although he had not been told why this was necessary. If it was true, I decided, the British could certainly claim that their involvement had been forced upon them, for, had they not acted, others more than willing to do so were already standing on the borders, both north and south.

Eccentric and grossly misunderstood as Said Bin Taimur may have been, neither East nor West questioned the fact that he had to go.

From great moments of history....

It was evening and I had gone across to the Oman United Agencies office in Ruwi to collect a copy of their monthly programme for Seeb Airport. An invaluable document, it listed the comings and goings of all international flights - and I was trying to decide when I should start and finish my first leave.

That morning, we had received a telex from Singapore confirming that Colonel Hassan Ehsan would be returning to Oman on tomorrow morning's British Airways flight. 'Arrives at 0400 hours' confirmed our movements staff, and his driver and the Moral Guidance Branch had been briefed. The former was to convey him to his house, the latter to ensure that his return would appear amongst the interminable parade of doings and sayings of government officials that appeared on Oman TV every evening.

It was a Tuesday and I recall that my eyes ran down the Seeb programme and came to a halt opposite the next flight from Singapore due in that evening. There was no flight from Singapore on a Wednesday and there was no way of checking back - Hassan had to be on that aircraft. I made a decision. Poor old Moral Guidance would have to make a fruitless journey to the airport, because I had no idea how to get in touch with them, but I could do something about Hassan's transport. I got into my shiny new Toyota and drove down to the soldiers' barrack huts, where I located cheery little Imam Bux. I explained the situation, adding, 'I cannot find the Colonel's driver, because he lives in Muttrah with his family, so you must go to the airport to meet Colonel Hassan. OK?'

The inevitable wide grin, salute, and 'Teekhai Sahib.'

The following morning, the storm broke.

Unbeknown to me, although not entitled to one, our Guards Lieutenant Colonel had always regarded Imam Bux as his personal driver, and he had instructed the little Baluchi to drive him to a party at the British Ambassador's residence that evening. My removal of Imam to the airport had ruined Dominic's evening, for his partying was grossly inhibited by the fact that he had to drive himself home.

The next morning he arrived late at the office in a foul mood and, purple with rage, marched into my office and told me how his evening had been a social disaster. I listened and replied that I felt little sympathy for him. Neither he nor Imam Bux had mentioned anything about their arrangement and so far as I was concerned, it was much more important that Hassan was met at the airport, than the fact that he was worried about his alcohol intake. He turned an interesting colour and as the realisation dawned that he could neither court martial me nor have me lashed to a gun carriage, he stormed out of my office, expressing his feelings by slamming the door violently. He was a big man and the noise of that door reverberated around the building.

Seconds later the door opened again and Dennis poked his head through. He looked startled. 'Somebody fired a gun. Are you OK in here?' His eyebrows rose, then his expression became hurt as I guffawed with laughter.

Such moments were precious to me in what was becoming a fairly routine daily round.

The weeks crawled by and my impressions of the place and the people bacme clearer. Bait al Falaj was an anachronism that could only exist in Arabia. A centuries old Beau Geste style fort, in a camp containing accommodation nearly as old, enclosed within a ramshackle wire fence in the middle of a rapidly burgeoning twentieth century city. Our office and the organisation it contained was almost as anachronistic, for none of the three services recognised the Joint Staff as having any standing and certainly no authority over them. Indeed, they regarded us as on a par with the MoD, which was personified in their eyes by His Excellency Saleem Al Ghazali.

Lord knows, both Peter Thwaites and Saleem Al Ghazali tried to obtain co-operation and recognition from them; the former on military matters, and the latter (usually) on financial affairs. Appeals for details of contingency or exercise plans from CJS or details of expenditure from the US usually went unanswered. It seemed that only in such routine matters as intelligence reports were we acknowledged by the receipt of a daily copy, and this, only so that we could act as a rather upmarket post office, and pass it on to the Palace Office.

I recalled my initial disbelief when I discovered that the major (and almost only) activity of one of our staff officers was to convert the signalled intel-information into a readable form, have it typed and forwarded by a driver. Later, I was to take over this task, and estimated that it occupied about ten minutes of my working day.

Under a conventional power structure, similar to that of the United Kingdom, the military are subservient to civilian authority in the form of a civil service with financial control, who are in turn, controlled by a civilian minister and parliament. Within this structure, there might have been some hope. As it was, each of the three service commanders, (CSOLF, CSOAF, CSON), HE the US and CJS were all of equal rank and each had direct access to the Sultan.

If his Excellency (or CJS) had an audience with his majesty at ten o'clock and asked him to confirm and impose some decision on one of the commanders, it was a fair chance that the commander would have an audience at half past ten during which would make an impassioned plea to reverse it. I was to see this in operation on a number of occasions and I began to suspect that the name of the game was 'Last one in gets the final decision'. This in turn led me to think about the Omanis themselves.

Totally unlike their arrogant neighbours to the north and west (the UAE and Saudi Arabia) they were a quietly spoken and courteous people. Among the younger officers there were a few who couldn't handle their liquor, but then, I reminded myself, there were plenty like that in the UK. This was the sort of thing Said Bin Taimur had been worried about of course, but that was hardly a reason for excluding medicine and education from the country. They exuded a genuine aura of friendliness and I found them easier to like and talk to than most of the nationalties I had met on my travels. It was to be a month or so however before I finally abandoned the British approach to business and came to accept their insistence on the formal salutations before the reason for the visit was introduced. I don't think however that I ever brought myself to enjoy the Arab love of rhetoric and their conviction that if something was said loud enough and often enough it would happen.

On the other hand, I suspected that my rather direct approach and speech offended them occasionally. Not that they ever showed they were put out, for quiet calm courtesy prevailed at all of my dealings with the Omanis; something that certainly could not be said about some of my official brushes with my British contempories.

There was much I admired in Islam and a devout Muslim was a person of considerable integrity, but the 'Insh'Allah' (will of God) mentality I found hard to accept, for many Muslims, both Omani and Baluchi, used it as an excuse for idleness or neglect. Later, as I got to know my less efficient staff better, I would reject their standard reply thus: 'Mahomet. Please take this letter to His Excellency's office immediately.'

'Insh'Allah.'

'Insh'Allah be buggered, do it now.'

This response showed considerable religous insensitivity on my part, but it invariably brought a high-pitched giggle and the orderly's rapid departure, which was what I wanted. Soon, they came to understand that I was not prepared to blame God for a twenty-four hour delay in a personally delivered message which had to travel two hundred yards.

One other grievance was that I found it impossible to reconcile my establishment knowledge with the ranks of our staff officers, who were all at the rank of lieutenant colonel when their level and workload justified a senior non-commissioned officer at the most. On consideration, a lot of young sergeants I had known in the past would have been very unhappy with a job as one of our staff officers, regarding the post as offering them no opportunity to shine or show initiative. There was only one argument for the lieutenant-colonel rank that I could see and that was status, the argument being that they needed the pip and crown to carry some weight in their dealings with SOLF, SOAF and SON. This was an argument that was rarely accepted in the British forces, because the major factors in determining the rank of a post was its job content and responsibility level. In the joint staff, job content was virtually nil as was responsibility level and as for status, the three armed forces of the Sultan deliberately had as little to do with our office as possible. It was becoming very clear to me that, whatever the reason had been for creating the joint staff, it had been 'sent to Coventry' so to speak by the three Commanders who saw its existence as a threat to their right of direct access to His Majesty. What I did not know then, in those early days, was that Peter Thwaites was trying to do something about it.

But how could anybody of lieutenant colonel rank spend his days doing so little and of such a trivial nature? I was to find the reason later.

I wondered whether there much point in trying to improve the organisation of the office? I had no choice I decided. While the office was there I had to try and make it run efficiently. But I was well aware that although my days were busy, the rank of my post was also inflated.

That evening I sat in the ante-room sipping my whisky and soda trying to decide whether I could be bothered to go to dinner. It was only a few weeks since my arrival but already I was beginning to feel some sympathy for those who shunned mess catering. The problem as far as I could see was that the evening meals were invariably the lunchtime meals reheated. In other words, if you wanted some reasonably cooked moist beef or pork or whatever, you ate at lunchtime. If you didn't object to dried out, reheated meat then you ate in the evening. Unfortunately I had always eaten my main meal in the evening and I didn't like reheated food. The mess did produce some very tasty toasted sandwiches at lunch time however and if you wished, they would fill them up with plenty of crisp salad. I doubted if I could ever be bothered to do my own catering so these sandwiches and the few local restaurants looked like featuring largely in my future diet.

Somebody sat down nearby and I glanced up. It was Stan Fisher, a truly delightful man recently turned sixty. Slim and always smartly dressed in a fawn or blue safari suit, it was easy to accept that he had been a lieutenant colonel in the British Army. Already, I was finding myself differentiating between what I called 'real rank' ie, one earned in the British Forces, and 'local rank' ie, one awarded in the Sultanate Forces for whatever reason. I already knew that merit was not a major consideration in local promotions.

Stan loved his grog but never allowed his drinking to interfere with his work in the Purchasing Directorate. His attitude to life could best be summed up by his reply one morning when I asked him if he was alright. He had clearly hit the bottle fairly heavily the night before.

'Didn't feel too good first thing,' he said, 'but when I put my legs back on again, I feel much better.' Unfortunately I didn't realise at the time that it was a passing reference to a terminal illness Stan knew he was suffering from and not a joking reference to the night before.

'Stan,' I offered, 'have a drink? '

'Certainly.' came the reply, and added, 'you look pensive old chap.'

Among my new friends, there was no better person to talk to I decided as I went to the bar. I started as soon as I returned.

'Stan. How can four half colonels sit in their offices every day, do next to nothing, draw their pretty fabulous pay and still look at themselves in the mirror every morning?' I was on my second W & S and got slightly carried away. 'It's almost obscene!'

He grinned. 'Not really.'

'What do you mean? '

'Have you been to one of your lieutenant colonel's hirings or married quarters yet? '

'No. I'm going to a drinks thing at Denis' next week though.'

'Good. Look around you when you're there. You'll be suprised.' He saw my raised eyebrows and explained. 'Service or civilian equivalent, the gap between the conditions of a major and a lieutenant colonel out here are enormous. If you're a major or below, it means living and eating in this mess,' he waved a derogatory hand as if brushing away a fly, 'sharing a batman who's probably straight down from the mountains and can't tell the difference between a broom and vacuum cleaner and seeing your family once every three months. Make that little step to half colonel and what do you have then?' he paused. 'You're accompanied by your family and given three or four bedroom luxury accomodation and you have two servants, a cook a steward and probably a driver as well for your larger car.' He grinned. 'And of course a socking great tax free salary on top of your pension from the British Forces.' He asked me. 'Would you worry if you had nothing to do? Would you rock the boat?'

I took his point and shook my head. 'No.'

He stood up wih his empty glass. 'My turn. Same again? 'While he was away another question came to mind which I put to him on his return. 'You're in the Purchasing Directorate Stan?'

'Yes'

'So you know a fair number of local businessmen? '

'A fair number.' he agreed.

'Well. You hear a lot of gossip round here. Are they really as crooked as people say they are?'

His initial reaction was a light laugh, then he thought for a minute. 'No. I don't think so. Like everywhere else in the world a few of them are crooked but most of them are honest by their code'.

'What does that mean?'

He sipped at his drink. 'Not easy to explain.' He sat down.

'Look, the first thing you have to appreciate is that the Omani, or rather the Arab approach to business is entirely different to ours. For them, being a trader is an honourable profession. Mohammed himself was one. It's more important that you understand the tribal concept out here before you can really appreciate their way of thinking.' He paused for a moment then continued. 'To an Arab, his tribe is his family. I suppose it's a hangover from the Bedu days, but wealth belongs to the tribe rather than the individual. You'll often find one brother selling cars, another brother selling electrical goods and perhaps another brother holding a high position in the government or the civil service. All their incomes are divided among parents, uncles, grandparents and so on. Wealth can also be distributed in other ways to relatives, by awarding them contracts, giving them jobs, etc. In other words, nepotism is a way of life and if there is a sin, it would be in not giving a job to a relative if he wanted one.' He concluded: 'So you can see, it is quite wrong to apply British attitudes about nepotism to the Arab's tribal way of life.'

'I see.'

'There's one final thing,' said my mentor. 'Oman is booming at present and everybody's out to make a fortune - and a lot of them do. I was talking to one of our drivers this morning. He already owns three houses and is buying a fourth. Mind you, I believe his wife's an Al Harthy, so that would help.' He stood up. 'Anyway, come across to the other side and meet some of the lads in the Bamboo Bar.'

It was an interesting way to finish the evening, even if my dinner did consist of only a few handfuls of peanuts.

Chapter 2

The call to prayer next morning penetrated my sleep like a dog's distant howling. I stumbled across the darkened room, switched on the light, then filled the kettle. Now, two more steps across my bijou residence and I could stand pensively in the gloom of my toilet disposing of the countless Whiskey and Sodas I had drunk the evening before. Having made the coffee and needing milk, I opened the door of the refrigerator. The cardboard box on which it stood collapsed and it fell to the floor with a crash. I cursed loudly, grabbed the milk carton before it spilt and finished making my coffee. I swore an oath that even if it did hurt Harvey's feelings I would insist on either a decent length of flex to reach the wall socket or a solid table on which to stand the bloody thing.

For two minutes of peace I sipped at my coffee, relishing its bitter strength, then I froze. From the dark outside came a scream which ended abruptly, to be followed by a succession of growls and crunching noises. There were many stray cats and kittens around the mess who existed by foraging in the swill bins. That sounded horribly like a pye-dog had caught one. Dear God, I thought, have some mercy. After last night's excesses, I do not need an excerpt from *The Hound of the Baskervilles*. The noise had stopped and I closed my eyes and listened thankfully to the reassuring rattle and bang of the air-conditioner. My mind wandered back to yesterday evening. I certainly wouldn't be doing that very often. It had been very entertaining and the company lively, but how many Scotches had I drunk? When I had packed it in and said my 'goodnights' the hard core were well into their stride and clearly set for many more hours.

Apart from Stan, who never appeared to be affected by his alcohol intake, the rest of the party had become progressively louder, noisier and more clumsy as the evening wore on. Glasses were spilt, many broken and many drunken apologies made to the Indian or Pakistani barmen. A few times I had had to remind myself this was an officers' mess and not an Irish grog-shop.

'Jesus!' I thought to myself as I watched the room take shape in the growing light. I've tied on a few in my time and I enjoy my Scotch sufficiently to worry about my health occasionally, but I'm a rank amateur compared to those lads.

Bill, for instance, was a desperately heavy drinker. I had gathered that he was something to do with the civil engineering department, and also looked after the camp. He had a very attractive young wife in Muscat, who was out here in her own right as the employee of a civilian construction company. With a wife waiting for him to come home, what the hell was he doing drinking himself senseless in the mess every evening? He was just one of the many, I was to discover later, who had their own particular devil riding on their shoulder.

Dave, a delightfully open-faced young man with a steady gaze, was in the same outfit as Bill, but clearly there yesterday evening because he was a sociable character and liked an occasional bust.

Ashley was a large and overweight ex-rugby international who I learnt was an Omani agent for a large tobacco consortium. He was a pleasant man who had a charming Indonesian wife and a large company-provided house at the end of the road past the camp. What was he doing here?

Lastly there was Robin, later to have his name spread across the front pages of every UK newspaper. He was another desperate drinker but an entertaining character until he passed his limit and became morose and objectionable.

Individually, I would have been happy to meet any of them again, but I had serious doubts about joining them as a drinking party. Boring though the ante-room company might be, I was pretty sure that it was a much safer place to spend the evenings than the Bamboo Bar. But I had never seen boredom raised to an art form before. Take Bill and Stan. They might sound like a comedy duo and rightly so, but they were a couple of middle-aged nags whose major topic of conversation was the food in the mess. However, their complaints were peculiarly slanted and not aimed at the quality of their own meal but at the quality of the meal their neighbour had just eaten. Thus:

'Did you see the piece of meat Richard had?'

'Yes. It looked beautiful.'

'Ha! Well! Richard is Mess President of course!'

'Oh yes. Of course.'

As the elderly, irascible members of a London club they could have presented a superb comedy sketch. As it was, I used to listen to them and wonder what had happened to the spirit epitomised by Lawrence of Arabia. Clearly, it wasn't in evidence at Bait al Falaj.

Another regular was Charles, whose sole conversational subject was the up and down movements of various exotic company shares or the Omani Rial/Pound Sterling. A typical chat with him as I left the mess would go as follows:

'Evening Alan.'

'Evening Charles.'

'Any papers in today?'

'I'm afraid not.'

'For God's sake! If I can't find out how 'Diamond Basuto' and the exchange rate are getting on how can I brief my broker next week?'

It was interesting to note that a lot of the long-serving contract officers, civilian and military, maintained an ongoing interest in the stock market. Later, as the Omani Rial (and therefore my salary) began to slide I too began to take an active interest in the exchange rate.

Sandy so rarely spoke to anybody that for a member of the officers' mess he was introvert enough to be regarded as eccentric. He spent a lot of his spare time trudging up and down the local mountains, and so was very fit. A demanding activity in those temperatures, it was known as 'Jebel Bashing' or, more decorously, 'Jebel Walking'. His room was only a few feet from mine and after months of non-communication I felt quite uplifted when a 'good morning' of mine was acknowledged with a smile. He was an ex-British Army officer I was told but nobody knew why he had become a social recluse. Sadly, he was evacuated to the UK with a heart problem and died in Haslar hospital after an apparently successful by-pass operation. I was even more saddened when I heard subsequently that his last few nights in the mess had been spent sitting upright on a chair in his room, this being the only way he could obtain some relief from the intense chest pains. Why, I asked myself, didn't he knock on my door? I could have given him some company and possibly talked him into going to the doctor sooner than he did.

In this category one other ex-British Army officer remains fondly in my memory. Peter's eccentricity was mild compared to some and indeed after some months of living in Bait al Falaj I began to doubt my judgement in the matter, for, I suspected that I was developing a few quirks in my behaviour.

Steve, however, was obsessive about security; at least that's how I can best describe it for his speech was frequently accompanied by sideways glances, quick looks over his shoulder and sometimes, a total silence when asked for a vital piece of information. Both of us were avid readers and one conversation we had will always remain with me:

'Alan, I'd be grateful if you'd let me have that book.'
'Which one is that?'
'You know.'
'No, I don't.'
Furtive glance over shoulder. 'It's about this part of the world.'
I never did find that book.

Totally different in character was Bill Foxton. A uniformed major and a complete extrovert, we would occasionally swap wartime reminiscences although his wars were quite different from mine. Fifteen years younger than me, he had served as a youth in the French Foreign Legion. He had drawn all of his savings from his Post Office account and gone to Paris to join up. It was as romantic as hell but he could not now recall the incident or the set of circumstances that made him do it. He had also served in the British Army before becoming a contract officer in SOLF, but it was his memories of the legion that interested me most of all.

He vividly recalled the appallingly hard training and his first patrol when two Morrocan insurgents were captured. His captain had glanced over the patrol and his eyes had settled on young Bill. The two prisoners had their hands tied behind their backs and he pushed them towards Bill. 'Take them to Algiers', he ordered and indicated a nearby dune. How far away Algiers lay he had no idea but he thought that it was in the direction the officer had shown and he assumed that before too long he would see the distant white buildings of the city. He and his prisoners had left the first dune behind and were surmounting the second when he heard a shout. He turned round and stopped as the sergeant came panting towards him.

'What are you doing for God's sake?' he demanded and an expression of astonishment crossed his face as Bill replied 'Taking them to Algiers'.

'Go Back', the NCO said to him and watched as Bill trudged away.

Bill had just rejoined his patrol when two distant shots sounded to be followed some minutes later by the reappearance of the sergeant alone. It was then that Bill understood what the expression 'Take them to Algiers' really meant.

Bill had a hook in place of a left hand (the result of picking up an unexploded shell in the Dhofar) and an outrageous sense of humour. This led him, on occasions, to supply the most appalling gossip about some of the personalties in the SAF. Because he had been around the SAF for a long time, however, there was often an element of truth in his stories. In time I came to refer to him affectionately as 'Rumour Control' a title I suspect he was rather proud of. He had lived in the Sultanate for some time and it was from him that I learnt about the graves outside my room. They contained the bodies of the men who had fought and died for the Sultan at the battle of Bait al Falaj in 1915. Three thousand dissident tribesmen from the Interior had marched on Muscat and were finally defeated around the camp. The story goes that the bodies of the tribesmen were left unburied.

The graves were now no more than small mounds of earth covering a few bones and the headstones, in the tradition of Islam, were any old lumps of rock stuck on end into the dry soil. One or two of the gravestones were shaped however and bore Arabic lettering. These I guessed, probably belonged to a few of the British and Indian troops who died alongside the Sultan's men.

It took no great flight of fancy to imagine the ghosts of those long dead warriors stirring occasionally for, as I mentioned earlier, they rested beside the camp's open air cinema. On three nights a week Indian or Pakistani films were shown and on the other three, British or American. It was hardly surprising (for the manager of the British Services Cinema Corporation knew his business and his audience) that most of the nightly offerings included fights or battles of one sort or another: Mongol tribes versus Indian Rajahs, cowboys versus Indians or simple heartwarming cops and robbers. Whoever the participants, my room was bombarded by explosions, shrieks and dying gurgles (for maximum volume was *de rigeur*) and the ghosts of 1915 must have wondered whether they were in some hideous time cycle, doomed to fight their last battle again and again.

That cinema also presented me with another problem. Most Indian films seemed to run for anything between three and four hours; usually nearer four. The heroine betrayed her mounting interest in the hero by an increasing display of eyelash fluttering and he showed his growing passion by facial contortions suggesting an acute attack of wind. This was not a problem for neither eyelid fluttering nor pained expression could wake me up. Occasionally however, these suppressed emotions proved too much and they would burst into song. Sometimes the song would have a rhythm and lilt which made it attractive to European ears but this was rare. Whatever the tune however, the audience always reacted with thunderous applause which had a tendency to wake me violently from a deep sleep.

My worst night however, occurred when I was awake and writing a letter. On the opposite side of my room from the camp cinema and equidistant, was the Muscateer Club and on two nights a week (Monday and Friday) a film show was held on its patio. On this occasion a cowboy film was being shown at the camp cinema and another cowboy film was on at the Muscateer. Halfway through my letter, the monotonous and garbled stereo drawling stopped and a battle erupted on my left, while a shoot-out on my right. For a moment I crouched in my chair waiting for the bullets and arrows to pass through my room from one window to the other. I was beginning to understand why some of the inhabitants of Bait al Falaj were a little eccentric.

The following morning I arrived at the office to find that another pseudo-battle had just taken place. This time it was between the SON and the Marine Branch of the ROP. I knew that the three services were only talking to each other when they had to and none of them were talking to the Joint Staff (except about trivia), but here was another force to be reckoned with - or ignored - The Royal Oman Police. Apparently they only talked to the SAF when the demands of the law forced them to, for example in cases of drunken driving, traffic accidents and so on. The ROP had a few helicopters for the usual policing and security duties and a Boeing 727 for transporting members of the force between the north and the south of the country. It also possessed a considerable number of armoured personnel carriers and riot control vehicles which made up a pretty impressive ground force and a quite substantial Marine Branch, both in size and number of vessels, ranging from the usual harbour launches to seagoing coastal patrol craft. There was no doubt in my mind that the ROP was a paramilitary force to be reckoned with, for it had well-maintained equipment and every one of its uniformed personnel were always impeccably turned out - an outward sign of the strict discipline that bound them together.

Returning to the near fracas, it appeared that one of the SON coastal patrol vessels was cruising off the northern coast early one morning, on the look-out for smugglers, infiltrators/ refugees from Iran and illegal immigrants from India or Pakistan, whilst a coastal patrol vessel of the ROP Marine Branch was doing exactly the same. There was also a certain nervousness about possible incursions from the Iranian Navy, so throats must have become dry on both vessels when the slim grey shapes glided towards them through the early mist. Both craft went on the alert and guns were manned. I never did find out how a catastrophe was averted and can only assume that one of the crew members was very good at ship recognition.

When I heard about the episode I found it difficult to believe and remember asking our naval staff officer: 'Do you mean that neither of them tells the other one what its ships are doing?'

'No fault of SON', he replied.

I found the episode, and the situation which allowed it to happen, almost unbelievable and I learnt that although SON were agreeable to close active co-operation with the ROP, the police were not. Whether it was the fear that the SON might eventually take over the entire Marine Branch, or the traditional desire to remain an entirely separate fighting entity, I did not discover, but the original concept of Sultan Qaboos and his advisors was beginning to create many problems. Change was becoming essential.

Having deposed his father in a *coup d'etat* , necessary though it might have been, Sultan Qaboos was well aware of the risk of being toppled himself in a similar manner. Indeed, I was told that a year or so after his accession a few young Omani officers made an unsuccessful attempt on his life. It was inevitable therefore that the national requirement to build and maintain a strong defence force had to be achieved with this risk in mind. The solution was simple. He had served in the British Army as an officer for some years and had a high regard for its tradition of service to civil authority, so he decided to ensure that most of his officer corps came from Britain. The other (perhaps more sensible) step would be to make sure that each of his defence forces would exist as a separate independent entity; each force would have its own commander, a British officer, and each commander would be answerable directly to the Sultan as Commander-in-Chief.

Later, he appointed his uncle, His Highness Said Faher bin Taimur al Said, as deputy Prime Minister for Defence and Security with responsibility for administrative affairs.

Apart from the security organisation itself, there was one more major military force - the Royal Guard regiment (later to become a brigade). A well equipped and well disciplined ground force, its loyalty was unquestioned for it existed solely to protect Sultan Qaboos.

One had only to reflect on this independence of the services, their refusal to co-operate closely (except during essential manoeuvres) and their dislike of the Joint Staff (as small and ineffective as it was) to wonder how they would give battle to an external enemy. As events later showed, I was not the only person who wondered about this.

By now, some of my colleagues had begun to assume recognisable personalities and behaviour patterns.

Sarah was Peter Thwaites secretary, a young slim girl who originally came from South Africa. At that time, it seemed to me that her reactions to the world about her were conditioned almost entirely by the current state of her love life. Her sometimes tense, almost rude behaviour meant there had been a tiff or quarrel. Relaxed and happy, she was on an emotional high. I had noticed this pattern before with young female staff, but tended to ignore it. Although proficient at shorthand and typing she would occasionally wander mentally during one of her 'lows' and incur the wrath of the Brigadier. This was an event worth witnessing (unless you were the object of his wrath) for he had a rich flow of invective and sex was no safeguard against his tongue. The first time I saw it, Sarah was the recipient and at the end of his tirade her squeal of 'Oh! Briggy!' reduced him to a stunned silence. It must have been a unique experience for him, as a brigadier, to meet with such a response.

It was through her that I gained my first knowledge of the pragmatic Islamic laws that were applied in the local Shariya Courts.

Ten years after Sultan Qaboos came to the throne and the modernisation of Oman had begun, many of its citizens were still unaware of the dangers of road traffic. This was doubly true in the case of elderly people who were visiting the Capital Area for the first time. Face to face with a highway, such as Qaboos Street, filled with onrushing cars, coaches and lorries, they were a danger to themselves and drivers for they thought that, protected by Insh'Allah and an up-raised hand, they could cross the road whenever they wished.

Sarah was driving to the office from the newly growing suburb of Medinat Qaboos one morning when a bent, white-haired ancient stepped into the road just in front of her. She stood on the brake pedal but still bumped him sufficiently to make him fall down. A sympathetic crowd appeared instantly and the bruised old man was helped to his feet. Two young and courteous Omani traffic Policemen noted all the details and waved Sarah on her way. 'This will have to go before the Shariya Court Madam, so that an assessment of the damages can be made. You will hear from us soon,' were their parting words.

At her first appearance in court she listened to the old man's son.

'He was a man of great agility and strength. Wise and full of good counsel he was much respected in his village. Sadly, he has been so damaged by the car that he is unable to attend this court and it will be many weeks before he can do so.'

While Sarah tried to reconcile her memory of the slack mouthed an-cient with the son's description, the judge spoke to the son. Clearly this was not a new story.

'I cannot pronounce on the matter of compensation until I see your wise and active father. This case is put away until you can bring him before the court.'

The son protested at the delay but the judge dismissed him with a wave of his hand. Sarah, conscious of her servile role in the Arab world meekly followed the grumbling plaintiff out of the courtroom.

Four weeks later she was summoned to appear again and this time the old man was present on the arm of his son. If he had ever been ag-ile and full of wisdom, his shuffling steps and quivering head told a different story now.

The son started to speak but the judge cut him short. 'I wish to speak to your father.'

A burst of gutteral Arabic followed, to be met by the old man's va-cant stare and silence. Eventually, after further questioning he answered with a short quavering mumble. The judge made his decision.

'I award this man's family the sum of one hundred Rials for the dam-age the old man has suffered.'

An outraged cry broke from the son's mouth and he launched into another speech about the inestimable value of his father to his adoring family and admiring neighbours.

The judge held up his hand.

'Enough. The old man is senile. If you say any more I will fine you one hundred Rials for failing to honour and protect your father. You should not have allowed him to walk the streets of the capital area by himself. Be gone.'

Such a dismissal recalls a phenomenon I was to see many times.

Most evenings you would find one or two officers sitting morosely by themselves in the ante room, usually with a large glass in front of them. If you were unwise enough to sit down beside them then you were treated to a monologue about their family and their home and how much they missed them. As I learnt, they would keep talking about the subject as long as you kept their glass filled. 'Christ! How I hate this place!' was also a recurring theme. Ultimately, I lost patience with this self pitying behaviour for they could always give three months' notice and leave provided they had completed twelve months. Even if they hadn't, they could always do a 'runner', a practice adopted by a number of ex-patriates. The truth was that although the wire fence around BAF may have given it the appearance of a stalag, it was no prison and they could leave when they wanted to.

In those days we all signed the initial contract of three years, although it later became two, and thereafter if the contract officer wanted to stay on he applied for a one year extension. If service was satisfactory, the request was granted. Each officer had to make a conscious decision whether or not to stay for another year and, for all their nostalgic talk and yearning for the domestic and silvan delights of Britain, most of them renewed their contracts, year after year.

There was a subsequent cycle to the renewal which was entertaining if only because the performer seemed unaware of his performance. It would start with a firm declaration of intent at the beginning of the new year's service: 'That's it. Come October (or whenever) I'm packing it in. I've had enough of this bloody place.' This statement would be heard less and less as the year wore on and after six months (when you had to apply for a further year) a sheepish silence would descend. Nothing more would be heard until the start of the next year.

If you were naive enough, as I was at first, to ask the individual why he had changed his mind you usually received one of a number of quite specious reasons. Examples: the wife had bought a new car or new house, or the children were at an expensive private school. You never received the true reason, which was that he was leading a life almost completely free from hassle. No boring worries about such mundane matters as paying the bills, heating costs, servicing the car, paying the school fees, disciplining the kids and so on. There was the little woman, little house and the little family to visit every three months or so like a benevolent uncle. These visits could be even less frequent if she had been a bit of a nag on that last leave, or if George, for example, had gone into raptures over his last leave in Bangkok.

Admittedly there were drawbacks to life in Oman. There were very few English women and competition for them among the younger uniformed contract officers was ferocious, but there was unlimited alcohol at a reasonable price in the mess. The climate, although excessively hot and humid for a few months of the year, was infinitely better than the UK. So the country was an intellectual and artistic desert - but who had come to the Sultanate seeking those cultural delights?

Ultimately, I came to learn that those who voluntarily terminated their service usually did so for some quite extraneous reason. For example: threats of divorce from the little woman at home who was totally fed up with running the household by herself, illness or the death of immediate members of the family, or occasionally, ill-health in the individual himself. The sad thing about the first of the above though was that often it was not the real reason, the truth being that she had met somebody who was a lot more available than her husband. Usually then, by the time he had given in, completed his service and returned to England, home and beauty, only England was left: beauty having left home and shacked up with the more accessible male, leaving the returned warrior to find himself not only homeless but jobless. This was one of the risks of the contract officers' life, whether he was a warrant officer teaching Omanis how to handle a light machine gun or a staff officer trying to explain to a more educated Omani why he shouldn't just give that splendid job to a brother.

Sometimes I toyed with the idea of displaying a large banner outside my office: 'NEPOTISM RULES, OK.'

George Kutty was our one and only clerk in the Joint Staff. He was a Christian Indian (as opposed to a Muslim Pakistani) and a good and intelligent worker. As with so many on the sub-Continent (as we referred to India and Pakistan) his English was not as good as he thought it was, and his method of filing left a lot to be desired. I knew from past experience that it would be a waste of time to try and get George to make the mental leap to another filing system, so we needed another clerk. I did not want to replace George because he and I had had to come back into the office every day for months past to try and bring some order to the shambles that currently existed. I needed someone who was bright enough to adopt and operate a new filing and information system in the office. George could be left to cope with the more routine matters, one of which, I was amazed to learn, consisted of putting away in the secure cabinet the file trays of our redoubtable Air Force representative. As the secure cabinet stood some three feet from Harry's desk I instructed George to stop carrying out this onerous task and refer Harry to me if he complained. So far as I was concerned, there was a limit to delusions of grandeur.

It was unwise to mention within George's hearing that I was going to recruit another clerk for within minutes there was a discreet tap on my door and George was besieging me. He had a brother who was a brilliant typist, an accounts clerk and had a diploma in commercial accounting from some unpronounceable college in Southern India. His brother was undoubtably the answer to my problem. 'He does not drink, nor does he smoke ... and he goes to church every Sunday sir.' I succumbed to my weakness for awful jokes and pointed out that this practice would not be very welcome here. On a Sunday, I would want to see a clerk in the office, not at church. George ignored this. His brother was not even married so he would cause no trouble by wanting to go home for family reasons. Then he administered his *coup de gras* and thrust a bundle of papers into my hand. 'Sir. I have here all of the documents relating to my brother.'

I took them and agreed weakly to study them later.

'Thank you Sir. Oh, Thank you sir.' said George as he shuffled backwards.

I did as I promised and his credentials were most impressive. I set the recruiting wheels in motion. This was a lengthy business and included the use of a recruiting agent in Bombay, so a couple of months passed before Thomson was proudly ushered into my office by his brother.

He was quite a few years younger than George, slim with a broad pleasant face and smartly dressed in the standard clerk's uniform of white shirt and black trousers. As I also discovered during this first interview, he had a quick intelligence. I was congratualting myself on a choice well made, when in response to my question, Thomson gave me his name in full. As I wrote it down I noticed that there seemed to be no family connection between him and George. I raised the point.

'Oh no sir', said George. 'He is not my brother like we have the same mummy, but he is my brother because we come from the same village in India and we both go to the same Church.'

I sighed inwardly and thought, 'Oh God, here we go again', but on reflection I decided I was wrong. Maybe Thomson did not come from the same 'mummy' but among the thousands and thousands of Indians and Pakistanis living and working in the Sultanate, to have a friend who came from the same village and went to the same church in that vast sub-Continent, was indeed to have a brother.

I welcomed Thomson and told George to take him on the usual round of the camp offices and report back to me if there were any problems. 'Otherwise, bring him back here to start work when you have everything sorted out.' I shook Thomson's hand and settled down to work again. I remembered the old saw: 'You learn something new every day'. Obviously the 'family' extended much further than I thought, but there was much comfort in the statement: 'He is my brother,' which clearly meant a lot to George, Thomson and their colleagues.

Unknown to me, Maurice had been suffering from strain and a medical condition for some time. Running a camp the size of Bait al Falaj with a staff of not-overly bright Baluchis was not an easy game and I could appreciate a hundred and one things that would make Maurice's daily round stressful. It was sad that Thomson's arrival possibly hastened his departure.

I suppose the youngster had been with us about a month when the problem appeared. Inevitably he was junior in rank to his brother and because of this he had to share a room with five other civilian clerks. They were all Pakistanis and Muslims and they jeered and cursed him when he knelt beside his bed and said his prayers every night. There were tears in his eyes when he spoke to me and I reflected, not for the first time, that contrary to what so many young demonstrators in London proclaim, racial and religious intolerance is not the prerogative of the white races. George was willing to make space available in his room for his 'brother' and it was a simple and obvious solution. Unfortunately accommodation for the other ranks was entirely the responsibility of the camp commandant, but I was confident that Maurice would agree to the move. I telephoned him and drove round to his office with George and Thomson.

Leaving them momentarily I went into Maurice and told him they were waiting outside. Protocol had to be observed however and they were escorted in by the warrant officer who ran the camp commandant's office. Something had upset Maurice recently. That was obvious for his normally red complexion was even more fiery. With the two 'brothers' standing at a sort of civilian attention in front of his desk he barked at them in a parade ground manner. 'Well? What is it? What's your problem? Speak up.'

Southern Indians are a slight and gentle people and if you want to reduce them to nervous gabbling wrecks then shout at them in a threatening manner. As I feared, they both began talking at the same time, and seeing that this was angering Maurice even more I held up my hand and they stopped. I then told Maurice the nature of the problem while the lads' heads nodded in agreement with my account. His reaction was dramatic; excessively so.

'What!' he bellowed. 'What! They dare to interfere with a Christian boy saying his prayers!' and still shouting he leapt to his feet, put both hands below his very solid desk and hurled it over. The crash was stupendous as the desk, telephone, filing trays, books and various military impedimenta hit the floor. George and Thomson, reduced to abject fear, retreated to the corner of the office where they held each other's arms for moral support. Both knew that the British had peculiar mental processes and sometimes, even more peculiar behaviour patterns, but nothing in their combined experience had prepared them for this. I took one look at Maurice's face and waved them out of the room. They almost fell over each other in their haste to leave. As they reached the door it opened and the warrant officer who had shown them in appeared again. Carrying a pill in one hand and a glass of water in the other he approached the Camp Commandant and silently handed them to him. Equally silently Maurice swallowed the pill and the water. A few minutes later his colour returned to normal and he rose to his feet. 'Let's get out of here Alan. It's stifling.'

I followed him to the door and accompanied him on a brisk circuit of the camp's perimeter fence.

As we marched we talked. Not about the recent episode, nor of Thomson's problem but of inconsequential things. Clearly Maurice had a health problem but it was not up to me to comment or enquire about it. I had already learnt that one rarely asked personal questions of a brother officer. We returned, I had a cup of coffee in his now restored office, and went back to mine.

Ten minutes later there was a quiet tap on the door and George entered. 'Sir?' he said plaintively and looked at me for help.

'Don't worry George.' I told him. 'Major O'Brien is not a well man. It was not your fault.' He beamed, then another cloud crossed his face. 'Sir. What about Thomson?'

I made my decision for the day. I was certainly not going back to Maurice with the problem again. To hell with areas of responsibility. 'Tell Thomson to move his bed into your room George.'

The more I knew of Maurice the more I admired him. As an ex-Guards sergeant-major he made a good practical officer in SOLF - and Lord knows SOLF needed them. Horticulture was a passion of his and the thriving trees and shrubs of Bait al Falaj were like a green jewel in the arid wastes of Ruwi.

I learnt that some years earlier Maurice had owned and operated a landscape and gardening business in the West Country back home and for a number of reasons beyond his control, the venture sagged. It was then that he received a letter from one of his former officers. Would he like to join the Sultan of Oman's Land Forces as a contract officer?

Here was the income he needed, and leaving his wife Rosie to carry on the business, he took off for the Sultanate.

It was now beginning to look as if his time was running out. It was no great surprise therefore when he was formally and informally 'dined out'. It was tragic and affected us all badly when, shortly after his return, one of his children who was about to be married was killed in a driving accident.

Dave was a near neighbour of mine, and as I have already mentioned, an occasional participant in the Bamboo Bar evenings, but not a 'professional drinker' in any way. Ex-Royal Navy and an electrician by trade, he was responsible for maintaining the appalling electrical system of Bait al Falaj, a responsibility he took as lightly as possible. This was just as well, for he could not be held to account for the frequent breakdowns in the camp, often caused by such well known electrical problems as overloaded three ton lorries carrying overhead powerlines, or the Omani duty electrician not knowing how to operate the massive standby diesel generators.

By now I was becoming reasonably well organised in my room. Delicate hints and totally unprincipled foraging on my part had now provided me with two comfortable armchairs, a long, low (and battered) coffee table and a bookshelf (of sorts). I doubted if Harrods would have wanted to store them, but I was beginning the uphill struggle which would provide me with a comfortable room. I was comparatively ignorant of electrical matters. As a result, I was slightly concerned when I invited Dave for a pre-dinner drink one evening and having entered and viewed my room he said 'Christ! I don't believe it!' I looked around. The place wasn't that badly furnished and I had already gone round with my brush and pan. 'O.k. Dave,' I said. 'What's the problem?'

He explained that it wasn't really good enough to have three table lamps, one radio, one refrigerator, and one toaster running off a single wall socket via a collection of two-way and three-way plugs. Whether it offended Dave professionally or aesthetically I never did find out, but I had discovered a new method of provisioning my room. The following day a Pakistani electrician and an Omani assistant arrived and fitted power points around my room as if an electrical famine was about to strike. I was delighted.

It was inevitable that the fitting of new wall sockets would damage the wall plaster. This was soon replaced, but the repainting of the walls became a matter for Harvey, the mess manager, to arrange. Ever helpful, he assured me that he would see to the moving of the furniture and the cleanliness of the room, but having seen the painting teams operate elsewhere I felt uneasy when I drove off to the office.

By ten o'clock I had convinced myself that I ought to go back to my room to see how they were getting on.

They were, in fact, getting on very well. The leader of the team, a Pakistani, sat at my desk with a can of Fosters lager in his hand and a wide beam on his face. On my bed sat his three Omani assistants similarly enjoying themselves. I looked at the *tableau* and could only manage a feeble, 'How's it going?'

44

'Oh very fine Sir.' said the team leader. 'We have finished our painting and now we are having the party.'

'The party?'

'Yes sir. The party,' came the firm reply.

'Oh good,' was my feeble parting shot and I retreated, closing the door.

What the hell's going on? I asked myself. I could hardly believe the total lack of embarrassment on the part of the unbidden guests. In fact, I was pretty sure that if I stayed a few more minutes, they would have invited me to join them. There must be more to this than meets the eye. Normally, they would not dream of touching anything that belonged to one of the officers. Where the hell was Harvey? I marched over to the officers' mess.

He was sitting in his office, relaxed and enjoying a cup of coffee. 'Hello Alan. How's it going?' came the cheery greeting. His smile slowly disappeared as I told him. 'You know they're forbidden to touch alcohol unless they're officers. If the ROP catch them outside they'll go straight to prison.'

By now, Harvey had a stricken look on his face. 'Oh God! It's probably my fault', he moaned.

'What do you mean?'

'I've got to stop them.' He rose to his feet: 'I gave them a hand to shift some of the furniture in your room before they started. When we moved your fridge the door came open. I saw some cans of beer in there.'

'So?'

'I made what I thought was a joke and said to them: 'you'll be able to have a nice party when you've finished'.'

I sat down and grinned to myself as Harvey disappeared down the corridor. I remembered a story I'd heard a couple of weeks ago. It was about a British contract officer who had been sacked and ordered back to the UK by Saleem al Ghazali last summer. It seemed that the officer had had one of the engineers in to repair his air conditioner. It was a steaming hot day and before he went to work he opened up his refrigerator, gestured to the contents and said: 'Have a drink if you get thirsty.' Perhaps naively, he assumed that as the man was a Muslim, he would only help himself to a Coca Cola or a lemonade. In fact he drank three cans of beer, drove straight out of the camp into another car, was arrested and finished up in prison for two months. In his defence, he said he had been given the drink by an English officer. The police reported it to Saleem al Ghazali and the officer received his marching orders. I heard that he was reprieved only at the last minute after some fairly high level intervention and the Under Secretary had been convinced that the invitation extended to the workman had been made in good non-alcoholic faith. Judging by the speed of Harvey's recent departure he had heard the story too.

Shortly after the workmen's party I became embroiled in the electrics again. Those who know me well would agree that I am not subject to attacks of hypochondria, but during the following two weeks I began to wonder whether I had been smitten by some exotic tropical disease. It seemed to me that every time I took a shower I developed a pleasant

45

tingling in my fingertips. At first this slightly intrigued me then, as the tingling grew in intensity I began to get a mite concerned. Then came the day when the tingling grew into a slight jolt whenever I touched the hot water tap. Slow on the uptake I might be, but I knew an electrical shock when I experienced one. I mentioned it to Dave and he sent along one of his men.

To cut a long story short, the tingling disappeared, then reappeared then disappeared and so on until the day arrived when I experienced what I can best describe as a bang from one of the shower taps. Clad only in a towel I marched along to Dave's room. He forestalled me. He had been taking a shower as well and had also been attacked. From what he said I gathered that there was now an officially recognised serious electrical fault in the system. The total effort of the Electrical Department of Bait al Falaj would be devoted to its location and eradication.

The effort was successful. Some wiring, adjacent to the water pipes, and even more ancient than most, was replaced. It was a month or so afterwards and I was recounting this story to one of our oldest inhabitants in the ante-room. A reflective look crossed his face. 'Good God! That reminds me,' he said. 'Can't quite remember now. Could have been four or five years ago. One of the blokes living in your bungalow was found dead in his shower. They said it was a heart attack.' He paused and took a sip from his glass. 'Makes you think though, doesn't it? Wonder if it was your shower?'

I shivered a little. 'I hope not. I'd hate to think of sharing my shower with a damp spirit.'

My companion wisely ignored my feeble joke. 'Wish I could remember his name.'

We both sipped a silent toast to whoever it was.

Occasionally, His Highness Said Faher would chair a meeting of the Defence Council. It was an event he looked forward to with little relish because some of its members (CSOLF, CSOAF, CSON, CJS & CRGR) were partisan and argumentative to a remarkable degree, even for senior officers. Some matters however, such as changes to personnel regulations, had to be given joint service approval before they could be implemented. It was just as well that these meetings were infrequent because, although the venue was always His Highness' conference room, discussion and argument about the date and time was nearly as tiresome as the discussion and argument at the meeting itself.

In the past I had attended many similar conferences, and reading the minutes of the Defence Committee it was abundantly clear that what was lacking was somebody with the rank to knock a few heads together. It was unreasonable to expect His Highness to do so, for discussion was frequently about items common to all the services but of little concern to him and, although he had the rank, he had to rely on inter-service agreement before he could grant his approval. Such agreement was remarkably rare and often the meetings would deteriorate into vehement arguments of such a nature that one boggled that such a minor matter could generate such a large amount of emotion. A typical if trivial example was on the subject of 'local leave'.

I had no idea who wrote this item of total confusion, but part of my contract stated that:

'For each year of service the Officer shall be entitled to:

(i) 60 days annual leave on full pay, etc, etc...

(ii) 7 days' local leave, which may be taken anywhere, without entitlement to free travel.'

Nobody knew what had prompted sub-sub-para 13 (a) (ii) in the contract, but the concept of 'local leave, which may be taken anywhere,' raised some doubts about the intelligence of the drafter, if nothing else.

When this subject came up, the approach of the individual committee members was typical.

The Land Forces Headquarters staff had a very relaxed lifestyle and their working week was remarkable for its brevity. Because of this CSOLF was also totally relaxed about the subject. Doubtless his British contract officers would take what local leave they wanted to whatever the regulations said.

The diminutive CSOAF ran true to form. I had heard that he insisted on knowing everything that went on in his air force, even to down to vetting spare seat fill-up (indulgence) passengers on his BAS 111 trooping aircraft. It was hardly surprising therefore that, so far as he was concerned, nobody was going to tell him what local leave his British contract officers could take. He and he alone would decide that.

The Commander SON was well into the Silent Service tradition. A slim and professional Royal Navy Commodore on loan from the UK Services, (as were CSOLF and CSOAF), he returned to his parent service shortly after the meeting and I never did quite catch his name nor his going. But his successor came from the same mould. They were both proof of the advantages of rotating the Commanders' posts every two or three years, for they did not regard SON as their own private navy, unlike CSOLF and CSOAF who had been in the Sultanate for too long.

CSON's attitude to local leave was also in the best of Royal Navy traditions; terse, tight-lipped comments which left you wondering whether they understood the question or, for that matter, cared very much what the question was.

The Commander of the Royal Guard Regiment was an ex-ranker from one of the ex-colonies. He was single-minded in his dedication to protecting the life of Sultan Qaboos and rightly, very highly regarded. Inevitably however, he was a man who tended, as a matter of principle, to take the opposite viewpoint to the other Commanders. As a bachelor with no home to go to, so to speak, he thought all of the British contract officers got far too much leave anyway. 'Get rid of local leave and cut down the annual leave' was his war cry. 'I don't allow my officers to take all of their leave anyhow. They get too much as it is,' etc. The other Commanders tried to conceal their horror at this heresy.

The meeting had been going on for an hour and a half and His Highness began to fidget. This local leave. What was the problem? It seemed that they did not want more, in fact, they wanted to stop it. This leave was a gift from His Majesty, so only Allah knew why they wanted to reject it. But it was a matter affecting British contract officers so it was up to the Commanders to agree among themselves. It was lunchtime and he was getting bored. It was under AOB at the end of the agenda so it couldn't be important. 'Alright,' he said as CRGR wound down. 'I understand that none of you are happy about local leave, so we will stop it.' He forebore to add, 'God knows why'. The members of the committee looked at each other. Yes, I suppose that's what we've been saying, was their unspoken thought.

After my years in the UK Civil Service, many of them spent negotiating with overseas trade unions, I was conditioned to two fundamental concepts: 1) you never gave anything to employees until you had to, and 2) you never ever took anything away from current employees.

Our Director of Personnel was an ex-RAF Group Captain who had devoted his life to the minutiae of Queen's Regulations and who seemed to be totally unaware of the concept of 'employees retained rights'. Within three days of that meeting and his Highness' decision I was advised that I had lost my right to local leave. I had never taken any and had no intention of taking any. Indeed, at that point in my career as a contract officer I would not have known what to do with local leave. Nevertheless, like anybody else in that situation I was miffed at having the privilege withdrawn in such an arbitrary fashion.

A few days later I had my first experience of a petition. Any Omani who has a grievance, justified or not, may appeal to the head of his tribe, village, company, organisation; whatever he feels he belongs, or is emotionally attached to. So far as I was concerned, in most cases they were soldiers who, having exhausted all of the usual channels, were appealing to the head Omani in the Sultan of Oman's Land Forces, in this case, Colonel Hassan Ehsan Naseeb. Sometimes however, the petitioners were not soldiers but relatives of soldiers, these occasionally being aged tribesmen who had walked God knows how many miles to Bait al Falaj in order to present the case.

In this case, as I recall it, the elder was unhappy about his son's unsuccessful efforts to join the Land Forces. I happened to be in the hallway when he arrived and went through the ritual greetings:

'As-salaam alaykum.'
'Wa alaykum as-salaam.'
'Kayf haalak?'
'Al-Hamdu lillah.'

He seemed very old. His dish-dash was filthy and he wasn't much cleaner himself, while his white stubble needed a razor badly. I reminded myself that it was his country and if you lived up in the jebel or out in the sands it wasn't easy to appear formally dressed on such occasions. I announced him and showed him into Colonel Hassan who rose from his desk and greeted the tatty old trooper as if he was a friend of many years. Clearly, age carried its own privileges and I couldn't help but feel admiration for the courtesy that had been displayed.

Our aged visitor presented his case, accepted a cup of coffee from Hassan and left on his fifty mile journey back into the Interior. He was happy now. He and done all that he could for his son.

Faqir Mohammed was a recent arrival among the Joint Staff drivers. He was tall for a Baluchi, had one of those very swarthy complexions which suggested he was permanently in need of a shave and did not possess the ever-ready grin that most of his brothers did. This was probably one of the reasons why I suspected his sincerity when, after a few weeks, he appeared in my office, saluted and handed me a grubby piece of paper.

Peering through the greasy thumb prints I saw that it was a telegram addressed to him. It came from his village in Baluchistan (so he said), it had been recently despatched and bore a ludicrously simple message.

'Wife serious,' it said.

My poor sense of humour came into action. 'What is she serious about?' I asked. He wisely chose to ignore this attempt to sidetrack him.

'My wife is serious Sir. I must go home,' he replied and his face crumpled to suggest that he was undergoing serious marital and emotional distress.

I decided to jolly him along. 'Come along Faqir. We don't know what's wrong with her. We've got to know a bit more than this before we can send you home on compassionate leave. I will speak to the camp commandant and he will tell me what is to be done.' I told him to wait outside and picked up the telephone.

Maurice O'Brien had left a few months earlier and I spoke to his successor Peter Greaves. Younger than Maurice, he had a similar background in that he had been a SNCO in the British Army, served with distinction during the Dhofar War and was, like his predecessor, a good practical SOLF officer. He listened to my explanation and laughed. 'Sounds like the usual try-on, but we'll have to give it a fair go.'

'How do we find out if it's genuine?'

'We have to signal our depot in Gwadur in Pakistan and get them to contact the headman in Faqir's village.'

'How long will that take?'

'God knows. Three days, maybe more. I'll send off a signal straight away anyhow.'

'Thanks Peter. I'll just have to tell Faqir to hang on then?'

"fraid so Alan.'

When I told Faqir, his expression denoted even more distress.

'My wife, Sir,' he moaned and twisted his beret in his hands.

'I'm sorry Faqir.' I picked up the grubby piece of paper and gently shook it as I explained. 'This tells us nothing.'

'But Sir. It said she is serious.'

'I know. But serious about what, or serious with what?' I could see that I had lost him and gave him back his telegram. 'Come back tomorrow. Maybe we will have some news.'

His shoulders slumped, he raised his hand in a half-hearted salute and left the room silently.

Peter had said that he would tell me immediately he got a reply, but I found that facing Faqir's accusing eyes every morning was beginning to tell on me. On the third day I witnessed a display of distraught anxiety that had me near breaking point but I held firm. 'Come back tomorrow.'

On the fourth day my nerve began to go and I rang Peter and asked, 'How much longer do you think it'll be?'

'No idea Alan,' he replied cheerfully and explained. 'I signal Gwadur. They send a telegram to the nearest town that's got a post office and they deliver it to the village headman. Could even take a week or two. God knows where Faqir's village is. Probably miles away up in the mountains.'

'But I can't keep the poor bugger hanging around day after day. He was nearly in tears this morning.'

'Let him go then.'

It took a minute for this to sink in. 'But the chances are that the while thing's a fiddle.'

'Probably,' was Peter's response. 'But as you said yourself, you can't keep him waiting around day after day. Think how you'd feel if his wife was really seriously ill and died before he got there.'

That settled it. My nerve broke. 'Thanks Peter. I'll send him down to you.'

I told Faqir to report to the camp commandant's office and arrange his flight to Gwadur and his face broke into a wide grin. 'Oh thank you, Sir, thank you, Sir.' He grasped my hands in both of his and shook them up and down. Then his shoulders snapped back as he stood upright and gave me the smartest salute that I had ever received from him. The sudden transformation from a broken, defeated soldier into the pride of the regiment was quite remarkable.

A few more days passed and Faqir had left my mind when the phone rang and I lifted it to find Peter at the other end.

'We've heard from Peter's village headman,' he said and I could almost hear the laugh in his voice.

'Oh good. What does he say Peter?'

'You're not going to believe this,' came the reply and he chuckled.

'Go on.'

'Wife very serious.'

'What?'

'Wife very serious,' he repeated.

'What the hell's that supposed to mean?'

'I've no idea,' he said, and as he burst out laughing, I had to join in.

'I've just had a thought though,' he added.

'What's that?'

'Faqir would be at home by now. He probably wrote this for the headman.'

It was about three weeks later when the subject came up again. We were having a lunchtime beer when Peter spoke. 'That driver of yours. Faqir.'

'Yes?'

'I called for his personal file and it arrived today.'

'Go on. Tell me the worst.'

'His wife was serious last year. Like all the Baluchis, he goes home once a year and six months later she gets serious.'

'I can just imagine what she gets serious about,' was my coarse reply.

Peter grinned and nodded. 'You've got to admire his style though. With both of us fairly new in the post he probably thought it was too good an opportunity to miss.'

He continued. 'One thing's for sure, though.'

'What's that?'

'He got away with it this time, but she can get as bloody serious as she likes next year, and it won't do him any good.'

A few days later, Harvey the mess manager telephoned me. I had chatted to him the evening before and found him entertaining company. His brother operated some sort of stylish restaurant and club in the foothills of the mountains near Conway in North Wales and Harvey couldn't wait for his contract to end next year so that he could join his brother in the business. I didn't realise then that it was a dream I was to hear every year for the next four years as he, like many contract officers, replaced the day to day monotony of life in Bait al Falaj with a fantasy of the exotic and exciting life they would lead when they left the Sultanate of Oman.

Essentially Harvey was a cheerful man whose dark good looks belied his age. He had a line of patter that was to earn him the soubriquet 'Suave Harve' and, typically, in the manner of a second-hand car salesman about to flog me an aged Ford, he expressed surprise and sorrow that I hadn't yet got a batman. He became even more surprised and hurt when I turned down the one he was offering.

'But who's going to clean out your room?'

'I will.'

'What about your laundry?'

'There's a laundry in Ruwi.'

When he finally accepted that I was not interested, the reason for his offer came out. A number of officers were of similar mind to me and the Omani staff in the camp labour office were unhappy that these posts, which could be filled by countless brothers, uncles and cousins, remained unfilled.

Our problem was that, unlike the uniformed officers who could take a soldier, already possessing some basic intelligence and military training and make him into a batman, we had to take a person who was virtually unemployable elsewhere.

A lot of them were old. No, let's be honest. A lot of them were very old. Many had glaucoma or incipient glaucoma.

Finally, many were making their first contact with such mundane articles as toothbrushes, bedsheets, shoe polish, toilet paper and showers, not to mention such exotica as radios and refrigerators. If you took one of these men, who was probably straight from the Interior, you had a massive training task on your hands; a task which was likely to be wasted for a number of reasons.

Some were literally untrainable, some became quickly bored with the tedious routine of rising early and going to work six days a week, most were never as reliable as an alarm clock at calling you at the same time every morning and many, for good tribal reasons, never really grasped the concept of private property as we understood it. Toilets, beds, toothbrushes and razors were all fair game. If half an hour's dusting tired you out what could be more sensible than to lie down on the nearest bed; if your bowels were about to move, why not use the lavatory immediately available? Admittedly, it was uncomfortable having to squat on that stupid round seat with the hole in the middle, but it could easily be done with bare feet.

The batman game was a heavily loaded lottery. One colleague told me of how he struck it lucky on his fourth batman. Another of giving up after two unsuccessful attempts. Yet another of returning to his room one morning to find his batman entertaining his friends over coffee - his coffee.

A few months after my arrival I learnt that I had been an object of envy among some of the mess members. Unbeknown to me, I had in fact bypassed two of the hurdles that most contract officers had had to surmount. Traditionally when you first arrived you were given a used car for your personal use and, after a year or so, graduated to the waiting list for a new car. In my case ignorance was bliss for I was quite unaware of covetous glances as I drove my glistening new Toyota. I was also oblivious of the fact that many of my colleagues who had arrived before me were driving bangers. Because of the lack of sealed roads and the salt and dust-laden atmosphere, banger status was achieved much more quickly than in Europe; depreciation usually being assessed at five years.

The other hurdle that I had yet to jump arose from the fact that I was living in what was classified as a 'stone bait' and had been from the day I arrived.

Scattered among the stone-walled bungalows surrounding the mess were a number of Portacabins. New arrivals apparently went into a Portacabin and, under a system known only to God and Harvey, graduated eventually into one (or more) of the rooms in the bungalow. I, however, had gone straight into a stone bait.

When I heard this and thought of my room and its furnishings I recoiled mentally from the idea of second class accommodation in the Portacabins. In fact, although badly insulated against noise and heat, they arrived well equipped with built-in furniture and were certainly as comfortable as my room. But to many of my colleagues it was clear that I had some sort of pull. With hindsight I realised that I did: I worked for Brigadier Thwaites.

One other problem about accommodation was that the only senior non-commissioned officers' (sergeants') mess in Bait al Falaj was occupied by Baluchis, Pakistanis, Indians and some Omanis and, unfortunately at that time, a few British contract officers whose jobs only merited SNCO status.

In spite of any mutterings that present society might make about racial prejudice, it was considered (justifiably in my opinion) quite unreasonable to expect a Brit (to use a racist expression), to live in a non-alcoholic mess and eat curry at every meal. They were therefore made honorary members of the officers' mess.

That title in itself aroused considerable discussion for there were many (mostly ex-officers), who argued that it should not be called an officers' mess. I had no strong views on the matter, but it was clear that all of Harvey's vigour and enthusiasm could not make up for his lack of professional training and knowledge. Whilst he could organise a good party, his handling of more mundane matters such as staff discipline, cleanliness and maintenance of furniture and fittings left a lot to be desired.

There were also times when I wondered whether Harvey saw the mess as a training ground for his brother's club in Wales, for he would often announce that 'we' had made a substantial profit the month before. As the mess should have been operating on a non-profit basis and nobody saw any improvements occuring, this impressed nobody. But it kept Harvey happy in a tedious and wearing job and was a small price to pay for having a mess manager who was cheerful.

One group of mess members who used the dining facilities with devoted regularity were the Egyptians. I had one good friend among them, Maurice Sousou, who worked as an interpreter for His Highness. A cultured and talented man, he had learnt the rudiments of his profession translating film sub-titles in Cairo and was very entertaining company. The rest of the Egyptians, mostly employed in the translating field, were a remarkable and overweight bunch who seemed to possess a deep-set racial memory of some long past famine. If you were at all sensitive by nature, it was not a good idea to sit near them for they would gather everything that was set out on the tables or buffet and heap it on to their plates. Then the mechanical shovelling would start.

It was no surprise to hear that at lunchtime Harvey had stopped the stewards from bringing round the dishes and salvers of meat and vegetables to the diners, for any one of them would try to empty an eighteen inch dish of carved meat on to his own plate.

Two aspects of this were noteworthy however. One was that, unsurprisingly, our translators were grossly overweight; the other was that Harvey had changed over to individual servings, not because their eating habits were appropriate to Cold Comfort Farm, but because they were ruining his catering profits.

One pathetic outcome to this scene however, was the news one morning that one of them had died during the night, apparently from choking on his own vomit.

It was about then that I enjoyed an evening of Harry's hospitality and recalled Stan's comments about the difference between the major's and the lieutenant colonel's living standards. It was also during that evening that I gained my first insight into Arab commercial operations. Stan was absolutely right. The accommodation provided for half colonels and their families was luxurious by any standards. Three and four bedroomed apartments and villas with the appropriate staff to cook, clean, drive, serve drinks and meals. It was no wonder that a lot of majors, squadron leaders and lieutenant commanders devoted most of their working days to scrabbling up that extra rung.

It was when I asked about the building which housed Malcolm, Harry, Ken and other senior officers that I began to understand something of the Arab's approach to commerce.

The building itself was known as either the 'Kodak Building' (because of the largest shop on the ground floor) or the 'Said Faher Building' because of the owner. To do business in Oman, any foreign company had to have one or more Omani nationals owning at least 51 per cent of the company's shares. Among the many firms in which His Highness Said

Faher had a majority share was a very large building consortium called Joannu & Paraskevaides (Oman) Ltd. J&P were a Cyprus-based that I knew well. Large and reliable, they had expanded away from their native island. There was even a J&P (London) Ltd.

There was an urgent need for accommodation in the early days of the Sultanate's growth, particularly for the growing numbers of European specialists and advisers, therefore it was highly practical of J&P (Oman) to build, among its many undertakings, a block of luxury apartments outside the military camp of Bait al Falaj. It was equally practical of His Highness the Deputy Prime Minister for Defence to rent them to the Ministry of Defence as accommodation for military officers. Although this would undoubtedly produce much tooth sucking in the UK, it was an eminently sensible arrangement by local mores. Another aspect of Omani life of which I was becoming increasingly aware was that, at this point in the country's progress, there weren't many individuals and families capable of becoming major shareholders in commerce. Inevitably, those with the power, money and influence to send their children to be educated abroad during the stagnant years of Sultan Said bin Taimur, were the ones who were now beginning to reap the benefit. 'Unto every one that hath, shall be given,' as the Bible says.

Chapter 3

As the months passed I came to know more personalities outside the purview of the Joint Staff and the Bait al Falaj mess and, inevitably, I began to divide the British contract officer in Oman into types. It seemed to me that there were three of these, each well defined by age and quality.

The young officer was good value and, in the main, seemed either to have come to the Sultanate as a disciple of Lawrence in search of adventure, or because of some minor 'naughty' in the British Forces. One example I found entertaining was of a young army officer who had given way to alcoholic temptation and stolen the wheels of a mayoral car when His Worship was an official guest at a mess function.

The older officer had already enjoyed a full career in the British services and loath to cease working at the comparatively young age of fifty plus, had come to the Sultanate bringing his valuable knowledge and experience with him.

It is difficult though to generalise about the middle group and its performance. In this category (the thirties and forties), were those officers who any regiment in the British Army would be proud to possess, plus those who were either totally incompetent or totally idle. These latter had diverse backgrounds; some who had left the British Forces in mid-career because they could see no further advancement ahead (in other words, the no-hopers) and some who had served in the Dhofar during the incursions and had stayed on afterwards. In this group were several who, having rested on their laurels since then, had become known, perhaps unkindly, as the 'Dhofar Deadbeats'.

It was noticeable that most of these existed in the Headquarters of the Land Forces, perhaps understandably, because whatever their standards the Air Force and the Navy usually demanded some degree of technical knowledge and competence whereas many regiments only demanded that a chap be an officer *per se* .

Why were these ex-Dhofar people retained? As far as I could see there were two reasons. One was that those who had participated formed a typically discreet British 'club' and looked after each others' interests; the other was that the Omanis, particularly the Sultan, had a strong sense of loyalty towards those who had fought for them. There is little doubt however, that it was a bad mistake to assume that an officer who had valiantly defended a sangar in the jebel would be a competent and well-motivated staff officer. In fact, the more I came into contact with the HQSOLF staff, the more convinced I became that it would have been better, in many cases, to have given these officers a handsome golden handshake and sent them home. Many of them, I concluded, were in the category of that officer whose annual report read: 'This officer spends much of the time pushing at doors marked 'Pull'.'

I discussed this possibly harsh assessment with Stan one evening. He agreed in general, but pointed out that I had overlooked one important factor and this was, 'the inefficient recruiting the incompetent'. He considered that too much of the Land Forces recruitment was done by word of mouth from those who, in themselves, were not of the brightest.

'And don't forget the five Dees,' he added. He laughed at my bewildered look and listed them.

'Debt, Divorce, Drink, Drugs, and Deviation. Scratch most British contract officers out here and you'll find one of those behind him,' he concluded.

It was also about this time that I had my first experience of the 'Pakistani Mafia'. Though difficult to imagine the small wiry hill tribesmen as black hatted and suited members of the 'Cosa Nostra,' nevertheless I soon realised the connection. Information about anything which affected the Pakistani members of the MoD or the SAF travelled throughout Oman with the speed of jungle drums and from previous occurences there was little doubt that the same fierce tribal loyalty also existed.

There had been an accidentally fatal shooting on one of the rifle ranges near Salalah in the south but, as we learnt, there was some doubt as to whether it had been an accident. According to the terse wording of the signal the victim had been lying on his stomach in the prone firing position when he was shot in the stomach. Bux was one of his names.

Less than 24 hours later, one of the privates (Jundis) stationed at Bait al Falaj camp disappeared. This was an uncommon happening for there was little to encourage desertion in the Sultanate and a Baluchi would find it almost impossible to make the journey back to his home without the approval and assistance of the Army Movements organisation.

The following day the Brigadier's driver went sick and Imam Bux was deputized to act in his place and drive CJS to a meeting. About four hours later, Sarah received an irate telephone call from Peter Thwaites. In brief, he had finished his meeting and there was no car waiting. Where the hell was Imam Bux? She asked if she should send another car and driver but the Brigadier demurred, for it was half an hour's drive from BAF to NAM.

'I'll give the little bugger another quarter of an hour.'

Nothing more was heard from him and he arrived just as the office was closing. It seemed that shortly after his call, Imam Bux had driven up accompanied by two other Baluchi Jundis.

Wide grins and many apologies for being late, Sir. The Brigadier silently climbed into his Mercedes and the two Jundis climbed out.

The following morning CJS had cause for further complaint. He had gone to put a parcel into his car and discovered blood on the floor of the boot. Apologies again from Imam Bux as he cheerfully cleaned up the mess. By general agreement nobody asked where the blood had come from or pursued the matter any further.

I thought I had seen nature at its most violent when a typhoon had destroyed all our squadron's aircraft in India during the war; lorries trundling along with nobody at the wheel, forty gallon oil drums passing like giant cannon balls three feet above the ground and finally, that moment when we, the crew, abandoned our attempt to hold down the roof of our bungalow and watched it soar away above the denuded palm trees. A few nights after my conversation with Stan however I witnessed a different display; different but even more destructive.

It was about half past three in the morning when I awoke, feeling strangely disorientated and wondering what was happening. The room was daylight bright but there was a strange uncertainty about the light, changing every few seconds from the light of a grey dawn to arc-light brilliance. There was no sound, just this flickering luminosity. It was impossible to ignore so I sat up, swung my legs out of the bed and onto the floor: and into six inches of water. As if to reassure myself I reached out for the bedside lamp but there was no electricity. This was hardly surprising. I had already learnt that it needed very little to upset the BAF power supply.

I must have gazed at the lake for a few minutes before I began to wonder where it had come from. There was no sound of running water from the toilet.

I looked around. There was a waterfall descending from the curtain. I waded across the room and pulled back the curtain and was immediately soaked. Over the years the wooden window frames had dried out so much that there was a quarter inch gap between them and the wall. Through this gap the rain was jetting, hitting the curtain and cascading on to the floor.

Even now, my strongest memory of that night is the flickering light and the silence, broken only by the waterfall, while outside the most appalling storm was raging. As a navigator I had learnt quite a lot about meteorology, but I had never met up with this phenomenon before; ongoing lightning without the usual accompanying thunder.

Ten minutes later the room began to darken and I decided that there was nothing to be gained by sitting on the edge of my bed like Canute. In those temperatures, without night clothes, such crises were simplified so I lifted my feet out of the water, dried them on the bottom end of the sheet I was lying on and went back to sleep.

When I woke at first light, the lake was only marginally deeper as I splashed over to the toilet. I had better go round to the mess to see if I could borrow a couple of stewards to help me bail out the room. What I should have suspected became immediately obvious as I walked across the rough, stony and now slimy ground; I was not the only one who had suffered during the night. The collapsed pylons and broken lines told their own story and, as I walked down the side of the mess I found myself climbing over large broken pieces of stone balustrade. They seemed familiar and I glanced up at the wide gap in the ornamental parapet that surrounded the flat roof of the mess. The TV aerial had been secured to one of the balusters and when it was blown down it brought many of its comrades with it. I carried on into the mess to find Harvey in a self-congratulatory mood.

'The mess got off lightly,' he said. 'The power's gone, but that's all.'

'Not quite,' I replied and took him outside and showed him the balustrade.

'Not too bad,' was his comment, 'soon have that fixed.' I was to recall that remark a year later. The aerial went back up on the roof that day and the broken bits of parapet were taken away a couple of days later. Twelve months later however, the gap in the parapet was still there. It was when I asked Harvey about using a couple of stewards that I began to realise that the storm may have been much more severe than I had suspected. All of the stewards, Jundis and labourers were needed by the camp commandant. It seemed that the office of His Highness, built on the same raised bank of the camp wadi as the office of the Joint Staff, was in some danger. Indeed, as I discovered later that morning, the collapsing wadi banks had buried some of his cars, and a few others left overnight in the wadi bed had disappeared in the flash flood which had followed the storm.

A couple of hours later I decided that I had done all I could to make my room habitable again and so I drove down to the office. It was not all that easy for the roads were covered in silt, foliage and pebbles washed down from high ground. Peter's lovely white-painted stones which used to mark the camp roads, the car parks and the helipad had all gone - a few pale khaki boulders the only evidence that they had ever existed.

I was the first at the office and although it had appeared alright externally, it was a very different story when I entered. Collapsed ceilings, saturated floors and daylight showing through the roof. I looked around me and decided that I had had quite enough. I had already done all of the drying and cleaning out I was going to do for the day. This lot could wait until the clerks, the cleaners and the drivers arrived. Supervision was the name of the game from now on.

I walked around the office and made some notes while waiting for the staff to arrive. There wasn't too much damage, except to the shrubbery, but the concrete facing of the mound on which the office stood was showing some ominous cracks. The quicker they were examined professionally the better. I returned to the front door and stood gazing at what had been a dry river bed ever since I had arrived at Bait al Falaj. If ever there was a raging torrent I muttered to myself, this was definitely an example. A pale brown, speckled with a creamy yellow froth, it raced through the wadi and very effectively sealed off the few married quarters bungalows on the opposite side. Eventually, the occupants had to get out of the camp through a break in the perimeter fence and walk round on the road, but this was not without hazard, for the road crossed the same wadi bed and the number of stalled and abandoned cars told their own story.

Standing there however, I found that it was the debris borne along by the flood that fascinated me. At first, branches, palm fronds, then tree trunks, palm trees (some of which must have stood for eighty years or more), stones, boulders, bedding, mattresses, furniture and household waste that must have been dumped years before. As the flood continued to roll however, a grimmer picture began to emerge; dead dogs, donkeys, a young camel and finally, a shining and slowly turning corpse swept through Bait al Falaj.

It was then that I suspected that the storm had inflicted a lot more damage than was evident in our small corner of the Capital Area. So it turned out to be. Factories, workshops, houses, farms and stretches of new roads were bombarded by trees, boulders and mud and swept away as millions of tons of water raced down from the Hajar Range and across the narrow coastal plain out to sea. Forty people died that night, trapped in their houses or their cars. Most pathetic of all was the news of the young baby asleep in her cot who was rescued as she was swept through Seeb village; the sole survivor of a family of seven.

The rescue and rehabilitation work carried out by all of the Sultan's Armed Forces and the Royal Oman Police was a matter for some pride, but some of the damage would take many years to repair or replace. In particular, the roads had to be redesigned and rebuilt to cope with the possibility of another storm of such ferocity - Insh'allah indeed.

There was an interesting aftermath. SOAF had three BAC 111s used mainly for commuting between the southern capital Salalah and the national capital Muscat. They were based at Seeb Airport and were damaged severely during the storm, two of them having been blown on to earth revetments. Saleem al Ghazali was incensed, claiming that none of the civilian aircraft had been damaged because they had been secured. Why had SOAF not taken similar precautions after the storm warning? Had SOAF Ops Room received the storm warning? There seemed to be considerable confusion. The Under Secretary demanded an enquiry; CSOAF in an audience shortly afterwards got the enquiry quashed. As a result, Saleem al Ghazali, no admirer of the British, disliked them even more.

I have been driving in the United Kingdom and abroad for some forty years, survived eight years living in Cyprus and even a visit to Beirut when it was an international playground and possessed the most lethal taxi drivers in the world. None of this experience, however, prepared me for Omani driving. Whenever I encountered stupidly reckless behaviour at the wheel I treated it with the caution and contempt it deserved. I had also learnt to be grateful for any courtesy and consideraton shown to me by other drivers. However, it was the quite remarkable mixture of the two that I found difficult to adjust to whilst in the Oman. The bad driving was probably based on a blend of ignorance and the Insh'allah concept, but it was certainly in the Sultanate that I met the one of the most dangerous examples of reckless driving that I have met anywhere.

I was making the routine journey between BAF and MAM along the dual carriageway, Qaboos Street, which is intercepted by a number of roundabouts. Driving on the right (which we did) or even on the left, it is not a good idea to enter a roundabout off the outside lane if you intend to encircle it. Presumably, this taxi driver was unaware of the fact.

I firmly believe that as your driving experience grows so you develop an instinct which warns you about other drivers. Certainly as my car (next to the median strip) and the taxi approached the roundabout neck instinct made me break violently, at the same time as the taxi lurched past my bonnet on his way round the roundabout. A glimpse of the white turbanned driver hunched over his wheel and the terrified face of the passenger made it plain that he knew the rules of the road, even if his driver didn't.

The other side of the coin however was the extreme courtesy often displayed by the Omani driver, in some ways nearly as disconcerting as the previous near miss. It would often occur like this. Driving back nose to tail from the Aqua Club, for example, traffic maintaining an even speed and the road clear ahead as far as the Watteyeh Stadium roundabout, there would suddenly be a succession of squeals as the cavalcade locked its brakes. Your immediate panic is to avoid hitting the car in front then, safely stopped, you peer ahead to see what caused the mini crisis. A bent, white haired old man in a grubby dish dash waits patiently at the side of the road. Probably, he wishes to cross the four lanes of traffic to examine the gardens around the stadium. He does not understand the traffic lights at the roundabout and that it is much safer to use them. However, one driver recognises the old chap's problem and, oblivious to the hundred cars behind, stops, smiles and courteously beckons the ancient across the road.

In a way, it was a relief to see this practice lessening when I left four years later. Not only was it a good recipe for a four or five car shunt, but I often used to wonder how many pedestrians, encouraged by a smiling driver, used to wake up in hospital later to realise that nobody had yet stopped in the other three lanes.

Sometimes, the courtesy went so far that it bordered on the farcical. Driving from Ruwi to BAF camp you went down a sealed two-way road and turned left on a dirt road into the camp entrance. There were no traffic lights at that junction so one waited for the traffic on the opposite side of the road to lessen sufficiently for you to make the turn. On this occasion I was stationary and waiting quite happily for the one car on the other side to go past when there was a sudden shriek of brakes and it slid forward half-way into a skid. It stopped inches from my bonnet, the driver flashed me a wide beam and waved me into my turn. I backed away from him and gave a nervous wave of doubtful thanks before complying.

Even the dangerous driving however could have its lighter moments. One young Omani Land Forces officer speeding home towards the Capital Area became irritated by the slow progress of the large black Mercedes in the outer lane. There was no response to his violent hooting and eventually he overtook on the inside lane, mouthing obscenities and making rude and violent gestures at the car's occupants.

If the young man had only thought for a moment he would have realised that only certain types of Omanis were chauffeur-driven in large black Mercedes. But he didn't think until a few days later when he was called in front of his commanding officer. A letter had been received at HQSOLF. His Excellency, the Governor of the Capital would, if an apology was forthcoming from Lieutenant X, restrain his anger at his rudenesss and dangerous driving and insist on only a minor punishment: one hundred Rials fine and the loss of his driving licence for one year. If an apology was not forthcoming, however, would the commanding officer then please put Lieutenant X into Rumais prison for three months.

I loved it. Mainly because His Excellency had done something that I had often longed to do.

It is probably true to say that in most countries, the vehicles on its roads give a fair indication of the sort of society that exists, and this was certainly true in the Sultanate. Over 99 percent of the cars had arrived since Sultan Qaboos assumed power in 1970 so one rarely saw the aged vehicles that existed in Europe. Large and dusty semi-trailers showed the dependence of the country on road-carried imports through the United Arab Emirates (UAE) to the north and the many battered taxis reflected the lack of skill of their mostly aged drivers.

Occasionally, however, one saw a car that displayed speed, luxury and wealth in every line. Porsche, Ferrari, Aston Martin and so on, and behind the wheel the driver would invariably portray the same attributes. These were the young scions of the wealthier and more influential families.

Qaboos himself owned several high performance cars and it was said that he burned off occasional frustrations and angers by high speed driving, so there was almost a Royal blessing on the activity, except for one major difference. The Sultan was in a position to have the roads cleared before he indulged himself so he was the only person endangered.

The young ones were going to be a problem though. The offspring of the wealthy were probably quite content with their fast cars, their girlfriends (Omanis or visiting air hostesses) and their evenings at the Intercontinental Hotel or the Gulf Hotel. These were not up to the nightlife in London, New York or Munich, but the climate was infinitely better and you were a big fish in a little pond instead of just another bloody foreign student (who had too much money anyway).

But there was also now a rapidly growing group of young students whose families were not particularly wealthy nor well-connected but thanks to Sultan Qaboos and his Ministry of Education, had been sent abroad to gain knowledge which would help their country's progress. Unfortunately for Oman, during their expensive overseas education they had also picked up other dogma as well; dogma which would not particularly help their country at its present stage of development. Simple unrealistic stuff which would appeal to unformed intellects like: 'Kings and Sultans are bad and only the people are good'; 'Kings and Sultans are rich and their money should be shared out among the people'; 'the white faces in your country are becoming rich at your expense. Get rid of them and take control of your own future.'

The first visible signs of the growing nationalism of the young Omani that came to my notice was the mini-mutiny aboard the sail training ship, *Youth of Oman (Shahab Omam)* .

Based in Mina Qaboos, the country's major port situated in the Capital Area, she was a three-master with hefty diesel auxiliary engines. Built in the UK for one of the sailing organisations devoted to teaching youngsters self-reliance, discipline and the spirit of adventure, she had been sold to the Sultanate with the same object in view; hence her name.

Unfortunately there were a few problems surrounding her. Structurally she was sound enough but at that time she was not allowed to make journeys offshore. As good sailing winds are rare in the Gulf of Oman or the Arabian Gulf, most of her time under way was spent under power. SON were administratively responsible for the ship and her crew, but did not particularly relish the job. They regarded her as an anachronism wasting time and money that would be better employed elsewhere; and her officers as a bunch of slightly eccentric enthusiasts who were definitely not from the same mould as the ex-Royal Navy British officers in SON. When I knew them, her four British officers and Pakistani crew were a happy bunch who looked forward to and thoroughly enjoyed their infrequent trips to sea.

On this occasion they had a party of teenage Omanis on board who were to be given a day's run up the coast and back. As usual it was blindingly hot with the temperature at 110°F and rising. There was no wind, the sea was pale blue glass and the humidity so high that it was visible as a thin vapour writhing above the surface. *Shabab* had not yet been fitted with air-conditioning and Mina Qaboos was its usual heat trap. It was an inauspicious start.

For three hours *Shabab* Oman rumbled her way up the coast but the youth of Oman were not impressed. Where were the magnificent and towering sails emblazoned with the Sultanic crest? 'Why are the sails not hoisted?' they asked the officers. 'Because there is no wind,' came the perfectly reasonable reply. Much muttering from the passengers. Like all sail training ships *Shabab* was designed to be operated manually, in the style of the old sailing ships. Power operated winches had been abandoned in an effort to develop the muscles of the youth of Oman.

'If they think we're pulling up all those bloody sails just so that they can have a look at them, they've got another think coming,' was the unspoken comment of the officers and crew.

A few of the young Omanis wandered on to the bridge and gazed around. 'Why are there no Omani officers?' they demanded. They were even less impressed by the truthful (but tactless) answer that there were no Omani officers capable of sailing *Shabab* - they were all too busy learning how to become officers on the SON fighting vessels.

Their irritation was becoming evident and in the hope of making them feel better it was pointed out that there were also very few British officers who were capable of sailing the three-master. It didn't work. An attempt was made to take over the steering from the Pakistani helmsman and tempers began deteriorating on both sides. It was decided to return to Mina Qaboos.

This pathetic display of nationalistic fervour reached its even more pathetic climax when the *Shabab* Oman came alongside her berth. As the longshoreman threw the lines on board the passengers threw them back. This continued until the youth of Oman realised that in conditions of no wind it achieved nothing at all except to infuriate the Omani dockside workers. They reluctantly allowed *Shabab* to be made fast.

An official report was made about the incident to SON Headquarters who doubtless heaved a weary sigh before making a complaint to the sponsor of the party, a senior Omani government official. He was not pleased and made his displeasure know to the embryonic mutineers. As the episode was discussed in the mess that evening, there was general agreement that although it fell far short of Bligh and the Bounty, it was, nevertheless, a decided straw in the wind. [4]

[4] It is a pleasant postscript to record that since those days *Shabab* Oman has been allowed to make voyages much further afield, culminating in

It must have been about this time when, on returning to the office from MAM one morning, I glanced into Peter Thwaites office on my way past. He was standing talking to an extremely tall man of about the same age. Although CJS was above average height he still had to look up into the face of his visitor and there was a noticeable deference about the way he held himself. I was intrigued. Sarah kept the Brigadier's diary and usually knew all about his appointments, but she had been told nothing about this visitor. A week or two passed before the occasional remark and telex pieced the answer together: General Sir Timothy Creasey WNO KCB OBE, ex-Commander Sultan's Armed Forces between 1972 and 1975 and now due to retire from the post of Commander-in-Chief UK Land Forces. On his way back to the UK from Salalah he had called in to meet CJS. A few more weeks were to pass before we discovered why.

Peter Thwaites had not been completely fit for some time and had decided that it was time he retired to England. This would provide the opportunity for the restructuring of command that the Sultan's Armed Forces so badly needed. No longer would there be a Chairman of the Joint Staff, of equal rank to the Commanders but with no control over them; instead a Supremo - a Chief of the Defence Staff (CDS). He was to be a four star General of considerably higher rank than the Commanders and, judging by what I had seen, a man of impressive stature and bearing.

Although most of us welcomed the proposed change, all of us were saddened by the pending departure of Peter Thwaites. A gentleman in the true sense of the word, I had developed considerable respect and affection for him. Inevitably, our half colonels began to worry. Would a job be found for them? Were the days of wine and roses disappearing? It was to be many months before the answers to these questions began to emerge. Meanwhile, another pending event began to occupy everybody's attention, not only in SAF but throughout the whole country - the tenth anniversary celebrations of the accession of Sultan Qaboos.

In terms of his reign I had arrived very late on the scene and was unaware that he was held in such veneration by his people. I was also unprepared for the lengthy, ongoing preparations that were being made for the massive celebrations to. As time passed however, it became impossible to ignore them.

For all of its thirty kilometres, from the Capital Area to the Seeb Palace, the lamp standards in the centre of Qaboos Street were festooned with garlands of fairy lights and portraits of His Majesty, all highly coloured according to Arab taste. On every inch of wasteground, scaffolding was removed to display giant illuminated pictures of Qaboos and aspects of Omani life made up from coloured light bulbs. At night, castles, camels, oases and the Sultanic crest twinkled everywhere. There was no doubt that the most popular display was the artificial waterfall created on a rocky pinnacle beside the Corniche which led from Muttrah to Muscat. Sea water pumped up to the top cascaded back to the sea over brilliantly coloured floodlamps concealed amongst the

the visit to New York for the Tall Ships gathering at the Statue of Liberty centenary celebrations in 1986.

rocks. It was a spectacle which drew thousands to the coast road every night and which many Omanis will tell their grandchildren about in forty years time.

The first ten years of Qaboos: under his guidance the leap had been made from the poverty, hunger and ignorance of medieval Oman into the modern world - with full bellies, education, health care and the recognition that the most lowly demanded as much respect and care as the highest.

Even our office became involved and a spasmodic sort of activity occurred; our Guards' half colonel began to pore over block diagrams of Wattayeh Stadium as he worked out the complicated manoeuvres involved in the ceremonial parade to be held before His Majesty. Our Air Force representative became even more pedantic as he discussed helicopter flights for the arriving media and our Navy man retreated more and more into Senior Service reticence, which usually implied disinterest.

Since I had been in the country for only a few months and had arrived only just before the proclaimed date, I was very surprised to learn that I was about to receive the Tenth Anniversary Medal and the Oman Peace Medal. Moreover, it was announced that all officers were to be given a commemorative wristwatch from His Majesty.

It was impossible to convince myself that I deserved any of the awards, however I had no choice but to shrug mentally and accept them gratefully, as I did the two rather special social events which followed.

That anniversary year His Highness, the Deputy Prime Minister for Defence and Security Said Faher bin Taimur al Said still made it a practice to invite new MoD contract officers to a meal at his palace in Muscat. Usually this occurred during Ramadan and the meal was the breaking of the day's fast after sunset. I had learnt all the rules of behaviour on such occasions and I refreshed my memory about shaking your cup from side to side when you'd had enough coffee, not exposing the soles of your feet to your host, and so on, but I need not have troubled. In deference to the month and the Omani guests present, no alcohol was served, but apart from that the occasion was entirely Western in its concept and presentation.

I gratefully accepted the offer of a lift to the function, for His Highness' palace was in Muscat next to the Royal Palace. Muscat had changed little in the last few hundred years and its streets were labyrinthine. The imposition of a one-way system had added to the confusion and there was no chance of me finding my own way there. The journey confirmed this.

As we drew up at the foot of the steps leading to the main door I saw that His Highness and his son (by a previous marriage) were waiting to greet their guests. We left the car and I jumped involuntarily as the Royal Guard soldiers lining the steps sprang to attention and presented arms. It was the one and only occasion on which I had been so greeted and I still treasure it. Pure 'Hotspur' and 'Boy's Own Paper' stuff.

Massive, ancient, castellated walls, narrow winding streets and alleyways. A full and brilliant moon in a star splashed sky and the rich uniforms and the gleaming rifles of the guard of honour.

Inside, the rooms were large, high-ceilinged and luxuriously furnished, however, I found the harsh white lighting in the entrance hall disconcerting until I realised that the arrival of the guests was being filmed on video. Later in the evening, it was even more disconcerting when, sitting on a settee and talking to Madam Virginia, Said Faher's attractive English wife, I glanced up to find the camera lens only three feet away. I was mildly curious about the filming until I heard later from a member of His Highness' staff that out host and hostess occasionally enjoyed a video replay of some of their functions.

The meal was a buffet of western and Arabic dishes set out on a table well over twenty feet in length which bore a magnificent centre piece about eighteen inches high portraying a group of horses galloping through an oasis. I was told it was sculpted in solid gold and my mind boggled at this and the other evidence of the Said Faher wealth: drinks coasters in the form of solid gold maple leaves, the gold plated plumbing in the bathrooms and, indicative of their style of living, the cigarette boxes. Probably naively, I had always thought of a cigarette box as just that, a box containing cigarettes; and not, as I saw scattered on various tables, leather, gold-embossed caskets, each one containing twenty assorted packets of cigarettes.

It was a delightful evening which carried memories I will always treasure. Only one other occasion surpassed it for splendour and that was the dinner given for the officers of His Majesty's armed forces at his Seeb Palace. Held as part of the ten year celebrations, it was truly the most magnificent function I have ever attended.

Those of us living in the BAF Mess made up small parties and shared transport for we had been told that the car parks outside the palace would be filled to overflowing. As I had visited Seeb before, I was elected driver for our group. The journey was simple: north out of the Capital Area, past Seeb Airport on the right and the massive sprawl of MAM camp on the left and continue along Qaboos highway until the last roundabout. This was easy to recognise for the four lane highway deteriorates into an ordinary two way road at that point, a road which continues for another four hundred kilometres to the United Arab Emirates in the north.

The last roundabout was the junction for the road to Seeb Palace; the last kilometre being a blaze of colour: floral, arboreal and electrical.

Just outside the palace gates soldiers of the Royal Guard directed us to the left towards the car parks. Unaware of the procedure I had left my headlights switched on as I approached and was blinded by a powerful searchlight beam. I hastily switched them off and the night went dark again. Clearly, the Royal Guard, who were to be seen everywhere, were not going to have their night vision impaired by any unthinking guest.

I parked the car and our small party, in company with other groups, walked towards the glow from the palace ground. The spectacle that greeted us was pure Hollywood. Across the wide lawns and among the trees were hundreds of guests in either dress uniform or white dinner jackets; a mix of services, regiments and races.

Five bands were playing in various parts of the grounds and, even among the brilliant colours of the uniforms, the scarlet of the Royal

Guard patrolling the walls and the white dish dashes of the serving staff were distinctive. At a cursory glance I could see some twenty or more tables, each loaded high with so many varieties of food that it was easy to believe that SOAF and the Royal Flight had been flying in many of the delicacies during the past few weeks and that Harrod's Food Hall had been a major contributor. All of this exotica was complemented and enhanced by the rows of flaming torches topping the palace garden walls.

In a central position a table had been laid and this was for His Majesty, his commanders and certain selected senior officers to sit and dine. For the rest of us, it was a buffet self-service (once the Sultan was seated). The food was delicious - although there was far too much of it - and a few hours later, when everybody had dined and the Sultan had retired to the palace, the tables were still half covered with untouched plates of oysters, smoked salmon, pâté, cold and warm meats and fruit. I could not believe that so much food would go to waste, and indeed I later found out that it did not.

It was the first time that I had been close to Sultan Qaboos and it was easy to observe him while engaging in the usual party chatter. As the many thousands of pictures and posters portrayed, he was a handsome man with silver streaked black hair, short trimmed beard and moustache. Although small in stature he was an impressive and dignified figure in full dress uniform and the respect he commanded was very evident.

Quite suddenly the bands fell silent and, looking around for the reason, I saw the black velvet sky beyond the palace erupt into a multi-coloured spray of light as a spectacular firework display began. With everybody else I watched the equivalent of thousands of Rials flare and vanish every minute and smiled inwardly as I recalled the fireworks which concluded the annual regatta at West Mersea where I used to live.

His Majesty departed during the performance and, realising that the party was over, we wondered how we would be informed that it was time to go. I was soon to find out.

I had been standing near one of the doors in the outer wall of the palace gardens when suddenly it opened and a jet-stream of Omanis poured through. I looked around and saw that the stampede was being enacted at other entrances to the palace grounds. Dressed in the traditional white gown and head-dress each new arrival carried a large plastic bag and, ignoring the formally invited guests, they raced towards the tables. I guessed they were friends and relatives of the palace staff and probably villagers from nearby Seeb. After some good-humoured jostling around the buffets the food vanished. I tried to imagine the same thing taking place at Buckingham Palace...

In those early days, there was no doubt in any of our minds that the personnel division existed solely to make life as difficult as it could for all of us. In fact, it was often referred to as the anti-personnel division by the more deeply offended and bitter of the contract officers. As I mentioned earlier, its director was an ex-RAF officer who I knew from my MoDUK days. He was a rule-book man then and he was now even more pernickety as D of P (probably in an attempt to train the Omanis on his staff away from their casual approach to personnel administration). Moreover, our lives were made no easier by the fact that his Deputy was an Omani who was totally NAAFI (No Ambition And F*** all Interest) and his senior Assistant Director even more devoted to the observance of regulations than he was.

It was a known and unofficially recognised practice in SAF that a British contract officer would start his leave on Saturday and, Friday being the Islamic weekend, he could then catch the Thursday night aircraft to London, thus gaining an extra day's leave. Practically speaking I could see no harm in this simple subterfuge, for the Friday would be spent at the Aqua Club or in the mess anyway and British servicemen have been adding Saturdays and Sundays to their leave for centuries past. Uniformed SAF officers in the MAM Headquarters or in camps and bases throughout Oman were beyond any control that D of P could exercise, but MoD staff officers were well within his range and this sneaking an extra day off outside the regulations was anathema. Avoiding their probing enquiries with various cunning manoeuvres became an entertainment which livened up many a dull day.

The foolishness of all this was exemplified when, on one occasion, I departed on the Thursday night London-bound flight and a friend of mine responded to the inevitable question by saying that I had driven to Dubhai (over 400 kilometres to the north) for a day or two and was flying on to London from there. By some weird regulational logic Dubhai was 'local' and my residence there on a Friday acceptable.

Many held strong views about the personnel division. They were understaffed said some. No they're not, said others, they'd be better occupied getting on with policy matters like recruiting and training, and delegate trivia like leave matters to the line managers. Certainly, some of the paperwork they were responsible for was remarkably out of date. My copy of 'Notes for Guidance of New officers' referred to social patterns that had disappeared, regiments that no longer existed and a war which finished five years ago; it was however, reasonably accurate about Oman's geography and climate which presumably was fairly static.

I learnt, however, that there was a variety of 'Notes for Guidance' in issue and the edition you received seemed to depend on the agent who had recruited you. This fact came to light in a most entertaining manner. As I mentioned before, every British contract officer was issued with a car (or Land Rover) on arrival and it was a very sensible provision for without personal transport and the ability to go swimming or shopping or whatever when you wanted to, I am sure the incidence of alcoholism and suicide would have been much higher. The heat (usually over 100°F) made walking more than a few hundred yards an unpleasant and arduous exercise, taxis were expensive and mostly dangerous and our salaries at that time (with a worsening rate of exchange) were such that buying a car of your own would have been a major financial undertaking.

It was in this environment that our Director of Personnel discovered an old (and presumably discarded) regulation which said that cars should be shared among junior officers - two or three to a car depending on rank. Even D of P quailed at the prospect of telling current junior officers that henceforth they would be sharing their cars, but he was ever anxious to implement any regulations he could, and he decided that he would impose it on new staff officers in MoD. It was unfortunate for him that the next junior officer to arrive was one of his own men, a new Assistant Director of Personnel, for Bill was a very large ex-army officer not about to accept any changes in the conditions of service he joined under. Moreover, Bill was in the final year of obtaining his LL.B.

The battle raged for a month or more. 'A share of a car, it says here' cried D of P, waving his new regulation triumphantly.

Bill put his pending LL.B. to work and took steps to sue D of P in an English court. Misrepresentation was the name of the game. Bill got his car and the regulation went back into the archives.

D of P's departure was a little sad, (ill health), but he collected a gong as well as his gratuity on the way through the door and both were well deserved for nobody had run themselves into the ground more than he had. His final charge against Arab pragmatism was a fitting last act.

The D of P lived in the mess and had been indulging in an afternoon siesta as so many of us did. On waking he had seen a young Omani officer leave his room across the way and, after a furtive glance over his shoulder, siphon some petrol out of an army Land Rover into a jerrican. He then took it across the compound and emptied it into his own car. D of P was appalled. Long before the episode had finished he had got his camera and taken innumerable photographs of the developing crime. To these he added a four page detailed report which adopted formal recitations such as: 'On the afternoon of Monday... at approximately...'

All of this was duly reported and, unsurprisingly, the senior Omani officers were much more intrigued by the fact that a senior officer should put so much effort into such a trivial matter than they were by the purloining of a few litres of petrol.

'In the name of Allah, our country sends millions of gallons of petrol abroad every week. Is the Sultan so mean that he would worry about one of his officers using a few litres of army petrol? What sort of a man do you think Sultan Qaboos is?'

Clearly, they had no idea about what was upsetting D of P.

I suspect that this was the final straw on D of P's back; soon afterwards the Personnel Division changed for the better. The naafi Deputy became Director where he continued to portray no ambition and zero interest and a new British contract officer arrived as Deputy. I had know Mike years before as an RAF officer in MoDUK and he was a good operator. A blunt-speaking and practically-minded Yorkshireman, his approach to his new job was summed up by his comments about the Thursday night flights to London. 'They can take off after duty on Thursday, so far as I'm concerned, so long as they're back on duty when they're supposed to be.'

There are one thousand Baizas in the Omani Rial and the rate of exchange between it and the Pound Sterling was beginning to worry many of us. When I started, my salary was over six thousand Rials a year, which, at 630 Baizas to the Pound, was over ten thousand Pounds. It was a good salary for it was tax-free, my accommodation and car were also free and food and drink could be bought at well below commercial prices. Added to that, I could take three weeks' leave every three months with fares paid. However, as the rate of exchange worsened and began its climb towards Pound/Rial parity there were many anxious faces around the camp.

There was no argument that for most of the year the climate was distinctly unpleasant, with intense heat day and night, invariably accompanied by a high humidity. mess accommodation was of a low standard and the food indifferent. Entertainment in those days was the camp cinema (three evenings a week), the Muscateer film show (twice a week) or excruciatingly poor productions on Oman TV. Books were very expensive and difficult to obtain and newspapers many days out of date (unless somebody returning from leave remembered to bring some with him). And if for any reason you wanted to make an urgent telephone call to the UK you had to walk across the road to the Ruwi Post Office, book and pay for a limited time call, then wait for half an hour for the use of a telephone in an open-sided cubicle. Can you imagine trying to make an international telephone call flanked by Pakistanis who believe that maximum volume is the only way to communicate with their nearest and dearest across the water?

All of this was bearable, but the mail, Dear God! that bloody mail! It was so consistently bad that it was a constant worry.

Unless you have been separated from loved ones for a long time it is difficult to appreciate how vital a good mail service can be. Without a regular correspondence to reassure you that everything is going well at home the imagination begins to play tricks, morale sags and, strangely enough, even knowing that the reason for the lack of letters is because the mail service is appalling doesn't really help. The UK forces have known this for many years and the British Army Postal Service is highly efficient, but, unfortunately for us, all of our mail arrived via the Oman Post Office - and the doubtful talents of the MoD Administrative Wing.

At its best, airmail took five days to arrive from the UK; at its worst a month or more and during Ramadan it could take two months. Even five days was difficult to understand though, because British Airways had a daily flight to Australia which called in at Seeb Airport. The reason, however, was simple. Gulf Air, which was the mail carrier for our part of the world, flew the mail to Bahrein where it was offloaded and sorted into Gulf States for forwarding again by Gulf Air. If it had then come directly to Muscat it would have been a help, but Oman's capital was the last port of call on a feeder service which could meander around Qatar, Doha, Abu Dhabi, Dubhai and Sharjah before coming to us.

None of this hastened the mail towards the officer's mess at Bait al Falaj, nor was it hastened after its arrival at Seeb Airport by being delivered to Muscat Post Office for further sorting and delivery to the

Post Offices at Ruwi, Muttrah, Seeb, Salalah and so on. Muscat had been the capital city of Oman for centuries; indeed, until comparatively recently, the country had been known as Muscat and Oman. Now, however, it was a collection of ancient houses and palaces huddled together well away along the coast from the real commercial and administrative centre of Ruwi/Muttrah.

Crediting the letters with human intelligence, they might have been forgiven for thinking that at Ruwi Post Office, one hundred yards from BAF Camp and four hundred yards from BAF officers' mess, they were near their destination. Not so. There were a number of Post Office box numbers relating to the Sultan's Armed Forces and their interpretation was critical. The most well-known one was undoubtedly the Ministry of Defence box number 113, Muscat and this was the number we had been told to use in our 'Notes for Guidance'. It did not matter that 'Officers' mess, Bait al Falaj' appeared on the letter, 113 was the trigger number and our mail went into the gaping maw of the Ministry of Defence internal delivery system. As it went round the divisions, branches and offices it would collect cryptic comments like: 'Try Eng Div,' 'Not SOAF' and (an inspired guess) 'Try BAF Officers' mess'. Then, and only then, would the dog-eared envelope arrive at its destination.

This couldn't continue of course and a real crisis developed, Big Jim being the catalyst which was eventually to lead to some improvements. He earnt his nickname for obvious reasons. He was dark and sported enormous mutton chop whiskers which did nothing for his appearance. His voice confirmed, if any confirmation was necessary, that he had been a Guards' sergeant-major and his laugh was an ear-shattering guffaw. There wasn't an ounce of real malice in him and I liked him immensely.

Jim had been recruited to fill the non-commissioned civilian post of Publications and Printing Officer and he spent most of his days operating a couple of costly Japanese photocopying machines. He often referred to himself as 'the most expensive trained monkey in the ministry'. He was a total extrovert, loud and much given to whistling both at work and at play. This did not go down too well with the senior British civilian (who was Personal Adviser to His Excellency the Under Secretary) nor with his two staff officers who occupied the offices next door to Jim. Neither did his piercing whistle and occasional bellow of 'Hallo Alan. How's it going Mate?' go down too well among some of the more traditional of our mess members.

It had been decided that Jim and the Ministry should part company because of that peculiarly English classification that 'he didn't really fit in'. Jim was understandably hurt and resentful because his work could not be faulted and none of his superiors had taken him on one side and told him of his weaknesses. I had tried to curb him once or twice but his natural ebullience always burst through and then that appalling whistle would start up again. Anyway, he was resigned to his fate and was looking forward to an entirely new venture in Los Angeles. It could only happen in the USA. On a previous visit (I believe he had a daughter living there) Jim had been befriended by a millionaire who wanted to start up a business renting out chauffeur-driven VIP cars. The cars were to be stretched Cadillacs with a bar, TV, refrigerator, telephone and so on, which would be used by film stars and movie moguls for premieres or similar occasions.

With his height, erect bearing and mutton chop whiskers, Jim was every American's dream of the perfect English chauffeur; and this particular American wanted Jim and was willing to give him a stake in the business to get him. It could only happen in the USA.

International phone calls between his benefactor, Jim's wife, and then Jim himself, had set up the agreement in principle and a contract was on its way for Jim's signature. There was a deadline however. The millionaire was a busy man and had programmed the business to start fairly soon. I was delighted for Jim. He was such an extrovert and such a nice guy that I could see him becoming a great favourite with the film stars.

It was about then that the mail stopped coming. I don't mean that it become more erratic or that the delays worsened; it just stopped coming into the officers' mess. This applied not only to air mail, but to surface mail as well - and it wasn't even Ramadan!

A week passed and the complaints about the lack of mail grew louder. Then a second week and the mess members began to realise that everybody else was suffering too. Big Jim was becoming frantic and Harvey was collecting an earful every day. It didn't matter to the mess members that Harvey had nothing to do with the mail except putting it in the pigeon holes in the entrance hall. He was the mess manager, for God's sake, and anything and everything connected with the mess was his fault.

'Why don't you do something about it?' was a fairly regular comment. I think Harvey knew that he could never win.

The third week without mail went by. Big Jim ('I'll lose that bloody job if I don't get that contract') and Dave ('My wife's expecting a baby') were becoming very angry. Daily visits were made to the Administration Directorate, but their questioning of the Omani orderly who collected our letters from the Ruwi Post Office brought the inevitable answer: 'There was no mail today, Sir'. Neither of them believed him and they went across the road to the Post Office and demanded to see the manager. He was delighted to see them for, as he explained: 'Nobody has collected your mail for three weeks, Sir and I was wondering if I should do something about it'. They gazed at him, then at the back of the post office box and the mountain of newspapers, packets, parcels and letters behind it. They telephoned Harvey and told him to send over a truck.

Big Jim drove straight back to the Administration Directorate and (fortunately), Dave accompanied him. They walked into the office of the Omani director and Big Jim demanded to see the mail orderly. He was brought.

'Was there any mail today?' Jim demanded.

'No Sir,' replied the sweating orderly who was hypnotised by the giant black whiskered figure. 'There was no mail in the post office today.'

'You lying little bastard,' howled Jim, picking him up bodily and shaking him violently. 'I've just been across to the post office. You broke the key in the lock three weeks ago and you haven't been back since.'

Dave prised him away from the terrified Omani and they returned to the mess. On that day the mess was going through one of its regular disinfestations, so most of us had a snack lunch in the Muscateer Club. In company with the rest I stopped chewing my sandwich as the truck drew up outside and my jaw dropped as stewards and orderlies staggered in under bundles of magazines and sacks of mail. Jim was still muttering: 'I'd like to kill the little bastard,' as he came through the door.

There was a slightly depressing sequel, however, that occured when I went to see the Personal Adviser to His Excellency the Under Secretary. Something really had to be done to improve this appalling mail scene.

'Oh no,' said the Adviser's two loyal British staff officers, 'we mustn't disturb him with trivial stuff like this.'

I began to understand the occasional Omani comment that: 'The British are no friends of the British.'

Ignoring them walked I past their desks and into his office. As I suspected, his mail was delivered directly to his office and he was unaware of the brouhaha surrounding the mess mail. He was appalled that such a thing could happen; the outcome being that the officers' mess was given its own POB number and Harvey was tasked with the daily collection from the Post Office. Poor old Harvey; he had collected yet another area of aggravation.

Big Jim made his contract signature just in time and, so far as I know, is still driving for the Newmans and Spiegels of that star-spangled world. Before he left however, Big Jim featured in one more episode which kept the Mess entertained for some time; this was Little Jim's 'Runner'.

I had just learnt that, apart from death, there were two ways of achieving a rapid departure from the Sultanate. One was to be 'Tin Budgied,' the other was to do a 'Runner'. The former related to those who were sent back to the UK in disgrace on the first available aircraft and was a facetious reference to the screaming falcon logo on the tail of the Gulf Air Tristars. The latter expression referred to those who had found life in the Oman no longer bearable and had caught the first aircraft out.

The barbed wire fence and guarded entrance of Bait al Falaj camp only existed to keep unauthorised civilians out and, providing one had a pass, there was no restraint on entry or exit. As I also learnt, there was little or no control on who left the country; only on those trying to enter.

If you wanted to do a runner therefore, all you had to do was buy a ticket, drive to the airport, fill in the embarkation form and present it with your passport at emigration control - sweating slightly all the while and hoping to God that nobody saw you who knew you and started asking questions. This was always a definite possibility because every

UK bound aircraft had its quota of SAF/MoD officers going on leave who were accompanied by friends who had driven them to the airport.

Little Jim was an ex-Ordnance Corps officer who now worked as a contract staff officer in the MoD Purchasing Directorate and he was unhappy about Oman in general and his job in particular. He had served as a contract officer in Saudi Arabia and was a man of considerable experience, but our Purchasing Directorate had an appalling reputation among the three SAF services for incompetence overlaid with corruption. I possessed no facts but had heard sufficient 'chat' to form an opinion - and I suspected that the suppliers of SOLF, SOAF and SON were indulging in that old game of 'pot calling'.

Be that as it may Little Jim was extremely unhappy. He hated the mess, its accommodation and its food and the lack of mail from home drove him frantic. Moreover, he had just bought a very expensive hi-fi kit from a shop which belonged to one of our main suppliers and the following morning he had opened the drawer of his desk to find the precise amount that he had paid lying there. He had tried to return the money to the shop and they had denied any knowledge of it. He had then received a telephone call which made his position pretty clear - he had been set up and his co-operation was required. Rather like the Director of Personnel, this was the final straw and he had decided to do a runner. 'Would you drive me to the airport please Alan?' he had asked.

Most runners kept silent about their imminent departure and drove themselves to the airport, so I was curious as to why Little Jim wanted me to do so. It seemed that he wanted to keep his 'take-off' a secret for as long as possible by leaving his car outside his room. I couldn't quite follow his reasoning for he would be missed shortly after 7.30 in the morning when he failed to appear in his office, but his aircraft left at midnight and meandered around the Gulf before heading for London where it landed at midday. I think that Little Jim had nightmares about a most unlikely scenario of being put back on the aircraft at LAP and flown back to Oman. Later, I was to appreciate that he had good reason for his nightmares. Anyhow, he was already extremely nervous, and, not wanting to increase his agitation, I agreed to take him.

Came the day, rather the evening, of his departure and a handful of his close friends gathered in my room for clandestine farewell drinks. Big Jim had joined me for a drink in the Mess earlier and I had little choice but to let him accompany me back to the party. When he heard that Little Jim was doing a runner and that I was driving him to the airport he insisted on joining us, seeing it as an unusual and entertaining way of spending an evening. 'Perhaps we can have a few grogs at the airport restaurant?' was his suggestion for making it into a lighthearted occasion rather than the 'Wooden Horse' episode that Little Jim envisaged.

It was late and dark when we drove out through the BAF gate. The trip along Qaboos Street to Seeb Airport went without a hitch in spite of Little Jim's occasional nervous glances through the rear window. At the departure hall, Big Jim got out and helped with the luggage while I parked the car. Ticket processing and seat allocation went smoothly which was just as well, for Little Jim's nervousness was very apparent. I suspected that the Gulf Air girl thought he was just one of those thousands of people who are terrified of flying. On into the final barrier - Emigration - where the ticket, departure form and passport are examined and stamped. If the passport was stamped there was no problem for the armed policeman at the entrance to the departure lounge just waved you through; unstamped however, there was absolutely no chance. I will never know whether Big Jim's behaviour at this point smoothed Little Jim's departure or not. What I do know is that it very nearly gave Little Jim a heart attack.

Big Jim recognised the immigration officer as a friend and his bellow of greeting reduced everybody in the emigration hall to a stunned silence as they looked around for the source of the thunderclap. The Omani officer's eyes rose from the passport he was studying and a beaming smile split his face. 'Beeg Jeem,' he cried delightedly.

Little Jim's knees had started to buckle at suddenly becoming the focus of everybody's attention but supported on either side he was ushered forward.

'Hallo Mate,' bawled Big Jim, shaking the Omani's hand, 'long time no see. Let me introduce a friend of mine who's going home to see his missus,' and he shoved Little Jim forward. His heart may have nearly stopped but from then on his departure was assured.

'Bloody funny that, Mate,' said Big Jim during our drive back to Bait al Falaj, 'Little Jim looked quite dicky for a minute back there in the emigration hall.'

There were some bizarre sequels to Little Jim's runner. Poor Peter was questioned at great length about his part in the affair by the Omani Director of Purchasing. It seemed that the guard at the BAF gate had stated that a white haired man had driven Little Jim when he left for the airport. It was unfortunate for Peter that his hair was as white as mine and he had been a colleague of Little Jim's.

Whether he knew something that we didn't I'll never know, but when his disappearance became known the Director of Purchasing sent off an immediate signal to the Royal Oman Police (who controlled immigration and airport security) calling for the immediate arrest of Little Jim and his return to Bait al Falaj if he was sighted.

The Director of Purchasing was a big hearty man, full of good humour and a frequent visitor to the Mess. His English, particularly the oaths, was impeccable. I recall him telling me once that his grandfather had been one of the last Omani slave traders to sail his boom (dhow) down to Zanzibar on business, so to speak. I remembered the story well when the Director of Purchasing subsequently disappeared into Rumais Prison for a considerable time. Because the Omanis were such a tolerant people the general opinion was that he must have been very naughty.

Whatever assets he possessed that had not been frozen were available to one of his wives and her children, but not to the other and there was no love lost between the women. Because of this, the Officers' Mess at Bait al Falaj collected some additional mess members. Dear old

Harvey. One look at those big black pleading eyes and Mrs Purchasing and her offspring would be home and dry.

For those officers who were unaccompanied it was, occasionally, a lonely sort of life, for no matter how much conversation and company you may have enjoyed during the evening, at the end of it, you were in your room on your own. There were one or two exceptions to this condition for there were unattached girls around. However, they were so few and far between that I was frequently reminded of the deer rutting season in Richmond Park. There, the stag, having made his conquest, spent so much time battling or warning off would be usurpers that I was always surprised that they had any time or energy for procreation. So it was in Oman; the classic example being James who was about to become engaged to Susan.

She had a job of her own and could not accompany him on his next leave, but there was a passionate farewell at Seeb Airport and James departed, committed to various tasks including buying and bringing back an engagement ring for Susan. After a couple of weeks James found the separation too hard to bear. He had bought the ring alright, but London was no fun on your own especially with the cold and the never-ending rain. He thought of the warmth that awaited him in Oman and decided to cut short his leave and catch the next aircraft back.

As usual it was an overnight flight and he caught a taxi from Seeb and arrived back at Susan's flat at six in the morning. They were already at the stage of intimacy where he had his own front door key and with no thought other than the look of delight on his beloved's face when he presented himself, he walked through the hall and into her bedroom.

Tom was a good eight inches shorter and three stone lighter than his opponent. The battle raged and, naked, bruised and battered, he conducted a fighting retreat down the stairs to the entrance of the block of flats. All might have been well (except for Tom's injuries) if Susan hadn't panicked and started screaming at the top of her lungs. Bewildered, wide-eyed and tousled Omani families appeared outside their doors and on their balconies. It was unfortunate that a senior Omani official in the Ministry also lived in the block.

All three of them were employed by SAF and all came within a hair's breadth of being 'Tin Budgied'. As it was they were marched in front of their individual bosses and given the gipsy's warning: 'If anything like this happens again...'

Tom's battle scars were bravely worn but he tended to stay away from the mess after that. Over drinks one evening I was tempted to tell him how much he reminded me of a Richmond Park stag but decided against it. I didn't really know him all that well.

But reverting to the predicament of the unaccompanied officer, I had decided that at my age and shape it would be a foolish and wasted effort to try and compete with so many glossy-coated young stags. A tot of whisky and a book brought more peace and comfort than a pair of rounded thighs. Moreover, a book had a distinct advantage in that you could lay it down and it stayed there, wanting nothing more.

I have always been an avid reader and so I had to have books. Apart from the usual pleasure one gained from them there were many nights when I would wake at two or three o'clock and only innumerable cups of tea and a book would do until the eyelids drooped again.

At that time, however, books were not easy to come by, there being only one bookshop in the whole Capital Area. Known as the 'Oman Family Bookshop' it had a passable selection worth browsing over and, perhaps buying, (provided you did not convert any book's price into its pound sterling equivalent).

Harvey eventually came to the rescue by starting up a new mess library. It was a good scheme for the present collection of books (I will not use the word library) consisted of a hundred or so Mills & Boone romance paperbacks, all bearing the rubber stamp of an officers' mess at Knightsbridge Barracks. I hesitate to rely too much on my memory at this point for fear of arousing the anger of some perfectably respectable 'Brown Boots' outfit, but I must admit to a certain amount of quiet incredulity when I first saw the collection. Either the Knightsbridge Barracks' chaps or earlier residents of the BAF Officers Mess had possessed decidedly off-beat literary tastes.

I had developed a habit of waking up at about five thirty every morning and, on the rare occasions I didn't, the muezzin call from the Ruwi mosque ensured that I did very soon afterwards. Every morning, a battery of loudspeakers would remind me that Allah was great and that there was but one Allah - although occasionally I felt like arguing the point.

A leisurely cup of tea, followed by ablutions, and by half past six I was dressed and making my way across to the mess. However, this was not for breakfast, for I had abandoned that meal many years ago, but for a leisurely cup of coffee, a cigarette and a gossip in the ante room with whoever happened to join me. It was a very pleasant part of the day for the temperature was at its lowest, the camp and the mess at their most hushed and one could enjoy the quiet company of a few colleagues of similar disposition.

Stan was a regular until he finished his contract and went home and died. Tony also, until he stressed a catering argument by pushing a Muslim in the shoulder with a leg of pork. Bill was a fairly regular participant as well and we swopped yarns and listened to each other with considerable interest for we had both lived through different times and different wars. I was as fascinated by his experiences in the French Foreign Legion as he was by mine in the Royal Air Force.

The time for CJ's departure drew closer and his wife left her business in London in other hands and came out to join him for his last few weeks. Peter Thwaites had spent a big slice of his life in the Sultanate, throughout the Dhofar War and since then, and there were many friends to be visited and places to be seen - possibly for the last time - culminating in a final Audience to bid farewell to His Majesty.

The Omanis, like most Arabs, valued personal loyalty and service very highly and it was a matter for some speculation as to what sort of farewell gift the Brigadier would receive form Sultan Qaboos. In the event, the gifts certainly confirmed His Majesty's reputation for generosity. I became involved in their insurance and had never seen such concentrated glittering opulence before.

Chapter 4

A few of us were enjoying a pre-dinner drink one evening when the conversation moved round to the subject of the Sultan's farewell gift to Peter Thwaites. I mentioned one or two items and their value and exclamations of 'Jesus!' and 'My God!' showed that my audience was suitably impressed. It was then that Charlie told us a charming story he remembered from his early days in Oman.

Fred was an irrigation expert who had spent most of his life working in undeveloped countries, advising them where to find water and how to use it to their best advantage. Although not a glamorous job it was an invaluable one which had brought life to millions of acres throughout the world. He had done excellent work during his years in the Sultanate, but his age and failing health made him decide to retire.

There was no doubt about the high regard in which he was held, for His Majesty had asked to see him before he left.

'In those days,' said Charlie, 'Qaboos was much more accessible and it was possible for him to take a personal interest in what was going on and who was doing what.'

Anyway, Fred was delighted with this accolade of an audience and, who knows?, he had heard all sorts of gossip about the handsome gifts some people had received on leaving. Perhaps he would be lucky.

He was unlucky. The Sultan was kindness itself and clasping both of Fred's hands in his he thanked him for his efforts on behalf of Oman and its people.

'He may have been a little bit disappointed,' Charlie continued, 'but he was a quiet guy who wouldn't have said anything even if he had been.'

Either way, it was a bright sunny morning when Fred walked out of the terminal at London Airport, feeling very much at peace with the world. At this point a man stepped forward, introduced himself as coming from the Oman Embassy and handed him a set of keys. 'A gift from His Majesty, Sir, with the wish that you enjoy many happy years of retirement in her.' He stepped aside and indicated a large and gleaming Rolls Royce saloon at the kerbside. Charlie finished the story.

'He was so choked up that he reckoned it was a couple of minutes before he could thank the man.'

Another arrival in the UK that met with an entirely different reception was that of Mike Lloyd - the same Mike who had welcomed me to the Sultanate. Totally in contrast to Peter Thwaites and his family, who were due to depart shortly in the luxury of the Sultan's own four-engined jet, Mike had decided to make his own way back to England by car. In fact, it wasn't really a car but one of those little mobile homes produced by Volkswagen - caravettes I think they called them. What Rosie and the two little children thought about the coming adventure nobody knew, but Mike had bought the caravette second-hand with the dealer's assurance that it would be completely overhauled, and he was sublimely confident. This was in contrast to his colleagues who foretold all sorts of mishaps and possible disasters. They did have some grounds however for their uneasiness, for Mike had a remarkably casual approach to life and its problems; just two days before he left he wasn't sure whether he required a visa to drive through Saudi Arabia. Harry's approach was of course completely opposite and his conversations with Mike were an entertaining mixture of black and white, thundercloud and sunshine.

There was the usual round of farewells and the day came when Mike said goodbye to us at the office and went along the road a hundred yards to make his salaams to His Highness Said Faher. It was a worthwhile visit as it transpired, for he came away with the gift of a solid gold Rolex wristwatch; one of the scores reputedly kept for such a purpose in one of Mac Mackenzie's tin trunks.

It must have been at least a couple of months later when a letter from Mike arrived at the office and it made entertaining reading. His sublime confidence had paid off. Any bureaucratic transit problems that might have arisen had vanished at the sight of Rosie and the children, for what man could be up to mischief with such a pretty wife and pretty young children accompanying him. There had been only one serious mechanical breakdown and this had occurred but a few miles from a city in Turkey where there was a main Volkswagen agent. Thereafter, all had gone well until Dover.

They had crossed on a ferry which had deposited them at the foot of the white cliffs in the early hours of the morning and this may have been the reason why the customs officer wasn't particularly cheerful. Nor, for that matter, was Mike. This was understandable after such a journey for he had now reached the stage where he just wanted to press on and finish it. Mike's irritation with the formalities may have become obvious for his opponent became less cheerful and even less co-operative.

Finally, the last documents were pushed across the counter for Mike to sign and as he reached forward to do so, the customs man caught a glint of something. He leant forward, pushed back Mike's sleeve and exposed the Rolex. 'Nice watch you have there, Sir,' was his opening remark and Mike, recognising disaster, became even more irritated. That barely concealed irritation cost him money.

Peter Thwaites was away on his round of leave-takings when I went into his office one afternoon on a routine security check. Testing the door between his office and that of Saleem al Ghazali I found it locked, which was unusual. Even more unusual was that my key failed to operate the lock.

I was puzzled and knowing that the Under Secretary and his staff had long since gone I walked around and entered his office from the outside. Walking past the desk of his Office Director, through the waiting-room and entering the long, luxuriously furnished office I crossed to the door of CJS's office. It had disappeared and in its place was a sheet of boarding which had been painted exactly the same shade of white as the walls. Moreover, a dark six foot high glass-fronted bookcase stood where the entrance had been. I was mystified.

Whether it was due to his abrupt manner of speaking I do not know, but Saleem al Ghazali certainly gave the impression of barely concealed contempt for the British although he had always seemed to get on well with Peter Thwaites. Perhaps he had decided that Peter's successor was not going to be able to walk in and out of his office as Peter had done; or perhaps he knew Sir Timothy Creasey and was making sure that he couldn't walk in unannounced. I mentioned it to the Brigadier on his return and he was clearly as taken aback as I had been, but with only days to go he was not going to become involved in something which was, after all, a problem for his successor.

Sarah had mentioned once or twice that when CJS left she would go as well and I had not paid over much attention to it, for so many of the staff had set target dates for their going and, when the date was long past they were still there. But go she did, among many rumours (often self-inspired) that this officer was heartbroken or that another was going to resign and join her in London.

There were a number of girls keen to succeed Sarah as PA to the Chairman of the Joint Staff and this was not surprising for it was a contract post with free accommodation, a car and a good salary. Hazel, who was married to an officer at the SAF Training Regiment, was the successful applicant and I met her when she arrived for the handover. She was a tall slim and pretty girl, not overly well dressed, but then for her part, no doubt, she would have seen a white haired, overweight man in desert boots, khaki slacks and a white shirt. I recall my clothes so well, only because it was my usual dress for the office. It was a classic meeting involving non-appreciation and non-recognition and neither of us realised that we were going to share so many traumatic months together and become such good friends.

It might perhaps be appropriate to mention Hazel's residential status for, theoretically, all officers of and below the rank of lieutenant colonel (or equivalent) were unaccompanied and yet her husband was a major. It was quite remarkable however, how many of wives of majors and captains there were in the Sultanate. Some were there because they knew somebody, some on a never-ending stream of visitors' visas (broken only by quick trips into the UAE) and some because they had found a local job and, hence, an Omani sponsor. Hazel came into this last category having joined her husband and subsequently become employed in the manager's office at the Ruwi Hotel.

Then came the morning when I drove to the Royal Flight and said goodbye to Peter Thwaites and his family. I liked him and was sorry to see him go but I was sure that he was doing the right thing for he had been taking increasing medication during the past month or two and Oman could not provide him with the specialist medical treatment he needed.

Back at the office and in company with the other staff officers I awaited the moves in the hierarchical game which would replace our departed Chairman of the Joint Staff. They soon came. Colonel Hassan Ehsan Nasseb became a brigadier with the title of Acting Chairman Joint Staff and a reluctant Ken became Deputy Acting Chairman Joint Staff with the rank of captain in the Sultan of Oman's Navy. Ken was reluctant, but with good reason for he was well aware that both promotions had been made to fill temporarily vacant slots and, whilst Hassan as an Omani had a good career ahead of him, Ken most certainly did not. There were less than a handful of captains' posts in SON, all of them filled and likely to be so for some time to come. When Sir Timothy Creasey arrived the ACJS and the DACJS posts would disappear and then what would happen to him?

He bore the stigma of Joint Staff, he was a captain and therefore would certainly not be welcome in SON. I felt some pity for him but no more than I felt for the other staff officers. Our Guards' half colonel (who was on loan) would return to his regiment and Harry and Ken had pensions from their service in the British Forces. This was hardly starvation but it's always difficult to withdraw your clenched fist from the honey jar.

Now that Peter Thwaites had gone, there was even less to do. It was pretty clear from the fall in correspondence (if such were possible) that SAF had mentally written off the Joint Staff. This suited me admirably for I was busy helping Hazel to find her feet, while in addition one new contract officer had arrived and a warrant officer was due to arrive. But I still found time to ruminate, with some bewilderment, on the average contract officer's violent reaction to being told that his time was up in Oman.

By the nature of the contract he signed, no contract officer had the right to expect anything but short-term employment. It was a two year contract capable of being extended a year at a time, and always terminable by three months' notice on either side. Except of course if the contract officer was Tin Budgied, put in prison, medevaced out of the country or unfortunately died. And, of course, the whole point of the exercise was that we were there to train Omanis and, as soon as possible, give up our chair to one. But so many British officers were desperate - and went to quite remarkable lengths - to hang on, that it made me ashamed. Sad to say, many of them were encouraged in their attempts by senior British officers who should have known better.

Inevitably there were muttered rumours that 'of course he's a mason' and 'of course he came from the same regiment as...,' but it really was remarkable how many contract officers who should have been sacked or allowed to go on contract termination were kept on.

One of the worst examples, bordering on the farcical, occurred in the MoD itself. Brian had a piece of paper which said that he was qualified as an auditor but, as so often is the case, he had no talent and failed to pass his probationary period with MoD. Given another chance, he failed again and was eventually transferred to a post created solely for his very basic clerical skills. When I left Oman he had completed nearly three years of service, all achieved on the basis of successive three month probationary periods. The theory that he was only being kept on because he was a freemason began to gain ground and I could certainly believe it, because one dear old British contract officer who held a lot of power, was cursed with a badly failing memory and kept giving me the secret handshake every time we met.

The new contract officer was Mike's replacement as Secretary Joint Staff. Called Roger he was a SOLF Major who had been promoted to fill the post. Shortly after his arrival he gathered the Indian clerical staff, the Omani orderlies and the uniformed Baluchi drivers around him and told them that he was a professional staff officer who would stand no nonsense and if you play ball with me chaps, etc. They all gazed at him in awe tinged with bewilderment and I was pretty certain that only the Indian clerks gathered the drift of what he was saying. I could perhaps have forgiven him his pompous prelude if he had not proved during the following two weeks that not only was he not a staff officer, professional or otherwise, but there were strong doubts about his ability as an officer.

Basically he was a good-natured man, but he was totally incapable of being positive and I was often to see him in a lather of indecision about everything, from which driver to use, to tea or coffee, sugar or no sugar. His first effort at recording the minutes of a meeting was a disaster and because there was some urgency about it he became quite incapable, even with the assistance of a tape recorder, of deciding what had been said and agreed. I took over the writing of the minutes from his scribbled notes and mentally discarded him from future Joint Staff activities. Where do they get them? I asked myself. It was bad enough to recruit them, but to promote them to lieutenant colonel! A couple of years were to pass before it was decided that he must go.

Bill's arrival was in marked contrast. A short, slim man in his late thirties he was a British Army warrant officer who had been posted on loan to us to start up the office of General Sir Timothy Creasey. He was a man of quick intelligence and quick wit who I liked immediately. Unfortunately, he did not suffer fools gladly and this was to do him no good at all for he could barely conceal his contempt for some of the contract officers he had to work with who he rightly regarded as his mental and professional inferiors.

Our Guards' lieutenant colonel returned from a duty visit to the UK and we learnt that he had been selected by Sir Timothy Creasey as his Military Adviser (MA to CDS). Clearly, he was going to have an important place in the new power structure. I had my own thoughts, but Bill made it abundantly clear that he thought little of Creasey's choice. 'A bloody woodentop' was his comment. I had not heard the expression before and was quite delighted with it, expressing as it did the majority view of the British Army about the intellectual capacity of the Guards Regiments.

I remembered that in the Royal Air Force we had thought of them as unsurpassed for discipline and bravery but lacking in grey matter. My brother, a Gunner who had gone through Dunkirk, had similar views. Privately, I suspected that the latter was an essential corollary to the former.

On the other side of the wadi from the Joint Staff office there were four old bungalows. Three of them were occupied as quarters and one had stood deserted and decaying for as long as I had been at Bait al Falaj. They had been built many years ago and had been occupied by senior officers during the Dhofar War when the MoD had been located within the Bait al Falaj fort. The prelude to the arrival of Sir Timothy Creasey then began, for the new MA to CDS announced that the decrepit bungalow across the wadi was to be the office of CDS. Various experts were summoned from the MoD Engineering Department and the MA, Bill and I walked them round the old snake and rat infested pile whose verandahs were overgrown with exotic creepers, orchids and cotton plants. The works and bricks supervisors (all British contract men) treated the exercise rather light heartedly until they discovered who CDS was, his position in the hierarchy and his probable date of arrival. They opened their mouths to protest, then thought better of it, deciding that we would not be interested in their problems. They were correct.

However, I was curious. 'Why on earth does he want to move into this place?' I asked the MA indicating the damp walls, the grimy windows and the numerous plants peeping out of the cracks in the cement floor. 'He lived here when he was Commander SAF during the Dhofar War,' came the reply.

I sighed. 'I suppose you can indulge your foibles when you reach four star rank.'

Back across the wadi in the offices of the soon-to-be-extinct Joint Staff, gloom and doom reigned for it looked as if our worst fears were about to be realised. Our 'Woodentop's' future as MA to CDS was assured and Hazel and I found ourselves totally involved in working for Brigadier Hassan Ehsen Naseeb in his new role as ACJS. Our new Secretary Joint Staff and the Navy and Air Members, however, were seeking reassurance about their future like an alcoholic in pursuit of his next bottle. Roger, who shared an office with the soon-to-be MA to CDS was desperate at the thought of losing his shiny new lieutenant colonelship and pleaded with our Woodentop to put in a good word for him with the Supremo when he arrived. The MA raised considerable doubts about his own judgement by agreeing to do so. Next door, the Navy and the Air Force were dealing with the problem in their own inimitable fashion. Ken, now a captain in SON, could almost hear the guillotine blade being raised and he decided that the only way to avoid sudden death was to make himself invaluable to the upper echelons. Unfortunately, the only upper echelon available was Hassan Ehsan and Ken made himself so invaluable that Hassan would put his head around my door in the mornings and say 'Is that Navy man here Alan?' Later, when he began to feel his power and rank he became much more positive and simply said: 'Do not let that man come here to see me.' Having gone through the usual diplomatic excuses the only recourse left was for Hazel or me to perform a rugby tackle when he came charging in. We both baulked at this, but, nevertheless his attempts at being invaluable caused an awful lot of aggravation to both of us.

The Air Force representative had clearly, and with some justification, decided to sulk. Amassing a tall barrier of files in his 'In', 'Out' and 'Pending' trays he sat behind it and announced at regular intervals: 'Don't ask me what's going on. It's the classic mushroom scene so far as I'm concerned. Keep me in the dark and feed me horseshit.'

I felt some sympathy for them both but it was to be some months before they learnt their fate.

Shortly afterwards Sir Timothy arrived and took up residence in his refurbished office on the other side of the wadi, to be joined by our 'Woodentop' as his MA and Bill as his Superintending Clerk in charge of his office. A number of events then occurred in rapid succession. Bill came and requisitioned all the Joint Staff clerical support in the name of CDS. It appeared that he did not trust the Pakistani Mafia too well, nor their ability to spread rumour and gossip. Christian Indians were the ones he wanted and I had cornered the market it seemed. I was a little miffed, but who argued with 'Top Cat' (as he was occasionally referred to). 'Farting against thunder' was an expression we had sometimes used on the squadron and it was very appropriate on this occasion.

Then Hassan Ehsan was told to abandon his title of Acting Chairman Joint Staff as he was to move across the wadi and become Assistant Chief of the Defence Staff. Creasey's Omani deputy in fact.

When he told Hazel and myself Hassan was rightly thrilled for he knew as we did that such an appointment could only be made with the approval of His Majesty. He told us that he had been ADC to Sir Timothy when he was CSAF. 'We were always arguing and fighting,' he concluded with a big grin. I was personally delighted to find that our senior Omani officer in the Sultan's Armed Forces did not walk around on tiptoe and speak of CDS in soft reverential tones as so many of our British officers seemed to.

'He wants me to move across the wadi and set up my office in his bungalow,' said Hassan, 'and I would like it if you and Hazel would come with me.' Both of us had become fond of him and neither thought of refusing. He paused. 'And I want a new desk and a new chair and everything,' he concluded happily. Another thought struck him. (Until then he had been using Peter Thwaites office and car). 'And I want a new Mercedes.'

Hazel and I looked at each other and told him we would start on it straight away.

Hazel knew the strong colours and the furnishings that attracted Omanis and I was pleased to leave that part of it to her. She was simply to walk into the showroom, take her pick, tell them it was for Brigadier Hassan Ehsen Naseeb and get the bill sent to the MoD. 'No problem Sir,' to quote one of my clerks. Unfortunately, the new Mercedes caused a slight problem because I had to deal with a British contract staff officer who had been reared in MoDUK like me. Our conversation followed a pretty inevitable pattern for he had not yet adapted to the Omani way of doing business:

'Good morning Jim. Alan here.'

' 'morning Alan.'

'You know that Hassan Ehsan has been appointed Assistant Chief of the Defence Staff?'

'Yes. I had heard.'

'Well. He wants a new Mercedes.'

A few minutes silence then: 'Why?'

'What do you mean? Why?'

'Well. What's wrong with his present car?'

'Nothing, so far as I know. It's a bit worn, but not too much.'

'You know the bloody rules Alan as well as I do. I've just looked up the records of his car. Used to belong to Brigadier Thwaites, didn't it?'

'Yes.'

'Well, that's it then. It's got no mileage at all for a Merc. I'm afraid that he can't have a new car.'

I let the silence extend for a bit. 'You don't really want me to tell him that, do you Jim?'

'Dear God! How can I keep within my bloody budget?'

'Sorry Matey. Many thanks. Light green like the present one.'

Strings had been pulled when Hazel joined us and she had collected a new Corolla on arrival. Sarah's tatty old saloon was still standing in the car park outside the Joint Staff office. It was covered in leaves and dust from numerous helicopter landings and one morning, before he was hijacked into the CDS office, George asked me if he could be taught to drive in her. 'Faqir has promised to teach me Sir,' he concluded.

I thought of Faqir's 'Wife very serious' and imposed a limit on the lessons. 'O.K. George. But you must not drive outside Bait al Falaj camp.'

'Yes Sir,' he replied and beamed.

A week later I drove into the office car park and saw Sarah's old car standing forlornly under a large tree. Somehow it had collected a remarkably deep dent in the roof running from the windscreen to the rear window. It looked as if somebody had dropped a very large crate on the roof. I visualised such an accident and discarded it. I called for George and asked him about it and felt a certain sympathy for him as he told me.

That old tree had some massive branches and one of them was about five feet above and parallel to the ground. He had decided to give himself a bit of practice the evening before, backed out of his slot and along under the branch. Being inexperienced, it wasn't until the car stopped and stalled that he realised something was wrong. He got out and found himself wedged under the branch.

I asked him why Faqir was not with him when it happened and got the answer I expected. Faqir had lost interest in giving driving lessons when he discovered that they were restricted to the camp. His plan had been to drive around the Capital Area and visit friends.

After further professional tuition George eventually passed his test and I told him to return the car to the Admin pool. Shortly afterwards came a phone call and a plaintive voice said:

'There is a big dent in the car you sent back to us Mister Hoskins.'

'Is there really?'

'Yes Sir. Do you know how it got there?'

'I've no idea. I'm sorry. It used to belong to the secretary to Brigadier Thwaites and she went back to England a long time ago.'

'Thank you Sir,' came the resigned acknowledgement that the enquiry was closed. Over a year later, it was still being driven around with its 'V' shaped roof.

I now began to have doubts about the MA's judgement, for on his personal recommendation Imam Bux became the driver for CDS. I had to comment:

'Not my business I know, but he's so bloody unreliable, he's always late and I don't think he's very bright.'

'Oh nonsense,' came the reply. 'He's a super little chap. Always cheerful and obliging.'

After the MA left I said to Hazel, 'Yes. He'll still be grinning all over his face when he tells you that he's run out of petrol.'

His career was very short lived.

One of the first of Sir Timothy's official engagements was with the head of the Oman Research Department (a pretty euphenism for the Sultanate's Security organisation). It was a hot day and while CDS was being shown around ORD complex Imam Bux was sitting, sweating, in the new, big, glistening Mercedes. He switched on the air conditioner. I doubt if the idea of keeping the battery charged by running the engine ever crossed his mind, or if he even knew it was necessary. In the event, when Sir Timothy was escorted out to his car and had climbed in, the battery could only raise a pathetic whine from the starter motor.

Imam Bux never drove CDS again and was relegated to general office driving. When Lady Annette joined her husband he became part of their household staff.

Hassan Ehsan was now installed in a large office at one end of the CDS bungalow with Hazel and I occupying his outer office. At the opposite end was Sir Timothy's office with the MA in his outer office. In between, in a gaggle of rooms across the middle of the building, the registry and typing services operated, supervised by Bill. At first my Indian clerks had found it difficult to cope with him for he had a quick temper and would vent his spleen by uttering the most terrifying threats. In time though, they realised that there was little real danger in statements like :'I'll stuff that typewriter up you arse; wrap that typewriter ribbon round your neck; stuff that carbon paper down your throat,'to quote a few of the more repeatable admonishments.

But the building had been designed as a home and the layout of the rooms/offices would have made a work-flow expert throw up his hands in despair. For example, should CDS want to talk to ACDS he had to leave his office, cross the MA's office to the far side, pass down a short corridor, cross the main hall, walk through the registry, skirting the desks en route, enter our office, cross that and finally enter Hassan's office. It hardly needs saying that the office intercom was a very popular piece of equipment.

The MoD engineers had made a good job of renovating the old place and inside it was difficult to believe that it had been a partial ruin a couple of months ago. Outside however, spidery lines of fresh cement and plaster showed old cracks with plants still struggling through the bricks and plaster in the darker corners.

But it took determined efforts by Hazel to prevent the creepers and shrubs surrounding the bungalow from suffering too much at the hands of our two Omani gardeners. They were not gardeners of course, but someone's aged relations who had been promoted from the rank of labourer and their knowledge of horticulture was (if it's possible) even less than mine. Their gardening efforts were twofold and simple: water everything that grows every day and, if it grows too well, chop it back without mercy.

Outside the window next to Hazel's desk stood a large box filled with a variety of cactus plants. Their vivid green colour and drooping stems alerted us and we caught the grubby ancient the following morning.

'Maafeesh Maa'i,' said Hazel and pointed at the cactus. The old boy grinned happily at her and played the hose back and forth over the box. 'Maafeesh Maa'i,' she repeated and turned off the tap. He shook his head in resignation and walked away. 'Oh God!' she groaned, 'now I've upset him and he's never going to water any of the plants again.'

Her fears were groundless for he returned with his hose the next morning and watered the cactus along with all of the other plants. He did cast an occasional furtive glance over his shoulder however as he worked his way past our office. Clearly, he was expecting the 'Inkleezee bint' to pop out again.

Hassan Ehsan had the well-earned reputation of being a good and hard-working soldier and it soon became evident that he was determined to become a good staff officer as well. He appeared in the office only minutes after Hazel and I did and slogged away, often staying on late or returning for a few hours in the evening. It was a pleasure to work for him for he was always appreciative of time and effort spent on his behalf. He was not fluent in English but spoke it quite well and could write it. A lot of the time in the first few months was spent in polishing up his drafts or, conversely, reducing some of the more voluminous letters and instructions we received into simple English. Later as he got to know and trust us he would simply call us into his office and say 'Please write to... and tell them that...'

Hazel's Arabic was already quite passable and got better for she had taken a couple of courses and often spoke it on the telephone and to some of Hassan's visitors. Apart from the salutations and a few basic phrases however, my Arabic was non-existent. I occasionally had attacks of conscience but excused myself by acknowledging that ninety-nine percent of my dealings were with British officers or Omanis who spoke English as a second language or in some cases, their only language. Strange as this may seem it was not that uncommon for, during the reign of the old Sultan, a number of families had sent their children to the UK or the USA to be educated and their first contact with Arabic was on their return to Oman.

Hassan was a veritable squirrel with paper however, and if a letter was important it paid to keep a sharp eye on its whereabouts. I first discovered this when we moved his office, in his absence, from the Joint Staff building across the wadi. A whole four drawer filing cabinet full of such gems as four year old laundry bills, pamphlets advertising guided missiles and ancient invitations to regimental reunions. I tackled him about the collection and he assured me that he was going to sort through them all one day. I saved him the trouble during the move and he never commented on the disappearance of his hoard. But any piece of paper which was not of immediate interest went into that four drawer cabinet which I now cleared out every month.

I'm afraid that Hazel and I gave the MA to CDS a hard time at first for he became increasingly arrogant making announcements - no, pronouncements - like 'Sir Timothy wants...' or 'CDS has said...' Having dealt with senior officers during a fair portion of my working life I was not impressed by his reverential tone and Hazel had an inbuilt reaction against pomposity in any form. Moreover, we were both fond of Hassan and the MA had an appallingly arrogant way of addressing him which set our teeth on edge. The inevitable happened one day and the MA, presumably under some pressure, walked through our office and into Hassan's unannounced to tell him that he was wanted by CDS. He did it what's more in front of an Omani visitor. There was already a growing sensitivity among the Omanis about the number of British in positions of power in the country and Hassan was rightly furious. He spoke to CDS at some length on the subject and thereafter, the MA never spoke to Hassan without checking with us first. I was beginning to appreciate Bill's comments about 'Bloody Woodentops'. Sensitivity was certainly not one of their attributes and the MA had been behaving as if the British Raj was still with us.

The number of petitions seemed to be on the increase and as our office was rather large, part of it had been set aside as a waiting area for those wishing to see Hassan. Visitors ranged in rank and position from almost the highest to the lowest and I always enjoyed seeing how some of the less sophisticated ones would sit on the edge of the settee, sipping their coffee and watching wide-eyed as Hazel operated the intercom and her electric typewriter. Plainly, this entertainment was worth the many miles they had covered to get to our office.

Some petitions had a touch of pathos and some were pure farce. The case of Dad Rahim, a Jundi (Private) in the Land Forces, was one of the latter.

Dad Rahim had been in the Sultan's army for sixteen years and at the end of that period he was still a Jundi. It seemed that his officers thought him willing but dim whereas his comrades reckoned he had been touched by Allah, or, in English parlance, he wasn't all there. When Hassan told us about the petition I was inclined to agree with his comrades.

He was greying at the temples but still had the lean shape of the hillman (apart form the small pot belly which most of them attained by their late thirties). Nevertheless he was still a good catch for any young woman and a pair of soft brown Omani eyes had captivated him. Her father had agreed a 'bride' price of three thousand Rials. Dad Rahim had saved that and another three thousand to put down as a deposit on a house and his officer had assured him that he would get the rest as a loan from the Housing Fund.

Dad Rahim had never trusted banks. You gave them all of your money and all you got in return was a little green book with that strange English writing in it. His friends had told him that his money would be safe but he was not so sure. Anyway, he was perfectly satisfied with his cache; nobody would think of looking for his money there. A track ran from the Nizwa road to the village of his bride-to-be. Halfway along, opposite the two camel thorns, his money lay safe, buried in a tin between the ruts.

Poor Dad Rahim. As Hassan recounted the petition I could almost forecast the ending of the story. The day of the wedding was approaching and he decided that on his next leave he would retrieve the money and pay the bride price and the house deposit. Two weeks later he jumped out of the taxi and turned to go down the track to her village. He stopped. Something was appallingly wrong. Instead of dusty wheel ruts winding their way through the scrub a newly surfaced road unrolled black against the yellow sand and gravel. He ran down it to find his worst fears confirmed.

All three of us found if difficult to keep a straight face, particularly when Hassan dictated a letter to Hazel seeking the co-operation of the Director General of Roads in this tragic case. Would he please authorise some minor work on the new road running down to the village of Muti.

I had known Fred during my MoDUK days, albeit not that well for he operated mainly in the Army Department. It would be more accurate to say that I had know of Fred, mainly through a namesake of mine who had worked with him. He had been sent on loan to MoD Oman to be their Chief Finance Officer and then, after retiring as an Under Secretary for the British Civil Service, stayed on as Adviser to the Omani Head of Finance. A very difficult job, considering the Oman mores. I had met him a few times since arriving in Oman and he was always a pleasant and courteous man.

One morning the MA entered our office and announced that CDS had promoted Fred to be Head of Resource Management (HRM). Hazel forestalled me in asking, rather coarsely, what sort of animal was a Head of Resource Management.

'In charge of everything except military matters. Works directly under Sir Timothy.' replied our pet Woodentop. 'Rather like the Under Secretary used to.' I seized on this.

'Used to? What do you mean used to?'

'Well, I don't really know, but I understand that he's packing it in fairly soon.'

'Who's packing it in soon?'

'Saleem al Ghazali,' came the reluctant reply.

'Does he know?' I asked.

'Of course he does,' came the indignant reply.

'Well,' I said facetiously, 'I'm sure it's all for the best,' and Hazel, who tended to overdo the humour on occasions joined in. 'Ah'm suah de white folks knows what they's doin' Massa.'

The MA gave us a look of disgust and left.

'What's Resource Management mean?' asked Hazel.

'I'm not sure, but I suspect it's a current trendy name for an old job. If he's in charge of everything except military matters it simply means that he's taking over the old job of the Under Secretary.' I thought for a minute. 'But with a very big difference,' and I almost groaned. 'He's in charge of all the resources but, unlike the UK where he answers to civilian government, out here he's going to be answerable only to the military, because he's on Creasey's staff.'

'Is that bad?'

'The worst. The establisher's nightmare. The military controlling the money. In other words they can indulge all their fantasies about super regiments, super ships, super weapons, super aircraft and as many people as they want.'

The concept of a Head of Resource Management very quickly became one of those lesser problems that hover at the back of your mind, for a much more immediate and personal problem arose.

There was a steady and ongoing deterioration in the rate of exchange between the Omani Rial and the Pound Sterling. When I arrived in Oman, the pound had been worth under six hundred Baizas. Now it was worth over eight hundred Baizas and worsening.

I had never applied myself to or tried to understand the manipulations of the foreign currency market but we were told that the Omani Rial was tied to the US Dollar and, because this was falling badly, so was the Rial - in sympathy. This was interesting, but hardly enlightening. From the parochial viewpoint however, we had all seen the value of our salaries in the UK reduced by over thirty percent in one month.

As the situation worsened so the number of 'Runners' and those failing to return from leave rose. On the whole, life in Oman was not that pleasant and for those of us living in the Bait al Falaj Mess even less so. The situation was bearable if your salary compensated for it to some degree, but if you were earning about as much as a farm labourer in East Anglia then there was little incentive to remain. As one colleague put it: loyalty does have its financial limits. For my part I had set a cut-off. If the Pound and Rial attained par and nothing was being done to rectify the problem then I would leave.

But on the gloomiest of days there was humour somewhere and Phil provided it by dropping into our office a copy of a 1960 letter he had discovered in his office archives. Relating to the search for an Omani National Anthem it is, in its way, very descriptive of how life must have been under the rule of Sultan Said bin Taimur. I reproduce it below without amendment:

Letter from the Consul General Muscat
to the Earl of Home, Foreign Secretary.

August 17th 1960

My Lord,

I have the honour to refer to Your Lordship's despatch No. 8 of the 29th July, in which you requested me to ascertain, on behalf of the Lords Commissioners of the Admiralty, whether the Bb clarinet music, enclosed with your despatch, was a correct and up-to-date rendering of the National Salute to the Sultan of Muscat and Oman.

2 I have encountered certain difficulties in fulfilling this request. The Sultanate has not, since about 1937, possessed a band. None of the Sultan's subjects, so far as I am aware, can read music, which the majority of them regard as sinful. The Manager of the British Bank of the Middle East, who can, does not possess a clarinet. Even if he did, the dignitary who in the absence of the Sultan is the recipient of ceremonial honours and who might be presumed to recognise the tune, is somewhat deaf.

3 Fortunately I have been able to obtain, and now enclose, a gramophone record which has on one side a rendering by a British

military band of the 'Salutation and march to His Highness the Sultan of Muscat and Oman'. The first part of this tune, which was composed by the bandmaster of a cruiser(*) in about 1932, bears a close resemblance to a pianoforte rendering by the Bank Manager of the clarinet music enclosed with Your Lordship's despatch. The only further testimony I can obtain of the correctness of this music is that it reminds a resident of long-standing of a tune, once played by the long defunct band of the now disbanded Muscat Infantry, and known at the time to non-commissioned members of His Majesty's forces as (I quote the vernacular) 'Gawd strike the Sultan blind.'

4 I am informed by the Acting Minister of Foreign Affairs that there are now no occasions on which the 'Salutations' is officially played. The last occasion on which it is known to have been played at all was on a gramophone at an evening reception given by the Military Secretary in honour of the Sultan, who inadvertently sat on the record afterwards and broke it. I consider, however, that an occasion might arise when the playing might be appropriate; if, for example, the Sultan were to go aboard a cruiser which carried a band. I am proposing to call on His Highness shortly at Salalah on his return from London, and shall make further enquiries as to his wishes on the matter.

5 I am sending a copy of this despatch, without enclosure to His Excellency the Political Resident at Bahrain.

I have the honour to be Sir,

(J.F.S. Phillips)

H.B.M's Consul General

(*) H.M.S. HAWKINS

In marked contrast to our decreasing salaries and the state of affairs in Muscat in the 1960's was a quite remarkable episode involving a Pakistani mechanic at the Royal Garage. I suppose he would have been earning about two hundred Rials a month; a derisory amount to us but given the appalling rates of pay on the Subcontinent a lot of money to him.

The Palace Garage was near the Watteyah roundabout in the Capital Area and very exclusive it was too, for it existed solely to maintain the cars of the Royal Family and senior dignitaries in the ministries. The popular belief was that they would not soil their hands on anything cheaper than a Mercedes. Whether this was true I do not know, but certainly all the cars I saw there spoke of considerable wealth. For obvious reasons, the government official in my account must remain nameless for, as Archie said when he told me the story, 'it's more than my job's worth if his name became public'. Anyhow, this official had apparently telephoned Archie at the garage a couple of weeks previously and, honest to God, the conversation had gone something like this.

'Archie. My car came in for some repairs last week. Have any of your mechanics found anything in the car?'

'Nobody's mentioned it to me if they have Sir. What sort of thing was it?'

'Some money.'

'Oh! How much?'

'Thirty thousand Rials.'

'Good God! I'll start a search for it.'

'I'd be grateful if you would. It was most careless of me to leave it there.'

Archie found out where the car was and walked across to the body shop. He was thinking hard and by the time he got there something had clicked. He called the foreman over.

'Do you remember telling me about the panel beater who disappeared last week?'

'Yes Sir.'

'And when you made enquiries you suspected that he'd done a runner and gone back to Pakistan.'

'Yes Sir.'

'Do you also remember telling me how surprised you were, because he was such a good and reliable man?'

'Yes Sir.'

'Well. I think I've got a bloody good idea why he took a runner.'

Ken decided that his campaign to make himself indispensable to the new power base was not going very well. Whenever he contacted CDS's office the MA made noises which were far from encouraging and Hassan Ehsan seemed to be becoming less and less available. All told, he increasingly found himself sitting with Ken in an office block which was like a morgue. And people who accidentally found themselves talking to them on the telephone made tactless remarks like 'I thought the Joint Staff died months ago' and, even more cutting, 'Good God! Are you still around?'

It was as frustrating as hell. How could you prove that you were invaluable if nobody gave you the opportunity?

Harry ran true to form and sat behind his barricade of files making such comments as: 'I wouldn't treat an airman, the way I'm bloody well being treated.' On the whole though, the lack of activity was not new and his only, quite justified, complaint was that nothing had been said to him at all on the official network. Discussing it with him I did try to make the point that at his rank, perhaps it was thought that he didn't need telling. It was assumed that he could draw inferences from what was going on around him. 'Rubbish,' was his reply. 'Common courtesy to tell me.' It was difficult to argue that. As he put it: 'One day I've got a job and the next day everybody's gone and there's just me and him,' jerking his thumb over his shoulder to where Ken had installed himself in Hassan's old office. 'And,' he concluded, 'nobody's said a sodding word.'

Almost inevitably, Hazel started referring to them as Tweedledum and Tweedledee.

Ken however had decided to do something to make his presence known and, unbeknown to Hazel or myself had had a direct telephone line installed between his office and Hassan's.

You could have been excused for believing that Hassan had some connection with NASA for his desk was almost buried under communication equipment. There was an ordinary telephone with an intercept facility for Hazel; an office intercom telephone for CDS and ourselves; a private 'outside line' telephone; a 'secure' telephone accompanied by an enormous scrambler box which weighed half a ton and lastly, a red telephone which was on the 'Palace Office Net'. At first, the additional telephone on the window-sill behind Hassan's chair escaped my attention but when I noticed it and asked him what it was for he looked bewildered. 'But I thought that you or Hazel had put it there.' When I eventually discovered its origin I said nothing and was not surprised to find it with its receiver permanently off the hook.

Unfortunately, Ken with true Nelsonian vigour, pursued his campaign until the moment I feared came along. He telephoned me one morning and said that he wanted to see Hassan and discuss something of importance with him. I asked him the subject and he said he would rather not discuss it with me. I said I would see what I could do and went and called on Hassan. I got the answer I expected. 'I do not want to see that Navy man, Alan.' I returned to my desk and passed on the message as kindly as I could and after a moments silence, the telephone was replaced.

Whether Ken thought that I had denied him access, or whether he thought that all would be well once he saw Hassan I have no idea. All I do know is that twenty minutes later he marched determinedly through our office and said over his shoulder, 'I'm going to see Hassan.'

Early morning was never a good time to present Hassan with a difficult problem or a difficult situation and, in that, he was very like his master Sir Timothy Creasey. I was halfway out of my chair with an unspoken warning on my lips when Ken entered Hassan's office and less than a minute passed before we heard the loud high pitch of what we called Hassan's angry voice. Ken reappeared and without a glance in our direction marched through and out of our office. I felt some sympathy for him; his application for a renewal of contract had been submitted some time ago and he was clearly becoming desperate. I glanced over at Hazel and she shrugged and spread her hands. 'He asked for it.'

It was shortly after that episode that she began to spend most of her working days out of the office. Hassan was moving into a lifestyle more in keeping with his new rank and position as the senior Omani in the Sultan's Armed Forces and she was tasked with supervising the move into the new house; the new house being CJS's old house. How long Peter Thwaites had lived in it I had no idea, but for most of the time, it had been as a grass widower. In any event, a fairly extensive repaint job was required, as well as new curtains, carpets and furniture. The building which housed the games room, a room which I had once remarked would comfortably accommodate four of the rooms I lived in, was turned into a guest annexe and, at Hassan's request a large fountain, that sight beloved of all Arabs, was constructed in the courtyard.

The next few weeks were entertaining as Hazel cursed furniture suppliers, curtain makers, builders, painters and tilers indiscriminately. 'Why don't the bastards do what they say they're going to do?' she would wail. 'I don't think any of them ever turn up on time, or, for that matter, can tell the bloody time.' I sympathised with her and quietly congratulated myself on not becoming too involved. Eventually the move took place with Hazel at one end and me at the other and everything was moved without too much damage, but, once again, the camp labour force drove us both mad with frustration. As this group of Omani worthies featured so often in our lives they deserve a few lines to themselves.

Peter Greaves, as Camp Commandant, had a bunch of about fifty labourers on his staff and they were used for diverse tasks, such as whitewashing the stones which delineated the roads, car parks and the helipad; cutting back trees and weeding (under close supervision); loading and unloading lorries; sweeping roads and so on. They were of all ages, shapes and sizes and certainly not the brightest members of the community. But there were ten or so, regarded as a cut above the rest and these were the ones entrusted with such delicate tasks as moving furniture.

But, as I often said to Hazel after watching them at work: 'Your mind boggles at what the rest of them must be like. You'd think these dull buggers would learn. God knows, they're been doing the bloody job for years.'

Not a bit of it.

They would lift a desk, turn it on its side, usually without intent, and watch open mouthed as its drawers slid out onto the floor; or they would lift an armchair and charge a door when the most cursory glance told you there was no chance of them passing through. I thought that they were totally thick but her comment that 'they have absolutely no spatial awareness,' was a more entertaining and certainly kinder way of putting it. They would arrive on their lorry, accompanied by a Raqeeb (Sergeant) in charge, but none of our anguished cries of 'Oh God! No!' or his Arabic screams of fury made an iota of difference to their lumbering performance and, unless you were on the *qui vive* all of the time, the furniture would be badly scarred and the walls badly dented.

In their way, they were a cross to bear, rather like the packs of feral dogs that occasionally roamed the camp. We were, however, allowed to shoot these.

My self-congratulation at not becoming too involved in Hassan's move was very short-lived. After a few days leave, during which he fluffed his feathers and settled into his new nest, he came back to work and two minutes after his arrival he called me in. The following conversation took place.

'Alan. I wish to hold a party for my new house.'

'Yes Sir. How many people do you think?'

'Oh. About a hundred or so. I will let you have a list of the names.'

I blinked a bit but rallied. 'Yes Sir. When do you want to hold it?'

Hassan glanced at his notes. 'On the eleventh I think. I go on a visit to Sudan after that.'

I gulped. Four days away. Over one hundred guests. 'Might be a bit difficult Sir. I don't know if the mess can handle it at such short notice. And we have to get the invitations printed.' I could see that he really didn't want to be bothered with such detail and I thought, I bet his missus put him up to this.

'See what you can do Alan,' was his final word.

I returned to my desk and sat there for a minute. There was food and drink to provide; a guest list; staff; invitations; and a map showing the location of the new house. And what about dress? There had to be a police guard outside which could control the parking. Good grief! I looked at my wrist watch. Four days. No. Three and a half to be exact. I looked at the ceiling for inspiration but none came. Oh well. If we couldn't fix it that was that. The key was getting staff to serve the food and drink. If Harvey couldn't provide it, that was the end of the matter.

It has long been a tradition of most officers' messes that if a mess member wished to hold a private party he could use the mess staff and facilities providing it did not interfere in any way with the comfort and service available to the other mess members. This was a very useful aspect of mess membership for such a party could be held at half the price of a similar function organised by a civilian caterer.

It was inevitable that in this area Harvey's enthusiasm really took off for not only could he make a lot of people very happy, but he could give his staff the opportunity to earn overtime and boost the sales of mess food and drink. It also became clear that his enthusiasm had gone over the top when complaints at the dinner table elicited the fact that half of the stewards were five miles away serving at a private dinner party. Eyebrows were again raised when it was learnt that the mess cooks were making birthday cakes for the children of Omanis who weren't even mess members. Birthday parties for children in the anteroom in the afternoon I could just about tolerate, providing the debris (including the children) was cleared away by six o'clock in the evening. However, my patience evaporated one lunchtime when I walked into the mess for a beer and was refused entry by a total (British) stranger who asked me for my invitation card. It appeared that a wedding reception was taking place. From that moment on I began to view Harvey with a somewhat jaundiced eye for it seemed clear to me that he was happily convinced he was really running a slightly seedy hotel. And running it well, for the monthly profits continued to climb.

It was with all this in mind therefore that I approached him about Hassan's house-warming.

At the prospect of holding such a large party his eyes lit up, but they soon dulled when he heard the date. I apologised for the short notice, assuming that this was the reason, but he assured me that this was not the problem. The problem was that he had undertaken to run a private party on that date. 'Who?' I asked. The name came. 'Good God!' I protested. 'He's not even a mess member. Am I supposed to tell Hassan that you can't do his party because you're doing one for that guy.

Jesus! He's not even in SAF. Hassan will go spare.' I rose to go. 'Still. You're the mess manager and it's your decision. I'll tell him you can't do it and hope he doesn't ask me why.'

Harvey rose as well. 'No. No. Alan. I'll do it.'

'How? You've got the other party on.'

'I'll manage. Don't you worry.'

I thought for a second. It won't do any harm I decided. A bit of pressure will do him good.

'Harvey.'

'Yes?'

'You do know who Hassan is?'

'Of course I do,' he replied indignantly.

'Just bear it in mind. He's the senior Omani officer in the SAF. Any cock ups and it's probably the Tin Budgie.'

I felt a little better as I left the mess office, but began to worry again as I thought how best to notify the guests. Many of them worked at BAF and these I would ask in person, the rest I would telephone with a promise that a written invitation would follow. I would have to see Maurice Sousou for an Arabic version of the invitation for the reverse of the card. I hoped the printers could run off a hundred and fifty gold embossed cards in time. Hassan had said that dress was semiformal - tie, long sleeved shirts and slacks for the Brits, National Dress for the Omanis.

Eventually all of the preparations were completed and the party went without mishap, but in the process one very large and dignified member of the Omani Royal Family developed an intense dislike for me. Hamed was an imposing individual, a senior civilian officer in the ministry who spoke the most beautiful, fluent English. He also possessed an unerring instinct for immediately grasping the wrong end of any stick and dealing with it in speech and on paper at great length. However, this unfortunate episode was not his fault in any way.

My telephone rang and when I answered it Hamed's sonorous tones rolled through. 'My dear Alan. How are you?'

'Al hamdu lillah.'

'Good. Good.'

'What can I do for you Hamed?'

'Ah yes. The invitation to Hassan's party on the eleventh.'

'Yes?'

'What does 'Tie' mean?'

'Well. Sort of halfway between formal, you know, jacket and tie, and informal. It means slacks, tie and long sleeved shirt.'

'Ah. I see. Thank you Alan.'

After I replaced the receiver I thought only briefly about our conversation. I decided he'd probably never come across the expression before and had just wondered what it meant exactly. What never crossed my mind was that he might be one of those Omanis who could not read Arabic and would not be able to understand the reverse side of the card which specified 'National Dress'. He was, in fact, the only Omani at the function who was dressed in slacks, tie and long sleeved shirt and I don't think he ever forgave me for the embarassment.

One further episode enlivened that day. Without warning there was an enormous explosion which had the building and the windows shaking for some seconds. We all ran outside and there, across the mountains towards Mina al Fahal, a thick column of yellow dust was slowly climbing hundreds of feet into the air. Our first thoughts centred on some disaster at the refinery but, as we learned, the truth was happily more mundane. Something was at last being done about the growing traffic congestion and a new multi-lane highway was being driven through the peaks to provide a direct route from the Capital Area to the rapidly growing industrial and government office developments along Qaboos Street. That explosion was the first of many to come during the next two years.

The departure of Saleem al Ghazali from his post as Under Secretary took place as forecast and he moved across to the Musandam Development Committee. This was a much more personally rewarding job, as I surmised. In his place came a charming ex- SOLF Lieutenant Colonel whose tribal name was al Mutassim. I never did learn his first name for two reasons. One was that I had little to do with his office, the other was that his tenure was very short. His English was very good and he was a sociable man, but why he left so quickly I had no idea. Plenty of theories were advanced of course, and because he occasionally dropped into the mess for a drink it was suggested that that might have something to do with it. As I pointed out with some sarcasm, if that was so, then most of the British contract officers would have been Tin Budgied long ago. Something was definately going on. Various events and postings were taking place and we could see the hand of CDS behind some of them but it was to be a few months before we worked out where we were being led. I should have known, of course, for the appointment of a Head of Resources Management on the staff of CDS was a clear indicator.

One morning we had a complete electrical failure in the bungalow. This was usually no problem and the Pakistani electrician and his Omani assistant arrived within ten minutes of my phone call. On this occasion, however, the cause was not easily found; the intercom was dead, so were the typewriters and the copiers and the low overhanging roof of the verandah encircling the building made it impossible to work without electric light. Tempers were getting short and I drove off to find Dave.

He was not in his office. 'No Sir,' said his clerk. 'I am not sure where he is. Perhaps he is in his room.' I drove off to find that he wasn't there either. I heard loud laughter from the civil engineers room so I knocked on the door and after a shouted 'Come in,' I entered. The hard core were at it. Only half past eight and judging by the filled ashtrays and the empty cans they had been at it for some time. Dave was there and I told him the problem and he jumped to his feet with obvious relief.

'I'll come in your car,' he said.

As we drove away I asked: 'What's all that about?'

'Don't ask me,' he replied. 'I only popped into Bill's room to borrow something and they were hard at it.'

'Jesus!' was my comment. 'It's not even nine o'clock yet.' Dave burst out laughing. I looked across at him. 'What's the joke?'

He smiled. 'That remark of yours. I don't know about Ashley, but Bill and Robin have been at it since lunchtime yesterday.'

I closed my mouth while I absorbed that. Over the years in and with the services I thought I had met some pretty devoted boozers but this was really big league stuff.

'Christ! Dave. It's nearly a twenty-four hour session. Nobody can drink like that surely?'

'You'd be surprised Mate.' came the rejoinder. 'Bill reckons that he's had a few parties that have gone on for forty-eight hours.'

'Dear God. What the hell must they feel like at the end of it?'

'Well,' came Dave's placid reply. 'I know Bill suffers quite a bit and usually goes to bed for a day or two. Robin usually goes down to the medical centre and gets a massive vitamin injection; C or D I'm not sure which it is, but it works wonders apparently. He used to be a medical student you know.'

'Who? Robin?'

'Yes.'

I drove on in silence while I absorbed what Dave had told me. I often thought that I drank too much, but I was an amateur against this sort of scene. There was something desperate about that sort of drinking.

It was a few days later when the first visible cracks began to appear in Hazel's marriage.

Her husband was an ex-Guards officer and she had come out to Oman and joined him some four years earlier when his SOLF regiment was stationed near Nizwa, a hundred kilometres inland. Later, they had moved to the Sultan's Armed Forces Training Regiment at Ghala, half-way between the Capital Area and Seeb Airport and, fortunately for Hazel's continued residence in the Sultanate, she had found a job in the office of the Ruwi Hotel - and an Omani prepared to sponsor her. This was the situation when she got the job as Sarah's replacement. With that job went a furnished flat with all services paid for and a car of her own.

I felt sorry for John and Hazel as the marriage started to collapse. Poor John was apparently totally unaware that he was no longer necessary to her continued existence in Oman for she now had a job, a car and flat of her own while at the same time poor Hazel saw what she referred to as 'the wasted years' disappearing behind her. I was surprised, however, at the first indication of the crisis for it appeared in an almost ludicrous manner in a casual conversation.

Hassan had gone to a meeting with Ali Majid at the Palace office. Colonel Ali Majid was, to give him his full title, First ADC to His Majesty and President of the Palace Office. He was probably Sultan Qaboos's closest and most trusted friend and a charming man who I had met a couple of times. In Hassan's absence, Hazel and I were having a cup of coffee and chatting.

'I went over to the Cold Store earlier on to get one or two bits,' Hazel started. (The Matrah Cold Store was a supermarket a few hundred yards from the camp where we bought everything from cheese to soap powder.) I nodded.

'They had some marvellous legs of lamb in the butchers. God! I haven't had a decent bit of lamb for years.'

'Well, didn't you buy one?'

'I can't. I haven't got any money.'

I thought about that. She had been paid only a few days ago, so why hadn't she got any money? It wasn't my business I decided.

'Do you want to borrow ten rials then?' I asked.

Her face brightened. 'Would you mind? I'll see if I can get the money out of John the next time I see him.'

'Out of John?' I repeated.

'Yes. I give him my salary and he banks it.'

I gave her the money and kept my mouth shut. It was not for me to comment I thought, but she must have been the first modern girl I'd known who gave all her earnings to her man.

When she returned the loan I gathered that it had not been easy extracting it from her husband. I found it amazing that a girl as intelligent and independent as her had to plead to get some of her own money. My thoughts must have shown on my face for it all began to come out. She was totally fed up at not being able to have her hair done, nor buy a dress or a pair of shoes when she wanted to. I had occasionally teased her about a tatty old pair of sandals she was always wearing; now I realised she had had no choice. It was bloody ridiculous she said, here she was earning a damned good salary and yet she had to borrow ten rials from me to buy some meat. 'And I'm not bloody well going out to Ghala this Friday,' she concluded.

I raised my eyebrows.

'I go out there every Friday,' she explained, 'and half of the day I spend cleaning out his room and doing the washing.'

'But Good God! Hazel. He's got a batman, hasn't he?'

'Yes. But he doesn't like to ask him to do some jobs, so they're left for me. Well, he can clean out his own room this Juma. I'm going to spend the day lounging around in my own super little flat, do a bit of sketching, listen to some music. Relax. I don't need him.'

I made sympathetic noises and she added: 'And after work I'm going to come round to your room and guzzle gin and tonic until it's coming out of my ears.'

She did and the alcohol enabled her to really let her hair down about the marriage. Over the next few months as she went through the worst part of the break up I became a ready shoulder.

Dissatisfaction had been growing for some considerable time about SAF pay. Not so much over the rate of exchange at present for this had improved somewhat, but the pay itself. Not only the British, Pakistani and Indian officers and other ranks but the Omanis in the Forces were becoming conscious of the fact that their pay did not compare at all favourably with the Forces of the other Gulf States.

As we had the capability of carrying out the exercise ourselves it was beyond my understanding why the newly created Head of Resource Management called in a team of experts from an expensive UK company to evaluate the situation. At the time, I suspected that it was simple ignorance of the resources he had available and certainly by the time I made the point it was far too late for they were already very comfortably ensconced in the Gulf Hotel - with their own hire cars - all these charges, of course, over and above the hefty company fee.

Many months and many thousands of rials later they produced a list of jobs, commensurate ranks and grades and recommended rates of pay. What they had performed was an exercise that I had often carried out for MoDUK.

I had to admit however, that their presentation of their findings in a glossy booklet printed in London was superior to the typed pages I used to produce, while their use of words such as 'matrix', 'macro' and 'micro' sounded, and was, much more expensive than the plebeian words I used like 'table', 'large' and 'small'.

Having presented their 'macro' bill the team then returned to London and an interminable series of meetings followed, during which HRM attempted to obtain agreement amongst the three services about a joint service case to be submitted to the Ministry of Finance. It was an appallingly tedious affair that went on for months and months, not helped at all by the amazingly parochial view taken by the three service representatives.

'If your divers are going to have an allowance of five rials a week then our parachute instructors should have six,' or: 'If your parachute instructors are going to have and allowance of six rials a week then our mine and bomb disarmament chaps should have seven.'

For my part, I could not have argued with any of them. Anybody that dives into the deep black, jumps out of an aircraft without having to, or dices with instant death with a screwdriver deserves all of the pay that he can get.

It was during one of these meetings however, that the conference room telephone rang and Phil answered it. An ex-RAF wing commander, he was a civilian staff officer to the Under Secretary and regarded very highly. His immediate superior had been another British civilian staff officer and Personal Adviser to the Under Secretary, a man who was the senior British staff officer in SAF. This 'rooster' had in fact received his marching orders from CDS some weeks before. After the meeting, I gathered that it was now Phil's turn. He was not to be sacked, but moved sideways to become one of His Highness's many personal assistants.

He appeared bemused by the news and could only shake his head in bewilderment when I asked 'Why?'

'Didn't you have any idea that you were going to be moved?'

He shook his head again.

I had another shot. 'Who's taking you place in the Under Secretary's office?'

'Nobody, so far as I can make out.'

'But I reckon His Highness has got personal assistants coming out of his ears. He needs another one like a hole in the head.'

Phil agreed. 'That's what worries me. I'll be going into a 'nothing' job.'

And so it turned out to be.

When I returned to the office the following day I discussed it with Hazel. Slowly but surely, His Excellency the Under Secretary was being denuded of all his senior staff. Where would it end? we wondered. We were soon to find out.

As a change from going to the Aqua Club every Friday I had made a number of trips out into the local countryside with friends from the mess. Readers should perhaps erase any mental pictures conjured up by the word 'countryside'. It was interesting and informative but certainly no more than that. What we saw were mile upon mile of arid stony plains with the occasional oasis in the distance. Quryat: a fishing village a hundred kilometres south of Muscat. Nazwa: an ancient holy city two hundred kilometres inland, Tanuf: bombed and rocketed to destruction by SOAF during the jebel rebellion in the nineteen fifties.

It was interesting that the numerous civilisations whose remains cover Cyprus stirred me, intellectually and emotionally, whereas the medieval and recent history of the Arab world in Oman left me quite unmoved. I wondered why.

Chapter 5

One morning Hassan was summoned to Sir Timothy Creasey's office and when he returned he had much the same bemused expression that Phil had worn. Having entered his office he pressed his intercom and said: 'Hazel, please make me a cup of coffee and then come in here with Alan.'

We walked in, he gestured to us to sit down then announced:

'General Creasey wants me to become the Under Secretary,' he announced.

It took a few seconds for the information to be digested then Hazel and I started to speak together. I waved to her to go ahead for I was fairly certain that she would be asking the same question.

'Who becomes ACDS, if you become the Under Secretary Sir?'

'Nobody.' Hassan grinned broadly. 'I'm taking on both jobs.'

'Jesus!' I couldn't help the exclamation. 'Both jobs?'

He nodded.

I thought hard. Admittedly, the ACDS job was largely protocol at present, inspecting this regiment, opening that new barracks and so on, but he was the senior Omani in the Sultan's Forces and CDS would have to use him more and more as time passed. The Under Secretary's post was a full-time occupation in its own right. When Saleem had been in the chair, there had been three British staff officers directly supporting him, plus another twenty or thirty in finance, contracts, audit, admin and the rest. And this was ignoring the thousand drivers, cleaners, clerks, labourers and Omani staff officers. On the other hand, the new HRM post was taking over a fair slice of the Under Secretary's responsibilities. Maybe it would work. Poor Hassan thinks he works hard at the present but wait until he starts collecting some of the US's junk. Anyhow, whatever my thoughts we mustn't discourage him. I put on a cheerful tone. 'You'll be quite busy Sir.'

'Yes, I know Alan. CDS said that he will give us more staff.'

I should bloody well hope so, I thought, we're certainly going to need them.

Later, discussing it with Hazel, I found she was as angry as a mother hen whose chicks are threatened. She knew as well as me how such mental effort and how many hours had been put in by Hassan in his efforts to master his new responsibilities; the reading of position papers, dealing with importuning weapons salesmen, petitions, promotions, courts martial - all of it in English.

'The poor soul's up to his eyes in paper work already. How the hell is he supposed to cope with all the Under Secretary's crap? What's Creasey trying to do? Drive Hassan into a nervous breakdown?'

'I don't think so Ducks. What he's doing is gathering all of the reins into his hot sticky little hands and getting rid of all of the civilians from any position of importance.'

'What about HRM though?'

'Fred is bloody good value, but he's Creasey's man. They knew each other years ago in the British Army. Anyway, Fred is not an independent civil service man any longer. He's just another of Creasey's staff officers.' I thought on a little. 'The concept's very attractive. A Supremo with all of the power in his hands and answerable only to Qaboos. He could carry out some really worthwhile reorganisation. But I'm doubtful.'

'Why?'

'It's an inbuilt establisher's suspicion of the military mind. They're profligate with money and their answer to every problem is more men.'

'Oh!'

'We'll see. The next few months are going to be very interesting.'

They were, for new staff, military and civilian began to arrive and they had to be found office space whether their contribution warranted it or not. One who did not warrant any accommodation was Raa'id Sami. Impeccable English, bearded, olive skinned and handsome, he came from a good, wealthy Omani family and did not like the tedium of daily appearances in the office. He also had a reputation for jet-set scrapes in various night clubs around the world. Rumour had it that his last, earnt him an eviction from a New York night club, publicity and the displeasure of His Majesty. Such displeasure however, had not changed Sami's carefree approach and 'Where's Sami?' became a fairly routine enquiry around the office and 'God knows' a fairly routine answer.

It was on a Thursday that the military called him to task and the error of his ways was put to him at great length. 'Your future career in SOLF is at stake. If you hope to make Muqaddam (lieutenant colonel) you'd better pull your bloody finger out and start applying yourself to your job. And no more days off just because you went to a party the night before. Get it?' As I say, that was on the Thursday.

On the following Saturday he appeared in the office resplendent in the formal civilian garb of a senior government official. Bisht (black and gold embroidered cloak) over his white dishdash and gold and silver khanja (ceremonial dagger) at his belt. He looked most impressive and relished the expressions of admiration he received. Particularly those from Hazel, who he had been trying to bed without success for years.

In reply to our questions he announced that he had just been appointed Director of Meteorology by the Palace Office and was on his way to take up his new post. With ill concealed pleasure he made a point of visiting the British senior officer who had lectured him on Thursday.

I knew him well and liked him as an amiable and totally unreliable rogue and had always thanked the Almighty that he didn't work for me or with me. I could not resist making the somewhat coarse enquiry: 'What the ... do you know about meteorology?' and he grinned as he replied 'I shall leave such boring detail to my staff Alan.'

His parting words were almost inevitable. 'By the way. I'm off to a world conference on meteorology in Rio de Janeiro next week.'

Ignoring the blatant nepotism, which is the norm anyway, there was some logic in his appointment as the Director of Meteorology of a country where the daily forecast is always: 'Mainly clear skies will prevail over most of the country'.

One of the new appointments, however, generated considerable agitation in the heart of Hassan Ehsan; that of his principal Staff Officer. Personally, I welcomed the appointment for I knew of Sid's reputation as a very able administrator. An ex-Royal Air Force pilot he had commanded his own Phantom squadron in days gone by and now served as a senior administrative officer in SON. So far as Hassan was concerned his new right-hand man was to be a captain in SON and memories of Ken's badgering were still fresh in his mind. It was a long, tedious and unsuccessful task trying to convince him that Sid was good value and I took the first opportunity to warn Sid of the problem he might be facing. In conclusion I remarked: 'Hassan's a very good man. He drives Hazel and me mad sometimes wanting fifteen different things at once but we're both very fond of him and I'm sure you'll get to like him as well.' Sid looked dubious and I realised that there was a certain understandable lack of enthusiasm on his part also.

In the event, after some initial skirmishing, both of them realised the considerable merit in the other and they settled down to a harmonious working relationship which lasted many years. With the Under Secretary's responsibilities as well as those of the Assistant Chief of the Defence Staff there was no doubt that Sid, as Hassan's right hand man, was the hardest working staff officer in uniform, equalled only, as I later discovered, by Fred as a civilian staff officer.

Other facets of our take-over of the Under Secretary's Department also began to appear. A Portacabin at the rear of the bungalow to house more translators, an embarrassing influx of stewards and orderlies, more clerks and typists and finally, the Office Director. This grandiose sounding post was filled by an Omani civilian staff officer who theoretically had responsibility for the running of the Under Secretary's office and the control of his staff. Unfortunately, like many of his contemporaries, he was a firm believer in Insh'allah and the idea of improving the efficiency of his office had never crossed his mind. Such concepts were the prerogative of British contract officers. For his part he firmly believed in not interfering in anything and doing nothing unless and until specifically instructed to do so by his new master His Excellency Hassan Ehsan Naseeb.

I first truly appreciated his doctrine of non-interference in his staff's activities when I used one of his typists. This very large and not very bright Pakistani wore a flat cap in the office for some inexplicable reason. I gave him some urgent typing, a letter of six lines and three hours later he had still not delivered. I went to the typing pool and discovered him, hat on head, pencil behind ear trying to erase a mistake on each of the four carbon copies.

I chided him gently, reiterated the urgency and pointed out that he was sitting in front of a one thousand rial photocopying machine.

An hour later I returned and he was erasing yet another mistake. My patience began to wear thin.

'For God's sake! Why don't you type one copy and use the bloody copying machine?'

He replied with massive dignity. 'But Sir. I was trained to use carbon paper at my typing school in Karachi.'

As the new Office Director settled into our rapidly expanding office, it was fascinating to compare his approach with that of Hazel's. He was a pleasant plump young bachelor and so far as he was concerned he existed solely to satisfy very whim of His Excellency. This was in marked contrast to Hazel and myself who saw our duties extending well beyond mere unquestioning obedience. If Hassan wrote or said something which we thought unwise or perhaps, not intended, we would say so and discuss it with him.

One morning Munir came into our office to see the Under Secretary and I asked him to wait a minute or two. 'Hazel's with him,' I explained, 'but she won't be long.'

There was a moment's silence then her voice rang out from Hassan's office. 'You can't say that Sir,' and there was a general murmuring then again. 'I don't think that's a very good way of putting it. Why don't you say...'

There was an expression of awe tinged with trepidation on Munir's face. Not only was somebody arguing with His Excellency the Under Secretary and Assistant Chief of the Defence Staff Brigadier Hassan Ehsan Naseeb but that somebody was a woman. He looked around once or twice and I suspected he was seeking the bolt of lightning which must surely enter and strike that lowliest of creatures talking to his master.

Another entertaining aspect of that period when Hassan and Sir Timothy Creasey shared the old bungalow was that Hazel and I were occasionally privy to comments that we were not intended to hear. It was at that time that I discovered that Sir Timothy Creasey had brought bigotry almost to an art form.

The serviceman's contempt for civilians is well-known and although mildly irritating it does little harm for it gives the military man a pleasant feeling of superiority in his sometimes dangerous and frequently boring profession. Civilians are never civilians to the military. They can be 'bloody civilians,' 'sodding civilians' and even 'f***ing civilians' but never, ever, plain civilians. Sir Timothy's favourite expression was the last one and he used it often, whether any of the breed, including Fred his HRM, were present or not.

I really began to appreciate the phrase 'the simple military mind' however, when I learnt that he used it about all civilians whether they had spent most of their lives in the armed forces or not. Most of the officers in the MoD had served in the forces or, like Fred and myself, had been in the forces during World War II and in MoDUK since then, but to hear a staff officer referred to as a 'f***ing civilian' when he had just completed thirty-four years in the Royal Air Force seemed to me to be a remarkably simplistic approach to categorisation. Did Sir Timothy, I wondered, become a 'f***ing civilian' the day after his retirement from the army?

As we said goodbye to Hassan when he left the office that Wednesday neither Hazel nor I appreciated how close we were to never seeing him again.

Hassan had gone to Seeb Airport to head a delegation of Omani officers visiting Cairo to attend an anniversary parade and march past of the Egyptian Armed Forces before President Anwar Sadat. My first intimation that something had gone terribly wrong was a phone call from Hazel. Because of our duties both of us had residential telephones and I had just had my afternoon shower prior to dressing to go across to the mess. I picked up the telephone. She sounded excited yet apprehensive.

'Alan, have you heard the news?'

'No.'

'It's on the radio. President Sadat has been assassinated. It took place during the parade. Some of the troops fired at the President's stand apparently.'

'Good God!' I absorbed the information.

'And Alan.' She sounded close to tears.

'Yes?'

'They were saying that a senior Omani officer was among those killed.'

'Christ!' I thought for a minute. 'It may not be Hassan of course. There were quite a few senior officers in the delegation.'

'I know.' She said no more but I could hear her sniffing.

'Look. I'll get through to SOAF Ops Room and see if they've got any news on the party's return. I'll get back to you.'

'Please Alan. I hope to God that nothin's happened to him.'

That goes for both of us, I thought as I dialled the SOAF number. However, they couldn't help. All they knew was that one BAC 111 was on its way back with the delegation and they had orders to send another one with a military escort to pick up a body; but they had not idea whose body.

Hazel lived at Medinat Qaboos, a ten minutes drive from Seeb Airport, and rather than sit around consumed with anxiety she decided to drive there and await the return of the BAC 111. It was late at night and she did not have an airfield pass to give her access to the VIP area, but through the iron gates she saw the aircraft taxi onto the parking pan and under the brilliance of the lighting gantries she was delighted to see Hassan emerge with his retinue. She was standing in the gloom and knew she would not be seen by Hassan, but filled with relief she returned to her flat and telephoned the good news to me.

I doubt if Hassan slept that night for when he came into the office to receive our warm welcome and congratulations on his escape he was still very high on adrenalin and unable to stop talking. We soon understood why. 'Bring your coffee and come into the office,' he said to both of us and proceeded to give us a frighteningly vivid account of the assassins leaping from their vehicles as they drove slowly past President Sadat and spraying him and those near him with automatic rifle fire.

As the story unfolded he unbuttoned his tunic and showed us the holes in the front of his singlet and his tunic where a bullet had entered and exited and ripped out the throat of the Omani lieutenant colonel sitting next to him. If Hassan had been leaning forward just two or three inches at that moment...

Muqaddam Khalfan Nassir Hamed al Ghammari was the Commanding Officer of the Muscat Regiment. A delightful and popular man with a great sense of humour his death at the assassination cast a gloom over all of the Land Forces.

On the lighter side, the country's first English language newspaper made its appearance. Called *The Oman Observer* it rapidly increased its circulation, for English was the common language of many Omanis and most Indians, Pakistanis and other foreigners who lived and worked in the country. Its success was well merited for it was an attractively presented and entertaining newspaper.

Some of the entertainment was unintentional however and, in that, it reminded me of the dear old *Times of Cyprus* which could always be relied upon for one good howler a week; one of its best which still sticks in my memory was a full page advertisement declaring in three inch high letters:

'WOLKSWAGEN - THE ULTIMATE IN GRAFTSMANSHIP'.

Although much of the *Observer* 's entertainment value was also to be found in the advertisements they were of a much more subtle nature than the *Times* in that they frequently left you convinced that you had either missed the point or the advertiser knew something that you didn't. How else can you explain the following:

'Mummy! --- Oh Mummy! Take me to Samrat. I love its mixed plate.'

'Jeyaraman and Krishnan. Nights of delight planned for Carnatic music lovers.'

and finally:

'I, Nagash Band, S/O Sargand holder of Pakistani passport No. A. 107544 and I.D. Card wish to change my father's name which was being erroneously written as Hassan Bacha to Sargand.'

I felt some empathy, although had little real understanding of the last advertisement but then I had recently been given a new Indian steward for the office whose name was Theiwanayagam Thiruselvan. It took me only thirty seconds to latch on to the last two syllables and I told him that henceforth his name was to be Selvan for I boggled at using his full name. Obviously this was no new problem, for he cheerfully accepted this.

A sneaky kind of amusement was also to be found in the cartoon section of the *Observer* for the editor had been brave enough to run that famous series called 'Beau Peep'.

This cartoon had long been a favourite of mine because of the entertaining antics of the hero, a particularly dim Foreign Legionnaire. One of his adversaries was an even slower Bedouin and, having followed the series in one of the London dailies, it provided much entertainment to note the absence of those episodes in which the Arab was being too outrageously stupid.

There was, of course, the other even more discreet kind of censorship that the editor had to impose. So far as I know there were no rules as such, but he was a good operator with a nose for anything which might not meet with the approval of the Ministers, the Palace Office or the

Royal Family. Moreover, he kept to a minimum the reporting of the endless and meaningless local rhetoric. He was an honorary member of the BAF mess and I was pleased to buy him a drink whenever he turned up.

An interesting and almost perfect example of the Arab approach to influence and power occurred about then. Rashid, the Head of Finance was a tall and imposing man whose Zanzibarian background was belied by his fluent and cultured English. Nominally under Fred as Head of Resource Management he was still an Arab at heart as his perfectly logical plan for raising the wind showed.

He authorised a loan for himself so that he could have a house built - a procedure he had carried out many times for other MoD employees. When the house was completed he rented it out so that he could repay the loan. He than authorised a handsome monthly housing allowance for himself so that he could rent a property to live in. The beauty of the scheme was that the rules did not ban such a practice, probably because the British staff officer who had drawn up the regulations never envisaged that anybody would have the nerve. Clearly, he didn't know his Omanis very well.

The Head of Resource Management tried to explain to the Head of Finance that his actions were bordering on the illegal, but he knew, as I did, that he was farting against thunder. Plainly Rashid did not know what Fred was complaining about, although, there were some who hinted darkly that Rashid knew exactly what he was doing. True or not, HRM had to acknowledge defeat.

It was now that Sir Timothy decided that he was facing a mountain and Mahomet situation. Clearly, it was impractical to even consider moving the three service headquarters from their shiny new buildings at Muaskar al Murtafa'a down to Bait al Falaj for there wasn't sufficient space, and land in the Capital Area was already at a premium. Therefore, he and his staff and Hassan Ehsan and his staffs would move to MAM as soon as the three headquarters had reorganised their accommodation and made room.

Initially, I thought, as did most people, that it was intended to move just the staffs, ie, CDS and his office and HE the US and ACDS and his office. This could have been achieved fairly easily and there was obvious merit in doing so. I was appalled to learn, however, that the intention was to move the whole department of the Under Secretary (over one thousand staff). In company with many others I asked why? The most cursory glance told you that the logistics would be appalling and would add millions of rials to the annual defence bill. And to what purpose? Maybe a few directorates should move to MAM, but a large proportion of the Under Secretary's department had their business in and around the Capital Area and moving them thirty kilometres away would help nobody. The Lands Office were constantly visiting sites and other ministries in the Capital Area, and businessmen were constantly visiting the Purchasing Directorate, the Tender Board and the Contracts Branch. Much of the Administration Directorate was concerned with SAF rented properties in the Capital Area.

The transport bill too was bound to be enormous. There was no domestic accommodation available at MAM so everybody working in BAF would have to commute out there every day. What was the cost of an extra sixty or seventy kilometres per day on four hundred officers' cars? How much did forty coaches cost? About two million rials (three thousand pounds) we were told. How much fuel would they use every year? The Omanis could make their own way into the Capital Area from the surrounding villages but there was no bus service out to MAM so they would have to be transported every day together with the Pakistani and Indian clerical staffs. This would also mean an earlier start and a later finish. The Omanis, the Pakistanis and the Indians were far from happy. Thank God there were no unions, otherwise we would never have got away with it.

Substantial overtime bills were going to be inevitable. In Bait al Falaj, the Pakistani accounts clerks would go to the mosque in the afternoon and, chatting amiably together, drift across to the air-conditioned cool of their offices to spend a leisurely hour or two catching up on the job of paying salaries or bills. It was a socially agreeable unpaid overtime scene. However, they made it quite clear that this practice would now cease. Their working day was going to be quite long enough with the two coach journeys and there was no way they were going back to MAM in the afternoon, unless they were paid very handsomely for doing so.

Finally, although it was not an immediate administrative problem, there was going to be a long-term morale problem for the present residents of BAF. Officers were issued with a car and were entirely mobile but the Pakistani and Indian clerks and domestics (known as 'X' category employees) had no personal transport. BAF was within easy walking distance of the Ruwi and muttrah sugs (markets) and the few restaurants and better class shops to be found in Ruwi and Muttrah High Streets. Out at MAM however, there was nothing.

The camp itself was a vast sprawling complex and transport (or unlimited walking capacity) was needed just to reach the main gates. Outside those gates though, Seeb Airport was two miles away and Seeb Village ten miles and the suqs and restaurants of the Capital Area some twenty odd miles beyond.

It seemed easier to leave things as they were, except for moving one or two offices where there was obvious merit in doing so. Nobody in the UK had ever suggested that there was advantage in moving the whole of MoDUK down to Aldershot.

So far as I know nobody had suggested to Sir Timothy that his concept was only attractive so long as you didn't think too much about it. At that time, there was a strong feeling that if CDS spoke, even God listened.

For my part, I tried to recall the quotation of that ancient Greek General which, in essence, stated that it should never be assumed that reorganisation necessarily led to improved efficiency. In MoDUK such a proposal would be gone over with a fine comb to see if the advantages outweighed the disadvantages. Not here however. The committees were already meeting; not to examine the proposal but to implement it.

Late one morning Hazel and I were discussing this when Bill walked in. He had just made his first visit to the house that Sir Timothy had selected for his residence and, as Bill put it, he didn't know whether to be impressed or depressed: right on the beach; bloody great house; bloody great grounds; tennis court; enormous swimming pool with changing rooms and bar; servants quarters; guest annexe. It was a bit run-down and would cost a fortune to bring up to scratch. The rent was about ten thousand rials a month and with the rial at that time worth just over £1.50 Hazel and I sat there and thought about it. 'I wonder if he's going to be worth it?' I asked and the only answer I got was 'God knows,' from one and, perhaps unkindly, 'Now I know why we're all bloody well moving to MAM,' from the other.

A month or two later I began to realise that my working days were beginning to drag. Hazel saw to Hassan's immediate panics, phone calls and correspondence; Sid saw to the policy side and, whether effective or not, the office director had responsibility for the staff. No matter how much I might yearn to get a grip on some of them myself, I kept telling myself that the office director was an Omani and unless he asked for advice or assistance, I should stay out of it. Bait al Falaj was just about tolerable as a place to live and work in providing I had a demanding job to do. Without it.....

I started to look around for another job.

I went through the Ministry of Defence directory. Perhaps somewhere there was a slot that I could fill and occupy my days. I looked at the office of His Highness the Deputy Prime Minister for Security and Defence but found nothing there; then the office of the Chief of the Defence Staff: the post of Inspector of Establishments. There was no name against it, therefore the post must be unfilled. It was some months before I made it. For the last nine months or so of the old Joint Staff I had worked on all of the SAF establishment records, so I had good current knowledge as well as my years of experience in the game whilst in MoDUK. There was a welcoming but subdued response from Fred. Through no fault of his own he had become involved in a bit of a scene over the poaching of one of Hassan's staff and he was loth to risk another contretemps. It was up to me to secure my release.

Like most Arabs, the Omanis are very strong on personal loyalty and Hassan was not pleased at my approach and did not really understand my complaint that I had nothing to do. I could certainly appreciate this for, at that time, he would have welcomed a day with little to do, but my desire to leave his service reflected on him and he found this difficult to accept. It took a lot of nagging, at well-spaced intervals, to achieve my release and, I think the key which finally obtained his reluctant agreement was when I explained that by sitting around doing nothing I felt that I was wasting the money of His Majesty. This, Hassan could understand.

Two years later I was to wish I had stayed with Hassan Ehsan, but I was not to know that.

It was about this time that Anthony Berriman arrived on the scene. He was in his late forties, plump with a most agreeable manner and we soon warmed to him for he was a sociable man who was plainly at home and knew how to behave in an officers' mess. One or two of us may have raised a mental eyebrow at his occasionally florid gestures and rather precious form of speech, but being a homosexual as a civilian was no crime. And so far as I knew it was not regarded as a serious matter in the Arab military world. Indeed, if it had been, their forces would have been decimated.

The saga of Anthony's career and downfall is worth recounting in its entirety, even though it means encapsulating events which took well over a year to occur.

He had been with us for a few months when it became fairly general knowledge that this was his second time around in the Sultanate; it seemed that his previous tour had been brought to an abrupt end by the arrival of the Tin Budgie. He had been a Royal Navy officer on loan as an administrative officer to SON and so far as we could make out his only crime had been a surfeit of ambition for he had amended and improved his own annual report. It was a classic Sod's Law event that CSON should visit the Admiralty shortly afterwards and that the Personnel Branch should question an apparent inconsistency in Berriman's report with him. 'I never wrote that,' was CSON's comment and the metallic rustling of tin feathers could be heard.

As Anthony's previous spell in Oman had been quite a recent one we all wondered for some time why we had laboured so long over our security questionnaires. It was beginning to look as if the Royal Oman Police and the Oman Research Department who were responsible for immigration and security still were not talking to MoD and SAF.

The second time that Anthony was Tin Budgied was, in its way, even more entertaining.

He now had a job as a civilian purchasing officer in the MoD and had attained a raffish reputation among the younger Indian and Pakistani members of the mess staff. After one or two of them had nearly lost their virginity in the process of delivering food to Anthony's room, Harvey had wisely placed his room out of bounds to all mess staff. This did not deter him too much for, leaving the mess one lunchtime, I came across one young steward pinned in the corner of the entrance hall by Anthony who was sweet talking like mad. The youngster looked exactly like a rabbit facing a stoat and at my deliberately loud 'Hallo Anthony' he took the opportunity and disappeared into the dining room as if it was his burrow. Anthony turned with the weary resignation of a man filling in his one thousandth pools coupon. But, as I say, to most of us he was a genial man, a popular member of the mess and one who kept his sexual inclinations at a reasonably low key.

The time came when a new mess committee had to be elected - an event which was always welcome for a mess meeting took place an hour before end of play and, as the bar opened early for the occasion, it made a welcome break in the routine.

Following tradition, the outgoing mess committee sat at a blanket covered table at one end of the ante-room and facing them, on rows of chairs, sat the mess members. A large proportion of these were 'living out' Omanis whose Directors thought that their indigenous staff should learn about this strange British ceremony. It was clear however, that most of them were understandably bewildered at the start by 'the reading of the minutes of the previous meeting' and 'the carrying of the minutes of the previous meeting'. To give the Omani officers their due though, they stuck it out and, in company with their British colleagues truly came to life when such portentous matters as the price of Black Label came up for discussion.

It was always interesting to observe the individual's approach to the meeting. There was the bewildered enthusiasm of the Omanis; the anxious involvement of the British contract officers who had never before been in an officers' mess and tried not to make it too obvious and the ex-officers of the British Forces who were determined to see that the ceremony was carried out properly and that everybody else in the mess was aware that they (if nobody else) had been proper officers in a proper military force. These were the three categories who were to participate in the election of the new members of the mess committee and, in spite of this difference, there was already general agreement about some aspects of some of the posts. Regarding the job of the Entertainments Member, there was total accord that we all needed more entertainment but only God knew how it was to be achieved. The title of Wines Member was really a euphemism for the mess committee member who was responsible for such critical matters as the price of beer, wines and spirits. Recent experience had shown that a good steady drinker was a must and Tim was elected unanimously. Well, almost. One or two cynics did suggest, perhaps unkindly, that most of his activities would be carried out from the floor of the wine cellar.

Then we came to the Catering Member and, once again, there was general agreement that the present committee member had to go. A pleasant lad, he was an accountant whose only contribution to enriching the life of the mess members had been to impose a charge on casual cups of tea and coffee. This had met with the approval of Harvey, for whom profits weren't growing quickly enough, but with the strong disapproval of the 'real officers'. As one of them put it rather acidly 'Christ! Not another bloody accountant. The next one will put penny-in-the-slot machines on the bog doors'.

Those of us who did not eat in the mess were not even considered as possibilities for the post and this we all accepted with heartfelt thanks. Whatever criticism we had heaped on mess food in the past, few of us had any idea how to improve it. For my part I felt proud when I produced palatable bangers and mash and I knew that Andy's strong point was beans on toast. This culinary information we had both spread around assiduously and we grinned smugly at each other when our names were not mentioned as potential mess catering members. Because of this we both voted enthusiastically when Anthony's name was called, and were delighted to see that he had majority support. We were totally unaware that we had attracted the attention of the Tin Budgie.

'Good for you Anthony,' we called and applauded loudly. I noted that Richard, President of the Mess Committee, was peering over the tops of his half-moon glasses. He was unsure how to deal with such vocal support but clearly felt that it was a bit offside for a proper officers' mess meeting.

Anthony accepted his election gracefully and I pondered for a minute or two. With his sexual inclinations he probably had enough stress in his life. I doubted whether he had any idea of the additional stress he would accumulate as catering member. Even as a non-diner I had heard comments ranging from the petulant: 'They never serve boiled eggs as I like them,' to the more serious: 'That's twice this week I've had snails crawling out of my bloody salad.'

Heaven knows why, but port was the target during much of Anthony's tenure in the post. I wondered about this and, after admitting defeat, concluded that there was a massive field open to those engaged in catering research. Last week it had been baked beans. The member concerned had earned himself the nickname 'Beans' by making an impassioned plea in the suggestions book for more baked beans. They were filling, he wrote, full of flavour and fibre and a worthy accompaniment to many meals, hot or cold. Before the catering member could make the standard non-committal reply that the comment had been noted, another mess member rushed into print. Rubbish, he penned, baked beans might be popular around cowboys' camp fires and in working mens' cafes, but they were not the sort of dish that should be seen in an officers' mess. In fact, he added, from his years of living in officers' messes he would go so far as to declare that baked beans were *de trop* . The catering member had wisely decided not to add any comment.

Returning to Anthony's field of battle and defeat, mess members were in fact fortunate to even see pork for all of the catering staff were Pakistani Muslims. They had been given special dispensation by their Iman, but even so, there were some limitations imposed and direct physical contact with the meat was out.

Poor Anthony. I imagine he went through seven different kinds of hell before he finally cracked. His love life had been depressingly inactive for some months and, unlike most of us, who knew that our sort of sexual activity was unavailable and, we might as well forget it or resort to other means, he saw desirable and attractive young men every time he visited the mess - frustrating.

I occasionally took breakfast and one morning another attack was mounted against Anthony over the pork scene. It was a move against him from his flank so to speak.

'I've never, ever, had any crackling with the port I've eaten in this mess,' said one diner plaintively.

'Funny that. Same with me,' said his companion.

'Must be something to do with the fact that the cooks are Muslim,' said a third.

'Or perhaps we don't buy any decent pork,' suggested a fourth.

The conversation continued as if they were unaware of the presence of the catering member. Anthony cracked.

'Alright!' he howled and stood up from the table. 'I'll get you your f***ing crackling,' and he marched into the kitchen and confronted the astonished staff. They looked at each other. This was bacon and eggs time and here was the sahib banging away about pork. There was an inevitable failure in communication and this didn't help Anthony at all. To make his point, he seized a leg of pork defrosting on a nearby table and thrust it against an elderly cook. The white haired ancient promptly burst into tears. It was at that point that our catering member realised what he had done; he had condemned the cook to an interminable cleansing ritual because of his contact with the unclean flesh. He drew away and immediately apologised, but it was already too late.

To give Harvey, the mess manager, his due, he tried desperately to play down the whole business, even getting Anthony to formally apologise in front of the mess staff. The aged cook was not far off retirement and close to returning to his village in Pakistan and he would have been delighted to forget the whole thing, but younger Muslims (Omani and Pakistani) were not about to forgive or forget this insult to their religious beliefs. Nor to be frank, to disregard this golden opportunity to administer a slap to a white face.

It was all a bit sad for there was never any intent to insult Islam, but inevitably by now, the whole affair had come to the notice of Hassan Ehsan and, in his role as Under Secretary, he could not allow the violation to go unpunished. Poor Anthony; the Tin Budgie again.

I had quite forgotten him when, a few months before I left Oman for good I had a conversation one evening in the bar.

'Guess who I saw today.'

'Who?'

'Anthony Berriman.'

'Good God! What's he doing out here?'

'I was down at the new university site and I gather he's working for one of the construction companies.'

'Did you talk to him?'

'No. He turned away when he saw me.'

'I'm not surprised. Probably doesn't want his previous careers out here made public. I should think being Tin Budgied twice is quite enough.'

At the beginning of Anthony's saga I was acting as secretary for the interminable series of meetings which followed the expensive study of our pay and conditions. The meetings were unutterably tedious, took place every other day and a running record of decisions and agreements had to be maintained. Because of this my days were spent recording, writing and typing, frequently until ten o'clock at night and I ceased attending the office completely. Eventually, to everybody's astonishment, inter-service agreement was reached and the case for the pay rise was submitted to the Ministry of Finance. Its basis was market forces. In other words, what are the other Gulf States willing to pay for this Pakistani leading seaman, this British flight lieutenant pilot and that civilian Indian clerk. The upshot of it all was agreement to an average increase of twenty-five percent with Omanis receiving more than the average and employees from the Subcontinent less. There was no doubt about the success of the exercise however for it led to a major lift in SAF morale and the overnight disappearance of our serious recruiting problems.

The fact that I had been absent for so long from Hassan's office supported my argument that I was no longer necessary there and I was pleased one morning to receive a telephone call from Fred telling me that Hassan had agreed my transfer and would I call on him as soon as it was convenient. I did so and I was to learn that my first task as the new Inspector of Establishments was to carry out an examination of the whole of the Department of His Excellency the Under Secretary.

It was a daunting task and whilst Fred talked I thought briefly of the old Establishment Committee days; the wing commander or lieutenant colonel, myself, the SNCO secretary and the myriad specialist officers who advised us. Sometimes it would be necessary for all of us to examine some small *prima donna* unit in Europe or the USA where only a handful of officers and men operated. The Under Secretary's Department had a staff of over one thousand, military and civilian, 'and,' Fred concluded, 'CDS wants a report in a couple of months' time. He's convinced there's far too much fat in HE's department. Far, far too many staff.'

One of the first lessons you learn (and I did) in the establishments game is to never start a review with preconceived ideas. They are certain to be wrong. I nodded non-committally. 'They could do the job with half of the staff,' was Fred's parting shot.

'How can he say that?' I asked myself. Nobody's ever looked at them to see what they do and how many people they've got in each office or directorate to carry out their allotted tasks. They're responsible for the four or five hundred vehicles that MoD operates; they pay all of the rents of hirings and see that they are maintained properly; they are responsible for the pay and allowances of all of SAF and MoD personnel; they let all of the contracts and buy all of the equipment that SAF uses; they provide all of the maps; they provide the recruiting facility; they provide the stewards, cooks and cleaners for all of the messes, hirings and married quarters. There were innumerable tasks which Fred and his master CDS were ignorant of. Unless I'm mistaken, I decided, the mouths of CSOAF and CSOLF lie behind those sweeping generalisations. They probably see the advent of Sir Timothy Creasey and his appointment of a soldier as Under Secretary as a golden opportunity to put the boot in. Certainly CSOAF would welcome the opportunity to emasculate the department. It would make them regret the fuss they had made over the storm and the damaged BAC 111s. So there was a new man in the top job: a soldier called Hassan Ehsan. Nevertheless the department hadn't changed; there were still too many civilians poking their noses into scenes they didn't understand. This approach would have met with the full approval of CDS whose opinion of the civilian breed was well-known.

As HRM finished I answered cheerfully, 'Well, we'll have to see what's going on, won't we?'

I suspected that, at that stage in our relationship, Fred would have welcomed a bit more of the 'Gung-ho' axe wielding approach from me; something more in line with his master's wishes. However, I was an Inspector of Establishments who had been pressured by unions from below and senior officers from above so often that I knew such efforts were counterproductive.

'I'll report back to you and to Hassan Ehsan about once a month. Let you both know how it's going,' were my parting words.

Shortly afterwards a letter arrived bearing the signature of Sir Timothy Creasey. In essence it stated that SAF cost too much and that too much of that cost went on personnel. By a target date of some months ahead he would be looking for a ten per cent reduction in the members of personnel in HE's Department, MoD, SOLF, SOAF and SON. Later, I was to wonder what had happened to that letter and indeed its theme.

Fortunately, the letter did not state whether the bodies should be real ie, persons actually employed, or establishment posts, whether occupied or not. If the latter, the reductions would be easy, for in every large organisation, a good percentage of all posts would be unfilled. In not specifying whether the staff should actually exist however, I began to suspect that neither CDS nor HRM (who would have drafted the letter) really understood the establishment business. Later events were to confirm this.

A brief diversion occurred before I could start on the exercise and this was a proposal to introduce a supply computer. Whether the idea originated in the services or within the Purchasing Directorate of MoD I never did find out, but in the same way that a small local variation in air pressure can be the trigger for a tropical storm so the computer idea generated a furore in SAF and MoD Oman.

At the start there was total agreement that the SAF/MoD supply system was hopelessly inefficient. Throughout the whole of Oman in all of the three services, military and civilian Pakistani clerks operated an archaic stock record card system which was probably introduced during the last century. Inevitably, they had no enthusiasm for any change which might affect their cosy undemanding little jobs nor did they welcome urgency. Indeed, there seemed to be little capability for priority in the system and the Purchasing Directorate frequently complained they were too often asked to supply something in two months when it was well-known that there was a lead time of six months between request and provision.

'Rubbish,' said the supply branches of the three services, 'we always give them plenty of notice but they never meet the target date. They're bloody useless'.

I had a number of friends both in the Purchasing Directorate and the supply branches and the major problem area seemed clear enough to me: poor quality of staff at all levels - a problem no computer was going to overcome.

I was asked my view on introducing a computer into the SAF supply system? My reply was a total negative and was based on the following reasons:

a) A military supply computer is an appallingly expensive piece of equipment which would cost many, many millions of rials to install and, to be effective in war, require hardened protection, security screening and standby power, all costing more millions. And without any of these, one bomb, air-dropped or hand-placed could completely destroy the whole supply organisation of SAF.

b) If we wanted to, we could employ hundreds more supply clerks and of a better quality than those employed at present for a fraction of the cost of a computer.

c) We could just as well improve the present ancient recording system and there are scores of better manual systems on the market, some of which would facilitate the eventual transfer to computer recording.

d) The Omanis are at the bottom of a very basic learning curve. It would be nonsense to expect them to grapple with a sophisticated computer system without the supervision of many very expensive computer specialists for several years to come.

I should never have made the last point because, as I later realised, it was a strong argument in favour of installing a computer, if it was a British one. The outcome was inevitable and two years or so later the computer was creaking into the initial testing stage and the British advisers were proliferating.

Whose interests are we serving? I asked myself. I was beginning to realise that it was a naive question. In later introspection I also asked - who are we going to fight? If it's to be a sophisticated enemy then the USA and the UK will be with us within hours. If it's not a sophisticated enemy then why are we buying Jaguars, Tornados, Chieftains and Exocets? I suspected that our weapons buying had little to do with potential enemies. No commander has ever been able to resist putting himself at the head of the largest and most sophisticated force that money can buy.

Tim's sense of humour was quick and often slightly acid. Without television and with only the occasional worthwhile film show, reading was a major recreational activity. Brigadier Akehurst had recently had his book about the Dhofar War published; entitled: *We Won a War*, a number of us had read it and were discussing it in the bar that evening. Although I always thought there was a faint note of surprise in that title, it was readable - unusually so for a book that had been officially vetted and approved before publication - although perhaps a bit too full of jolly good chaps and bounders across the border for my taste.

Somebody then commented on the number of books written about the Dhofar War. 'I bet the buggers spent most of their time in their sangers scribbling in their notebooks,' came one remark.

'I object to it being called a war,' came from one member who had served in tanks in WW II. 'When you read about it you find it's nothing more than a series of border incursions.'

'Whatever it was, there've been too many bloody books about it,' came from another.

'Akehurst? What regiment was he?' asked Robin.

'The Authors' Rifles,' came Tim's swift reply.

A month or two had passed and at last, back in the old Joint Staff office, things were beginning to move for our three abandoned warriors.

Captain Ken's fears about termination came within a hairs breadth of reality. CDS had made it clear that he regarded him with little favour and Hassan Ehsan had briefed Hazel and I to act as an early warning system should Ken show any signs of approaching his office. And yet somehow he attained a position in HRM's office with a special responsibility for building expenditure. When I left three years later he was still in that slot, still with his exalted rank of captain in SON. I had no doubts about Ken's ability but I was intrigued to see that a man, so out of favour with his superiors and surplus to requirements in 1981, was still going strong in 1984.

Wing Commander Harry's constant grumbling behind his static pile of files reached quite alarming proportions as the weeks went by and, during a social visit to his old office one morning, Malcolm as Creasey's Military Adviser decided to bring the situation to his master's notice. The outcome of this was a meeting between Sir Timothy and Harry at which he made it plain what he thought about the appalling personnel management scene which could leave him languishing in his office doing nothing for months. I doubt whether he recognised that in reality, this was no different to his lifestyle in the days when the Joint Staff existed.

CDS must have been impressed however, for he passed the problem onto CSOAF who came up trumps. 'Just the job' said Biggles, 'our Budget Controller is leaving and you can take over his job. Go along and see him'.

It was then that farce entered the scene.

The Budget Controller was an ex-RAF officer, a pleasant man in his late fifties whose job was to calculate and forecast the SOAF financial requirements for the coming years and monitor expenditure during the current year. It was a job which required foresight.

With the advice and assistance of an old RAF friend he had recently discovered Australia and in particular the beauty and delightful climate of Queensland. He was so impressed that he paid eighty thousand dollars for a superbly located house in a ten acre property just inland from Noosa. It was then he learnt that the immigration laws were quite strict and the only way he could live on his new property was by leaving Australia every six months. I would have thought this no big hurdle for he could afford a day or two away in Singapore, or the Phillipines or New Zealand twice a year, but it was sufficient to make him and his wife baulk and abandon their plans. So it was that when Harry arrived at the Budget Controller's office I was to learn that he was no longer leaving - indeed he saw a future for himself in Oman for quite a few years to come.

When he learnt of this change of heart CSOAF did not hesitate. No question of 'Sorry Harry. Looks as if you'll have to go.' On the contrary, it was a much more agreeable arrangement: 'We'll have two Budget Controllers'. This method of dealing with surplus personnel certainly boded ill for my future as Inspector of Establishments. It was however, inevitable that the two controller system should fail. Budget Controller A saw Budget Controller B as an ever present threat and divulged as little information as possible. After two years even CSOAF was forced to admit that his idea was not working and Harry left.

It was arguable whether Roger fared any better. His plea for help from Malcolm proved successful and he was appointed Army Member of the CDS Secretariat, thus proving that Malcolm was an even worse judge of lieutenant colonels than he was of drivers. Given an obscure post in the Land Forces Headquarters Roger might have survived unnoticed against a general background of sloth and mediocrity, but in Creasey's office....

The Secretariat trio were regarded as a joke by the staff of CDS and HRM, for not surprisingly, like their predecessors the Joint Staff, they were ignored by nearly everyone and had about as much to do. Ostensibly the three were in post as the representatives of the commanders in the office of CDS, but the commanders made certain that there was as little input as possible into the CDS office and conversely, CDS ensured that the Secretariat trio were ignorant of the activities of his office. This was not difficult for they seemed to have no natural curiosity about what went on around them and were quite content to do little or nothing. But even with this minimum of work Roger could not escape the occasional contact with Sir Timothy who was not a man to suffer fools gladly. Even so, he lasted two years, which was two years longer than any of us had expected. It was suggested that Sir Timothy was mellowing; certainly he showed remarkable forbearance, for Roger's indecisiveness worsened under pressure - and any contact with Creasey was pressure. One morning he was called upon to give a verbal briefing to CDS and the commanders about a reported military border incursion. Poor Roger, he came close to fame as the man responsible for starting General Sir John Hacket's 'Third World War'. Possibly unaware of the political difference between the north and south borders and certainly even more unsure of himself in front of all the red tabs and gold braid, he became totally confused and told the gathering that the incursion had been across the southern border. The southern border fronted the People's Democratic Republic of the Yemen and was where the Dhofar War had taken place; the northern border was an indeterminate line between Oman and the United Arab Emirates and wandering, usually lost, UAE border patrols often crossed into the Sultanate.

The meeting was galvanised into action and the decision taken to send a bell helicopter recce before committing the Hunter ground attack aircraft to a warning pass or two and possibly, more decisive action.

When they were contacted, Southern Oman Headquarters expressed considerable surprise. 'First we've heard about an incursion,' they said. 'How come you know about it up north and we don't?'

The confusion was soon resolved, but I suspect that Roger's military career started to decline at that briefing. It still surprised me however, how long some British staff officers survived considering their lack of professional ability and their appallingly anti-social behaviour. After all as contract officers they could be given three months' notice, or pay in lieu, and sent home.

P.G. was a classic example. One of our more notorious Dhofar Deadbeats he was a major who had spent most of his Omani career in a state of total intoxication or near intoxication. Whether his Dhofar War activities had been anything to write home about was open to question, but those of his contemporaries who knew him at that time told me that most of his war had been spent 'pissed out of his mind'. He had been placed in a number of staff posts when I knew him and in all of them he had been either absent or unproductive. But he was known personally to CSOLF and CDS as an ex-Dhofar warrior and led a charmed life.

As he went through the earlier stages of getting drunk he could be very entertaining but as he drank more so there would be sneering references to 'f***ing coons' and 'stupid bloody nig-nogs' and then the darker side of his character would emerge - his laughter would become manic and he would lose all control over his tongue. Most of us tolerated him but were amazed that he had survived so long on the story of his participation (drunk or sober) in the Dhofar War.

Inevitably he insulted the wrong man. Hilal was a pleasant, reserved young Omani and he had brought a friend into the mess for a quiet drink one evening. The friend, a good-looking youth, suddenly found PG's arm around his shoulder and an invitation being extended. 'Come back to my room and come to bed with me. I've got some porno films we can watch.' PG was dragged away but Hilal was infuriated by the insult to him and his friend. The PMC tried to have the affair hushed up but Hilal was out for blood and took the affair to Hassan Ehsan.

Rumour had it that Creasey had wearied of protecting PG, but my information was that Hassan Ehsan knew PG's reputation well and was not to be diverted. PG climbed onto the Tin Budgie - but he had survived for over twelve years. I thought it a pity that the 'white faces' should need Omani pressure to get rid of their rotten apples.

It was a foregone conclusion that when the committees tasked with organising the move of Creasey, Hassan and their respective departments to Muaskar al Murtafa'a came to grips with reality, they would be faced with quite appalling practical problems and steeply escalating cost estimates. The daily transportation of staff proved to be very expensive, but much worse than that, examination showed that there was a chronic shortage of accommodation at MAM. A substantial and costly construction programme would have to be started. This would include a new officers' mess plus accommodation for two to three hundred officers and office accommodation for the Signals Regiment and various other units who would have to be evicted from the headquarters blocks. What the total bill would come to I could only guess, but over the years, the capital cost of having all of the service headquarters and the MoD (Oman) conveniently placed for any potential enemy in one large complex must have topped fifty million rials. There had never been any serious attempt to cost out the projected move and set the figure against the potential advantages, if any. I had done this many times in the costings Branch of MoDUK and it had often been the main reason for killing off a number of half-baked proposals such as this.

Initially, there was considerable opposition to the move from the three commanders and they and their staffs found innumerable reasons why their tranquillity should not be disturbed. Eventually Sir Timothy lost his temper and told everyone to get on with it. Now ensued a highly entertaining series of 'pecking order' battles as majors fought to retain their own offices (to which they were not entitled) and lieutenant colonels struggled to hang on to their own office suites (to which they were similarly not entitled).

Eventually majors found themselves sharing offices and lieutenant colonels found themselves occupying just one room. A very ill wind was blowing through the headquarters but CDS had won the day and at least he and his staff could move to MAM. It was to be some months before HE the US and ACDS could move his office and personal staff and, a couple of years and much spending of money before buildings were built and some of his department could follow him. Even then, a sizeable proportion remained at BAF for solid practical reasons.

Said Faher however, not only refused to move himself and his staff to MAM, but accentuated his refusal by having a magnificent office block built next to his office at BAF. Beside the wadi it was designed to have the appearance of a tall, tapering but traditional Arab fort and it made an appropriate and handsome accompaniment to the ancient square fort a few hundred yards away. This was now undergoing a total renovation and conversion into a museum for SAF and the military history of Oman.

The old fort, whose drooping naval cannon had been the bane of Maurice's life, had a fascinating history and was going through a turbulent period at that time for its conversion into a museum was a difficult exercise.

It was an imposingly solid white structure squatting on an area of level sand in the middle of Bait al Falaj camp and, to quote some officialese: 'It is a square fort with a tower at the opposing north-east and south-west corner ... external walls extend about 25 metres from corner to tower ... the principal entrance is central on the north face ... the central court is 10.5 metres square and contains a well connected to the falaj. Built about eight centuries ago to protect the trading port of Muscat it had sat astride the passes leading to and from the interior. Many historians however believe that because of the unlimited water supply a fort of some sort had probably existed on that site for centuries before then.'

When I first set eyes on it, it was in a neglected condition. It had been occupied and used as the MoD during the Dhofar War and extension offices, external balconies and partitions had been added and were still clinging haphazardly to the exterior walls. In many places, the creamy white plaster which coated the walls had come away, exposing the stones and mortar beneath. This was its condition when John and Carole arrived on the scene.

John was employed by the Ministry of Defence Engineering Division (MoDED) but I never did learn what his profession was. I guessed he was probably a surveyor or a civil engineer for he was of senior rank (equivalent to lieutenant colonel) when he was given the task of restoring the fort to its original 'shape' and turning it into a military museum. Whether he was professionally qualified to undertake the task I had no idea but he plunged into the project with considerable enthusiasm and was obviously an educated man, for he eventually amassed a large library on the subject of museums, preservation of artefacts and so on. He also moved himself and Carole into a few rooms inside the fort so he could cut out commuting time and live 'on the job'.

It was a happy arrangement for a year or more because the courtyard with its encircling verandah was a pleasant spot and, standing there with a drink in your hand listening to the rustle of nearby creepers and palms under a star-studded sky provided a romantic environment.

I was not a close friend of the pair, but occasionally chatted with them when they called into the mess in the evening to restock their cellar. John was an Australian who had left the country as a teenager and never returned and Carole was a Londoner like me. She was a very kind soul who felt much pity for Robin with his marital and drink problems and she often invited him back to the fort for a meal. This was good for he ate solid food and had to restrain his drinking. Perhaps a psychologist can offer an easily understandable explanation for Robin's giant benders but to me, as a layman, they seemed to carry some sort of death wish for he would carry on his alcoholic gulping long after any enjoyment stage had been reached and passed.

One evening Robin asked me to guess at his latest bar bill one evening. I was out by hundreds of pounds and began to realise the size of his problem. Later I wondered how he could afford such outgoings when he was paying for three children at boarding schools in England on top of his own expenses. Traditionally in Oman however, it was a case of shrugging your shoulders and deciding that personal problems of that kind were no concern of yours. Certainly you would not be thanked if you tried to interfere as I discovered ultimately in John's case.

It is always a mistake I suppose, to reach conclusions about a situation without knowing all of the facts and I certainly had no idea what John's briefing had been when he undertook the museum task. In those days, MoDED saw itself as a sort of civil construction company that happened to be working for a military organisation and it is quite possible that he had been told not to let the military interfere too much. If this was the case it was to prove his undoing.

In the meantime there was a deadline a few years hence for its completion and formal opening by Sultan Qaboos. There were weapons to be gathered in, heavy and light machine guns, an armoured car or two, a Provost (jet or piston-engined) aircraft and other memorabilia from the Dhofar War. Whenever I saw John at that time I got the distinct impression that the exercise was proceeding at a fairly leisurely pace and that he was using many of his connections among the local building companies to get much work done at minimum cost.

It was an idyllic existence in its way. Carole was happy working as a teacher at the Sultan Qaboos school at Seeb, John was totally engrossed in his new task and their daughter was content in her boarding school in England.

Unfortunately, as I discovered, John did not seem to know, or want to know, the rules of the game he was playing. In MoDED I assumed, he had been given many various tasks to do and, in carrying them out he had been protected by understanding superiors who knew the construction business well. In the BAF Fort exercise he worked on his own and reported directly to an elderly British brigadier in His Highness' office and, working in Bait al Falaj, he came within the boundaries of interest of Hassan Ehsan.

In previous days when he wanted a piece of equipment he went and got it from store and bought it, no questions asked. Now certain material, such as the mortar required to face the walls, might entail a journey to the Interior or, the need of a specialist book might call for an order on a London or New York bookshop and John, following past practice, simply got on with it. Unfortunately, never having served in the forces and having little regard for the military he neglected to keep his boss (the brigadier in HH's office) in touch with what he was doing. All that the Brigadier was aware of was that he was in receipt of a fairly constant flow of bills on his desk without any idea of what most of them were for. He was unimpressed.

Waxing more enthusiastic about the fort and its future as a museum John sent out a call to all SAF units asking them to send him any spare weapons or Dhofar War memorabilia they might possess. Within months he had amassed a sizeable armoury in the fort and had to scrounge an elderly Baluchi warrant officer to clean and categorise the weapons. The Brigadier became concerned at the idea of a small uncontrolled arsenal in the camp, particularly as many of the weapons were usable.

John was elected secretary of the Oman Historical Society and this was a good leap forward in his new career for he acquired many influential Omani friends who provided much valuable, historical knowledge and a considerable amount of influence in many areas. Eventually, one or two of his new friends learnt about his growing store of rifles in the fort and at parties he was often shown many vacant places on sitting room walls just begging for a rifle to add a touch of glamour and tradition. Anxious to please - particularly as he had far too many rifles anyway - he usually obliged his hosts. The Brigadier became even more concerned. His Highness was Deputy Prime Minister for Security, as well as Defence. God alone knew what he would say when he learnt that John was distributing rifles like lollipops.

I had to visit London to attend a conference of establishment officers in MoDUK and, at John's request, called on the curator of the Army Museum in Chelsea. He was a charming and helpful man and he gave me much useful advice about the sort of support staff the Oman Military Museum would require. I also gained from him considerable knowledge about the professional career structure of museum managers. At this point in time I think that John entertained hopes of becoming our museum's first curator but having seen the qualifications and experience required in the UK for such a post I had my doubts. He was full of enthusiasm however, and worked damned hard. I decided to leave his future in the hands of the Brigadier and Hassan Ehsan. If they asked me I would have to tell them the sort of background required of a curator, but the museum was small and I felt sure that John was bright enough and enthusiastic enough to run it well.

When I returned to Oman, the fort's exterior had changed considerably and the extensions and the balconies added to house offices in its MoD days had been torn down. It was unfortunate that the most badly affected area was the south wall for it fronted the road through the camp which led to the office of His Highness Said Faher, the Deputy Prime Minister and the office of His Excellency Hassan Ehsan, the Under Secretary. The fort was now an eyesore for great areas of the wall had lost their facing and below it, piles of beams, bricks, stones and shattered plaster were spread across the ground.

I noticed this with some distaste but assumed that John would soon have the debris cleared away and some scaffolding erected to enable the workmen to replaster the wall. Weeks later the rubble was still there but I had other things on my mind and convinced myself that there was probably a good reason for it. There may well have been, but he was obviously unaware - as was I - that every working day His Highness and His Excellency were driven past the fort and noted its derelict appearance with growing displeasure. They also knew that the museum was a special project authorised by His Majesty Sultan Qaboos and he was quite likely to visit the camp incognito (as he had done a few times since I arrived) to check on progress. He would not be impressed.

As I say, I was unaware of this aspect until I called on His Excellency to discuss the forthcoming review of his department. Everything went well until somehow, John's name came up and Hassan's expression darkened. Hazel and I knew that look.

'I do not like that man,' he stated vehemently.

I was a bit surprised for as far as I knew Hassan had never met John. 'Why do you not like him, Sir?'

'The fort looks bad Alan. It looks worse now than when that man started working there. I am not happy about it. Nor is His Highness.'

'Good grief' I thought.

'There is a lot of rebuilding work to be done Sir. The conversion will take time.'

'I know all that,' he said a shade irritably, 'but why has all that rubbish been lying around the fort for months?'

'I'll speak to him Sir. Get him to tidy it up.'

Hassan grunted. It looked as if more than a tidying up operation was required to mollify him. With hindsight, I suspected that he also knew about the rifle scene and John's days were already numbered.

I left Hassan's office, drove straight to the fort and caught John in his office.

'Hassan's very unhappy John. If I was you I'd get that mess outside cleared away and then invite him down here for a visit. Show him what you've done so far and what you intend doing. Like you showed me some months ago. Get him on your side.'

As the answer came I knew that he did not understand that he was no longer working in the protected environment of MoDED. Nor did he realise where the real power lay in Bait al Falaj - and in Oman for that matter. 'If the bloody man can't understand what I'm doing here, then I can't waste my time explaining it to him.'

I opened my mouth but he spoke again. 'I'm fed up with the bloody military and the Omanis poking their noses in.'

John's contract was not renewed that year and he and Carole went to Australia. As he philosophically remarked just before he left.

'If you're going to be unemployed you're better off in a decent climate.'

Chapter 6

The abandoned three had finally left their old offices in the Joint Staff building: Ken to go the HRM's office; Roger to the CDS Secretariat and Harry to his new appointment as Budget Controller B, or whatever he was to be called. The rooms were quieter than ever as I walked through them. I decided that my old office would be fine for the interminable reports and recommendations that I would have to write and Peter Thwaites' old office, with its large conference table and ten chairs would be ideal for interviews. If any director or manager wanted to bring his senior staff along to advise him then this would present no problem. Another week or two and I should be able to start on the establishment review of the department of His Excellency the Under Secretary.

I had given a lot of thought as to how I was to carry out the exercise. There were over a thousand staff involved and there was no way that I could interview them all, or indeed, would want to. One room orderly did much the same work as another room orderly and I knew what their duties were. At that skill level therefore it was a question of how many were employed in the officers' mess and how many officers, and of what rank, did they look after. With due allowance for holidays, religious festivals, sick leave, local lethargy (particularly during Ramadan) and the 'my brother is a poor man and needs the work' factor, a simple calculation would tell me whether we had far too many room orderlies or whether our excess was acceptable.

Proceeding up the scale of ranks and gradings, similar equations and my personal experience could be applied to all sorts of tasks. How many pay accounts and how many pay clerks? How many stores and how many storemen? and so on. In many areas of activity however, particularly at the expensive British contract officer level, it might well be necessary to carry out an on-site examination. I already knew most of the ground that HE's Department covered, so in many cases it would not be necessary to visit individual offices. 'And thank God for that,' I murmured.

It had become clear however, that I would have to interview every officer, both military and civilian - as long as it wasn't in their office. This was a lesson that I had learnt many times over. Once in the office you could be talking to the officer concerned and an Omani friend or colleague would wander in. Five minutes would pass of: 'As salaam alaykum,' 'Wa alaykum as salaam,' 'Kayf haalek?' 'Khayr, al Hamdu lillah'. Then you would be introduced to the friend and another five minutes of 'As salaam, etc.' would drift by. Then would come the question of coffee, and the choosing and ordering of it and, by the time you returned to the purpose of your visit, all the meaning and direction of the original conversation had departed.

In future all of the interviews would be conducted in the now deserted old Joint Staff offices and I would have the telephone in Peter Thwaites' old office disconnected. The object was to get the interviewees in there, sit them down and get on with it. Interviewing that number of people was going to be wearisome enough without allowing local social conventions to enter the scene.

I wrote a letter explaining the purpose of my establishment review (to improve the organisation and trim it if necessary), how it was to be carried out (personal interviews with each officer) and I asked for their co-operation in providing me with staffing details. This latter information was most important, for whilst the establishment told me what staff they should have, only they could tell me what they had in reality. I also asked for work loading details (where appropriate) and personally written job descriptions. This last exercise was often helpful to the individual in clarifying his own thoughts about his duties and responsibilities. English and Arabic copies of the letter went to every officer.

The major Omani attitude to the exercise was one of helpful curiosity whereas the British contract officer was deeply suspicious of me and my motives, regarding me as a hatchet man, pure and simple. Some even went as far as to provide me with details of their domestic and financial commitments back in England. As so often was the case, there was confusion in their minds between themselves and the posts they occupied. Once again I found myself repeating the establishment officers' creed across the table, a creed which I had stated hundreds of times during the past twenty years:

'Officially I am not interested in you as an individual; my interest lies in the post you occupy. Is there an authorised and necessary job to do? Can one man carry it out or does it need more than one? Can it be done by somebody else with time on his hands? You must try to separate the post from you, the man who is filling it. If I decide that your post is no longer necessary it doesn't necessarily mean that you will get the sack. Often the solution is for you to replace some other contract officer who is finishing. Similarly, if I decide that the responsibility level of your post demands a higher civilian grade or military rank it doesn't necessarily follow that you will get promoted and stay on in your post. It's always a possibility that somebody else will get promoted and take over the job from you and you will be transferred.'

How often this message got through I could not be certain but my success rate was higher with the Omanis than with the British contract officer. This was understandable for the Omani had no prejudice against this, their first ever establishment review and no Omani ever got the sack.

The establishment officers' creed which I repeated during the first few interviews spread like wildfire. Not the essential part about separating the post from the man, but the much more attractive information that I had the power to upgrade posts. It was a classic example of only hearing what you want to hear. Now another factor began to govern the attitude of some British contract officers; I could help them surmount the unaccompanied/ accompanied barrier.

Many British contract officers who had achieved the rank of major or its equivalent grade of 19, were desperately keen to make that extra step to lieutenant colonel or grade 21, thus being able to bring out their wives, own a larger car, have servants and move into a large house or flat. I now discovered that as well as seeking the reality of their job I had to sift through a load of inflated responsibility garbage that they produced. But the review ploughed on with me holding more interviews, writing the reports, making the recommendations and circulating these for comments and/or objections. It was a tedious business, but I had no choice for the exercise had to be carried out in the lengthy and laborious manner of the MoDUK Army Department instead of in the quicker style of the Air Force Department where the establishment officer had executive authority. For all of my experience nobody was going to give me that sort of power. Much better, if any of my recommendations were contentious, to let them be discussed on paper for a year or two. But, tedious as it was, the review still produced a number of very interesting and indeed, highly entertaining moments; enough to make me greet each day with renewed enthusiasm.

Invariably I would finish the formal part of the interview and then ask the man across the table whether he had any points he would like to make or any questions he would like to ask me. This was no bad practice for it relaxed the individual, put the discussion on a more friendly and informal basis and often led to both of us gaining a better appreciation of each other. Many such chats produced amusing stories and one I recall involved my old friend Dad Rahim, (he who buried his bride price).

Nick was an ex-Dhofar warrior who had earnt his rank of lieutenant colonel for he was an excellent staff officer. Tall, slim and always immaculate he was respected both by his staff and his superiors. He knew that I had met the infamous Dad Rahim and he could hardly contain himself as he recounted the Jundi's latest petition.

Nick had gone to see Hassan Ehsan and found Dad Rahim in the outer office. He knew him well, having had him under command years ago and on this occasion, the Jundi was very clearly excited. His voice was getting louder as he spoke and it was far too loud for the outer office of Brigadier Hassan Ehsan Naseeb. The quiet placid Office Director was becoming agitated. As I say Nick was an imposing figure in his uniform and as he entered the room and saw the situation he barked: 'Dad Rahim'.

The Jundi looked round and, reacting to his years of service, closed his mouth and sprang to attention. 'Sir!'

'What is the meaning of this Dad Rahim? Why are you making all this noise outside the office of Brigadier Hassan Ehsan?'

Still at attention Dad Rahim recounted his petition. The Sultan owed him much money and now that he was a married man he needed the money. He touched off a wave of sympathy in Nick's heart when he said: 'My wife is young Sahib and wants many things.'

'Continue,' ordered Nick and the story came out.

When he joined the Jebel regiment twenty years ago the recruiting sergeant told him that he must wait four weeks before he could put on the soldier's uniform and start his training. He returned to his village to wait. Two weeks later another sergeant came to the village recruiting for the Muscat Regiment. This sergeant told him that he could put on the uniform immediately, so he joined the Muscat Regiment. For twenty years he had not received any pay from the Jebel Regiment and this was a great wrong.

Nick thought for a moment, then he spoke. 'Dad Rahim.'

'Sir.'

'I was at the Royal Palace in Muscat this morning and I spoke to His Majesty Sultan Qaboos about you.'

The Baluchi's face lit up expectantly. 'What did he say Sahib?'

'He said to me, tell Dad Rahim that he cannot be paid twice for there is only one Dad Rahim and he serves me very well.'

The Jundi's face fell slightly, but not too much, for the highest authority in Oman had spoken well about him and this was worth more than money. He saluted Nick smartly and, back straight with pride, marched out of the office.

As Nick told me: 'I could have talked about the ethics of double pay until I was blue in the face and I still wouldn't have got through. The Sultan is the beloved father of the troops out here and Dad Rahim will gain enormous status when he tells his mates what I said.'

Dad Rahim's latest exploit was certainly entertaining, but other episodes ranged between the frustrating and the farcical, depending on your degree of involvement and sense of humour.

Most of the Omani officers were a delight to interview, particularly the young ones for usually their English was good and they possessed alert and enquiring minds, although I occasionally found that the tedium of routine quickly weakened their enthusiasm. But they were fascinated by the concept of the review and they welcomed the opportunity to air their grievances and pass on their worries, regarding me, I suspect, as a white-haired and interested uncle who was not involved in the tribal scene.

Within a month it became clear that many of the younger Omani officers in the ministry had two major worries and both were matters of justifiable concern. In brief:

a)   Having joined the Ministry of Defence, it was many months before they began to learn their way round, what their own office did and how it fitted into the activities of HE's Department.

b)   Far too often they saw friends and colleagues getting promoted because their superior was either family related or came from the same tribe. Conversely, you could find yourself working for a superior who didn't like you and you could stay in his office for years with no hope of promotion.

It was difficult to maintain a serious face whilst listening to this latter complaint because, as in all Arab countries, nepotism was a way of life and what the youngsters were really protesting about was that they personally were not working for a blood or tribal relative.

There were simple solutions to both problems however, which had been introduced into the British government service Lord knows how many generations ago. A two or three day induction course with talks by senior MoD officials dealt with the first problem and a decent annual reporting system plus posting to a new job every three years dealt with the second; and this would also widen the experience of the younger officers.

I listed these two problems with my solutions in a report to His Excellency Hassan Ehsan and he reacted promptly. It was bad luck that he passed my letter with a request for early action to Hamed or 'He of The Tie'as I occasionally referred to him. Although Hamed's English, spoken and written, was impeccable and his Arabic minimal, his great weakness was an infallible instinct for rapidly grasping the wrong end of the stick and then talking and writing about it at great length.

My induction course solution required no more than a few of our brighter MoD officials giving short talks to new recruits. My second required no more than the introduction of a sensible annual report form and a BF (Bring Forward) system on each officer's personal file to ensure that they were moved around regularly. These were simple economical changes. Hamed's reply to His Excellency however, was inevitably long-winded and pompous. Yes, he wrote, he had given much thought to this serious problem many years ago. He was convinced that the answer lay in the creation of an 'Omani Careers Office'. Headed by a British contract officer of the rank of lieutenant colonel (or civilian grade equivalant) and supported by a staff of twenty or so, it should be able to deal with these problems very satisfactorily. His interest in this matter was so close to his heart in fact that he would be prepared to take this new office under his wing.

Because of some recent organisational changes his office had lost some of its responsibilities and his growing isolation from the mainstream of activity was becoming obvious. This undoubtedly prompted his bid for control of an 'Omani Careers Office' but it also effectively killed off my proposals. I had lost far too many battles over the years to become too upset or to take the matter personally but I decided that I owed it to the cause of efficiency to take a close look at Hamed's little organisation when the time came.

The Finances and Purchasing Division was one of the largest in the Department and its Controller was Rashid - the one who authorised himself a loan with which to build a house which he rented out, whilst paying himself a housing allowance to live in rented accommodation. He was supported by a few British contract officers, four of whom featured large in my examination of the Directorate. As I drew up a list of interviews I little realised that I was walking into a minefield and that my actions would be partially responsible for the Robin Walsh affair exploding into a major scandal on British TV and in the newspapers in two years' time. I did expect this part of the review to be difficult however for the Division was large and covered such diverse activities as budgets, accounts, contracts, purchasing, tender board and pay.

The first intimation of trouble ahead came from a telephone call. Andrew was a young accountant that I had met socially a few times and he asked me to call round and have a drink with him that evening. I did so and sat, holding a whisky soda and listening to a diatribe against the senior British contract officer in the Finance and Purchasing Division. Andrew was Rashid's right hand man; if a half of what he and Andrew said was true in his outpouring of bile, Jeremy had the approach and sensitivity of a wounded buffalo and was creating fear and confusion among the staff for he interfered in everything that was going on and criticised brutally anything which did not please him. 'He has reduced me to a state of impotent fury,' Andrew said, 'and is going a fair way towards doing the same with many others.'

I made a mental note of what he said and thanked him for the drinks but I had some doubts about what he had told me. I knew that he had served in the British Army, that he was a qualified accountant and an intelligent young man. I also knew that his very pretty wife was expecting a baby. All in all, he might be a little unduly sensitive to too much pressure. I decided to keep an eye on him from a distance and to resolve this possible problem area by interviewing the senior British staff as soon as possible.

I never even considered trying to interview Rashid for past experience told me that when it came to possibly unpleasant interviews Rashid made the Scarlet Pimpernel look like a British tourist with a knotted handkerchief and braces on his first visit to the Costa Brava. At the slightest suggestion of anybody wanting to discuss any subject which might be embarrassing - and that included work - he would disappear. 'He is on his farm up north Sir,' - 'He is in London/New York/Paris Sir,' - 'He is leading the Omani Delegation to the United Nations on Desert Reclamation/Conservation/Camels/ Horses/Sheep,' and so on.

The first three interviews were very enlightening.

Anthony was sad. In his first few sentences he introduced the subject of the very good schools he had attended (although he was in his late forties), implied (accidentally but probably truthfully) that he had been sacked from his last job, developed an embarrassingly bad stutter and convinced me that he had learnt nothing during his year in MoD. I felt sorry for him. On one occasion when he gave me an honest answer to a question he spoilt the effect by immediately putting his hand to his mouth and exclaiming: 'Oh! Jeremy will kill me for saying that. I'm supposed to say just Yes and No.'

It was almost inevitable that I had to telephone his office and ask them to send someone to collect the papers he had left behind in the interview room.

The next one to be interviewed was Len, an ex-RAF supply officer who I had met before in my MoDUK days. He had not changed much and obviously now considered the fact that he had attained senior officer rank in the British Forces made him an invaluable asset to MoD Oman.

I was intrigued to see how he would behave at his interview. He didn't. Plainly, he had taken Jeremy's briefing to heart for no answer extended beyond: 'Yes,' 'No' or ' Perhaps'. After ten minutes I closed my notebook and said to him: 'I'm not wasting any more time with you. You have clearly decided not to co-operate with me and I must take this into account in my report.'

The last one was Jeremy himself. Tall, solidly built and with thick-rimmed glasses on a square jawed face he told me within minutes of sitting down that he had attended the Harvard Business School, possessed degrees in this and qualifications in that and was 'undoubtedly the most highly qualified British Officer in the Ministry of Defence.' I look impressed but noted that he had forgotten to mention that he had no military experience of any sort. In a roundabout way I introduced the subject of working in the military as opposed to the commercial world. He saw little difference which surprised me - and disturbed me a little. So far as he was concerned the Finance and Purchasing Division was going to operate the way he wanted it to and because of that it was going to operate superbly. I made a quick note and wondered if he ever had any doubts about anything.

Before discussion started he presented me with a sheaf of typed papers neatly stapled together and on leafing through them I saw that he had written job descriptions for all the British and Omani officers under his control. They were very well written and provided much detailed information and I thanked him for them but added that I did prefer individuals to produce their own job description as it often cleared their thoughts about their duties. Jeremy brushed this aside. 'Half of them don't know what they're bloody well doing,' was his reply. He chose to ignore my final comment: 'That's really the point of the exercise.'

The interview was very informative. I tackled him about Anthony and Len's behaviour and he replied without any trace of embarrassment: 'Oh yes. I told them both to leave it to me. I said that I'd deal with you for all of us.'

I pondered this for a few minutes. He really did come across as a very strong personality who had little regard for other people's feelings. Did he even consider, I wondered, that telling the others to leave it to him was mildly insulting? The implication was that they couldn't be trusted to say the right thing in an interview with me. Len, I knew, must have had many establishment interviews during his RAF career. I was beginning to understand Andrew's comment; working for Jeremy would be a wearing business. I decided to change tack.

'There's one aspect I'd like your views on.'

'Yes?'

'Each of the three services has a Budget Controller who works out how much money his force requires and, when he gets his allocation he monitors its expenditure.'

'Yes.'

'Fred as the Head of Resource Management has now got a Finance Manager in his office and they are the ones who decide how much each service is going to get.'

'That's right.'

'Then where do you and the Budgets Directorate figure in this new scene?'

'What do you mean?'

'Well, what does the Budgets Directorate do?'

'We negotiate the annual amount each service asks for and then we monitor their expenditure.'

'I'm sorry. I don't agree. Negotiating the annual amount allocated is the job of HRM and the Finance Manager. Monitoring the expenditure is the Budget Controller's job.'

Jeremy got excited. 'You can't let the services monitor their own spending. They haven't got a bloody clue. They're bound to get it wrong.'

I began to harden my line. 'If the Budget Controllers can't do their job, then the quicker they're found out and sacked the better. They're lieutenant colonels or equivalent. They're being paid very well for doing their jobs.'

From then on the interview deteriorated as it became clear that he was not prepared to tolerate any view that did not coincide with his own. It was a shame for there was no doubt in my mind that he was very intelligent and strongly motivated. If only he would relax a little and concede that other people were not necessarily stupid because they disagreed with him - and might even have a good reason for their point of view.

Subject to some more research it was beginning to look as if I would have to recommend the closure of the Budgets Directorate and I wondered what would happen to Jeremy. He would not be easy to place elsewhere for his abrasive personality was becoming widely known. As for the other two they had done well to survive so long. I was glad however that any decisions about their futures would not come from me. My own decisions were difficult enough on occasions without having to consider the personnel problems which might arise. It was inevitable however, that one thought about them sometimes.

Later, as my experience as Inspector of Establishments in MoD Oman grew, I was to come across quite a few odd people doing odd jobs. (In this context, I am using the Concise Oxford definition of 'odd' as being 'left over when the rest have been distributed.') Unlike the British Forces, where every individual or unit was carrying out a task which had been approved at a higher level, one never knew in Oman whether the individual, or his task, was necessary or had been authorised; at least, not until a thorough examination had been carried out. Depressingly often I found the job had been manufactured to give old so-and-so something to do. I could never understand the reluctance of the British management to tell individuals that their time was up. Maybe I had been made insensitive by my years as a staff inspector, but it struck me as ridiculous. We had all joined as contract officers and knew exactly what that entailed - two years initially and then renewable one year at a time - yet I had seen one middle-aged SON officer pleading, with tears in his eyes, to be allowed to stay on; not, I knew, because he had heavy financial commitments at home but because he realised that the UK held no future for him. Unfortunately, the drink had got to him and he had upset too many of his superiors.

It is worthwhile placing on record at this point that, in my experience, the Sultan of Oman's Navy were totally professional in disposing of their rotten apples. I thought about this and decided that it was because the SON Commander was a Royal Navy officer on loan who was replaced every two or three years and carried his parent service standards with him. Not so it seemed for CSOLF and CSOAF. They had been there far too long and the Air Force and the Land Force were cosy little clubs and, like most cosy little clubs, the members had to behave in a truly appalling manner in order to be booted down the steps onto the street.

Bill was an obvious example of the sort of thing you had to do.

Bill was an ex-paratrooper in the British Army. He had served well in the Dhofar War and eventually was placed in a staff officers job at HQ SOLF. He found the daily round to be boring and, like many before him, took to the drink. He was a dangerous drinker in that he became increasingly morose and bitter as the evening wore on and the empty cans grew. On this occasion he had gone through the afternoon and the early evening and God knows how many beers when an elderly civilian and his wife were escorted into the bar by one of the mess members. It later transpired that the man was a civil engineer and had arrived in Oman that morning.

Bill brooded, decided that he disliked the man immensely, the way he stood and the way he talked, shrieked the paratroopers' battle cry of 'Geronimo' and, hurling himself across the room punched the man on the jaw and knocked him to the floor.

It took some pressure but eventually CSOLF agreed that Bill had qualified for the Tin Budgie and he was evicted from the club. He was lucky, although I doubt if many people realised it. If the elderly civilian had so desired Bill could have been charged with assault and whilst awaiting trial in a civilian court would have spent quite a few months in Rumais Prison.

It was about then that I had a farewell drink with Ray. He was a half colonel in the US Marines and had just completed his tour as Defence Attache at the American Embassy in Muscat. He was the classic 'Leatherneck Fly Boy'. An ex-operational pilot in his late forties he was lean, fit, bronzed and with close cropped grey hair. Hazel and I were convinced that he had been reared on a diet of John Wayne and *The Sands of Iwojima* for his every action and spoken word was from that era. He had a great sense of humour but it excluded jokes about his service and his heroes. It was a rather infantile prank that made us realise this.

Hazel and I had been discussing him one morning for he was due for a meeting with Hassan Ehsan. When he walked in I assumed a deep John Wayne American drawl and rumbled: 'OK, youse guys. Hit the beach,' whereupon Hazel slapped her desk and cried out in a high falsetto 'Naughty beach. Naughty beach.'

We both exploded into laughter but Colonel Ray's expression was wooden.

The next stage of the review was the Purchasing Directorate and when I started to interview the British and Omani officers who worked there I realised what murky waters they swam in. I had carried out a tour of duty as a contracts officer in Cyprus in my MoDUK days and I knew how dirty the game could be played for I had been accused of accepting large bribes on two occasion by contractors who had rightly lost grossly inflated incomes from the British services. The rules in Oman however, were not only broken but not even acknowledged as existing for, as family and tribal interests were actively pursued, there were almost as many involved parties inside MoD Oman as there were outside. And what was the point of holding up our hands in horror and deploring practices which had existed for centuries and seemed immoral only to us?

Many items of supply ranging from office equipment to food were supplied under contract by local businesses and shops and most prices carried a substantial mark-up from the original, imported price. The reason for this was practical and inevitable, for, from the moment the container was offloaded at the docks family connections ensured that as many as possible benefited from the goods on their journey towards the customer. Discreet enquiries made by some of the British staff officers disclosed what the original manufacturer or exporter had charged and, appalled at the difference in price, a few had tried going to the source for their requirements. When the source heard who was enquiring however, they quickly lost interest. Why should they break up a perfectly satisfactory arrangement with their Omani agent/importer so that the MoD could save money. Everybody knew that the military threw thousands of rials away every day. Also, everybody knew that Oman was one of those wealthy Arab countries.

Even if the manufacturers had been co-operative, such a system would have been impossible to introduce, for the importers were a close-knit club and the introduction of direct supply would have almost guaranteed the sudden disappearance of other, equally important provisions. Anyway, everybody knew that Sultan Qaboos wanted nothing more than to see his people happy, well-fed and earning a good income. To abandon a practice which kept so many of the population contented was almost an insult to His Majesty; or so the argument went.

Added to this it was impressive, although fairly common knowledge, that a couple of major participants in this and similar cosy arrangements were the Director of Purchasing himself and, let's be brutally frank, His Highness, the Deputy Prime Minister for Security and Defence.

Said Faher was a charming man who, after only a brief acquaintance, I admired tremendously, as I did his lovely English wife; and although his majority partnership in the Toyota agency (who supplied all of the MoD and SAF staff cars); J & P (Oman) Ltd (who built garrisons, barracks, roads, forts, married quarters and blocks of flats for hirings around the country) and Electroman (who seemed to be into everything else) raised many British eyebrows, the simple fact was that he was only doing what came naturally and very successfully too.

There was little doubt that the cause of much aggravation later on was that British commercial interests did not feature in His Highness' arrangements and inevitably, CDS did not approve of this.

This disapproval developed into a covert war, which later was to envelop poor Robin Walsh as Secretary of the Tender Board. At that time, however, the covert war passed comparatively unnoticed except when the battle over some particularly juicy plum reached even our ears. This conflict was to last a few years and Sir Timothy Creasey scored a few notable victories such as the British Scicon computer contract and some British weaponry including the Chieftain tanks. However, even these deals came under fairly savage attack in the *Observer* a couple of years later when the Robin Walsh Affair was at its height; and words such as misappropriation, financial neglience and opportunities for fraud and embezzlement were being thrown around. Even when Sir Timothy's contract ended [5] and he returned to England, His Highness Said Faher remained very firmly in control of the battlefield and CSOLF who succeeded as CDS was not the same man as his predecessor. He had been in Oman too long and was not about to engage in commercial warfare with the man who had been his master for many years.

One interesting side issue of the contracts battle arose from the efforts of CDS to obtain contingency plans from his commanders. I do not know if he was ever successful but I doubt it, for the nagging, prevaricating and stonewalling went on for so long that we all lost interest, as, I suspect, did CDS.

Provision of contingency plans is a simple and sensible military precaution. If you know your potential enemies, how or where they might attack you and what their weaponry, personnel and logistics capabilities are, then you are in a position to draw up your own plans. Armed with this information you can also best decide about your own weaponry, personnel and logistics requirements.

There were many friendly arguments in the office as to why the commanders failed to provide contingency plans. Some said that each one of them was so devoted to fighting his own war that he would not make his plans public; others said that the commanders had not got the staffs with the experience and intelligence to produce contingency plans. Personally, I suspected that the answer lay somewhere in the middle. By now I was developing little regard for the commanders and was beginning to wonder when Sir Timothy was going to achieve the task he was recruited for, ie, to weld the three forces into a fighting unity. I recalled a recent letter from Peter Thwaites in which he mentioned having lunch in London with Sultan Qaboos and General Creasey; the letter closed with the comment about Sir Timothy that: 'I am sure that he will provide the clout we so sadly lacked in my day.'

Two months passed before I finished my examination of the staff of His Excellency's Department - a period during which I met a number of personalities, pleasant and unpleasant, and learnt some more Omani facts of life. I have already commented on how difficult it was to remove British contract officers and cited Bill's assault as an example of what you had to do to get evicted from the club. However, I still had a lot to learn, as I realised when I tried to get Rashid sacked.

Rashid was an office orderly and God or Allah alone knew how he had got the job. He joined us during the last couple of months of the Joint Staff's activities and he moved across the wadi with Hazel and myself when we opened up Hassan's new office. Rashid was dirty (grubby and unshaven in his person and permanently wearing a grey and grimy dish dash); he was lazy (threats and a gentle nudge with the foot were necessary to get him to his feet and out of the office) and he was totally unreliable (one never knew whether he would arrive for work - thankfully, usually not).

---

[5] The original plan was that when Sir Timothy Creasey's contract ended he would move into the Palace Office and become the Sultan's adviser on military matters. Sadly, Sir Timothy developed cancer and he died on the 5th October 1986.

I was loth to take any disciplinary action because I suspected that I would be wading into very muddy waters, but one morning my patience snapped when I challenged a recent absence and was given an insolent reply. I made up a report listing his faults and misdemeanours and sent him back to the Director of Administration with a request for a replacement. Rashid disappeared for a month and no replacement arrived; but then he was so totally useless that his absence was noticed only with relief. Then he reappeared, washed and shaven and this time in a clean dish dash. In his very broken English he told me that he was now a good man and the Director of Administration had spoken to Hassan Ehsan who had agreed to give the reformed character another chance. The reformed character lasted about a week.

Twice he had walked through our office and into Hassan's without a by-your-leave and both Hazel and I had assumed, naively as it transpired, that he was on some special errand for His Excellency. We were wrong. His second visit lasted about ten seconds and as he reappeared in our office he was followed by Hassan who was in a towering rage. Rashid's first visit it seemed, had been to plead for a job for his brother; his second was to plead for a loan to build a house.

'Get him out of here,' howled His Excellency. 'I do not wish to see him ever again.'

I personally drove Rashid back to the Director of Administration and made it pretty clear that if he valued his own job he'd keep the horrible little orderly away from Hassan Ehsan. I concluded: 'If you take my advice you'll sack the little bugger. He's absolutely useless.'

But nobody ever seemed to annotate anybody's personal records and a few weeks later I looked up from my desk to see Rashid standing in front of me, smiling, albeit a little nervously.

I scowled to set the tone for the conversation. 'What do you bloody well want Rashid?'

'I wish to see His Excellency, Sir.'

'What about?'

'It is a personal matter, Sir.'

I stood up. 'Come with me,' I said and led him firmly by the arm outside and into my car. Having arrived at the Administration block I escorted him in a similar manner into the office of the Director. He was a new man and recently promoted. He looked up. 'Can I help you Sir?' I listed Rashid's unpleasant history. 'If I had let him into His Excellency's office,' I said, nodding at the disconsolate figure beside me, 'I'd have been on the Tin Budgie and you'd be back in you old job by tomorrow morning. Keep him away from Hassan Ehsan for God's sake.' The Director nodded nervously and thanked me. As I turned to go I added: 'By the way. What's he still doing around here? I suggested that he be sacked, then I heard that he had insulted one of your Omani lady officers and I thought that would be the end for him.'

'Oh, it was Sir, but this man petitioned His Highness, who said that because Rashid supported a large family he should be given one more chance.'

I sighed. 'Oh well. Keep the little grub away from His Excellency, otherwise you'll be the one petitioning His Highness.'

It was during one of my interviews with the officers of the Administration that I learnt that dirty, lazy, unreliable Rashid was still around and being moved from office to office with monotonous regularity.

But, thank God, Rashid was very much the exception and, unsurprisingly, the counterparts of the hundred or so officers I interviewed would have been found in any large commercial organisation or ministry in the United Kingdom. Certainly I knew a number of female equivalents of Huda al Ghazali for she was attractive, vivacious and with a bright intelligence. From an old, wealthy and much travelled Omani family she was a living advertisement for the Sultan's edict that the women of Oman should be allowed equal opportunity with their menfolk for she had already reached senior rank at a comparatively young age. I had certainly met Hamed's duplicate in MoDUK many times, in and out of uniform. Large, pompous, verbose and with an unerring attraction towards the wrong end of the stick.

In due course the interviews finished and I made my final liaison visit to His Excellency and gave my final debriefing to Fred. All that now remained was the collation and summation of the individual reports into a brief summary for submission to Hassan Ehsan as the head of the Under Secretary's Department and Sir Timothy Creasey as head of the Sultan's Armed Forces.

Of the eleven hundred posts in the department some two hundred were unfilled and had been for a long time. These were removed from the establishment on the simple basis of what you've never had, you won't miss. Another fifty or so posts which were filled I had recommended for disestablishment for a number of reasons, ranging from the obvious one that the occupant had no work to do to the more contentious claim on my part that their removal would improve the efficiency of the organisation. Into this last category came Jeremy and his cohorts and Hamed and his staff.

One of the less pleasant parts of an establishment officers' task is, at the end of the day, to tell the personnel he has been examining what he is going to recommend about their jobs. I was not looking forward to debriefing either Jeremy or Hamed. The former because he had already displayed no tolerance towards an opposing viewpoint and the latter, because he was 'Royal' and I had this irresistible picture of him trotting off to the palace after my chat. In the event, possibly because they suspected what was coming, neither of the interviews went off as expected.

There was a certain wide-eyed disbelief in Jeremy's reaction to my recommendation that he and his Budgets Directorate be closed down, but this may have been because he found it hard to credit that anybody would suggest such a thing. He was wearing a superbly cut lightweight fawn suit and our chat ended abruptly when he spilt a cup of coffee over it. Unlikely as it was, I felt sorry for him as he left me in his sodden and stained outfit to carry the news to Anthony and Len. (6)

(6) It is worth recording that Jeremy obtained his revenge on the organisation that dared to get rid of him when the Robin Walsh scandal came alive in the British press and on television in the summer of 1984, for, on TV he added a sinister dimension when he talked of leaving the Sultanate because of 'the danger from harassment' and accused the MoD Oman of financial negligence,

Giving similar news to Hamed was going to be a different scene I decided. I knew my place. I was not about to summon a member of the Omani Royal Family to my office to tell him he was out of a job; the least I could do was to visit him to pass on the bad news. I did so and was astounded at its reception.

'I am delighted Alan,' he said. 'As long as they make me ambassador to Timbuktu or somewhere, I shall be very happy.' We spent a few more minutes finishing off the inevitable coffee and going through the social niceties. As I closed his door I shook my head. You never really knew what was in the minds of people you talked to. It was possible that Hamed was aware of his fading authority and was more than happy to bid farewell to his present position; equally, being the sort of man he was that beaming smile could be hiding a seething interior. Anyway, I decided, thank the Lord that that's over and only He knows what they'll do with Hamed if they close his office [7] for he had already failed in the commercial world and they would have to keep him on as a Ministry of Defence employee for earlier approaches had shown that the Ministry of Foreign Affairs were not overly enthusiastic about Hamed's ambassadorial potential.

His Excellency Hassan Ehsan and Sid, his Principal Staff Officer, received my news about the review with no surprise for I had kept them briefed as it progressed. Sir Timothy Creasey however, would clearly have preferred me to have found the grossly inflated bureaucracy he had been told existed in HE's Department. Obviously, my credibility was going to suffer, for the more senior the officer, the less they appreciate being told what they don't want to hear. In the event, the implementation of my report was Fred's concern and I gladly left it to him. For my part, I saw another Ramadan approaching and everything was about to slow down. No matter how eagerly motivated you were, within a few days there would be no enthusiasm and even less co-operation from the Muslim (Omani, Baluchi and Pakistani) members of the staff.

I was now into my third year in the Sultanate and, may Allah forgive me, finding Ramadan an increasing bore. Ramadan is a lunar cycle of twenty-eight days during which neither food nor drink must pass the lips of the believers between sunrise and sunset and the effect of those days on the life of Oman (and the other Arab states) is truly remarkable. As the moon waxes then wanes, so everyday life slows down until, by the time Eid Al Fitr (the holiday celebrating the end of Ramadan) arrives the country's business, both government and commercial, is virtually at a standstill.

The Omanis, being the tolerant people that they are, allowed us 'Christians' to follow our usual eating and drinking habits providing

weak cost control and providing opportunities for fraud and embezzlement. My own footnote to this is that whilst the financial accusations had some merit, the harassment danger existed only in his imagination.
[7] Hamed moved on and on and is now in charge of a map office. It is possible that he has finally found his niche for, supported by specialists and knowing nothing of survey technicalities, he will find it difficult to become too involved in the daily operation of his office.

such activities were kept from the sight of the 'Faithful' but, inevitably, mess life became even more tedious for during daylight hours the dining room became a gloomy curtained cavern and in the evening, the bar, operating on restricted hours, served only soft drinks. Fortunately, the mess 'cellar' was opened for half an hour each day and you could buy beer or spirits for consumption in your room or your home. I found it entertaining to watch the furtive pre-Ramadan preparation of many of our Muslim officers as they loaded up their cars with crates of beer and cases of Black Label in preparation for the religious siege. It was comforting to see that Islam had its backsliders as well.

The 'Faithful' who lived in the mess had to be fed before sunrise and after sunset and this involved a breakfast (usually curry) at the impossible time of 3.30am and an evening meal (curry again) at 10pm. It was inevitable that with the prospect of no food or liquid for eighteen hours or more, the Islamic officers would stuff themselves to bursting at that appallingly early breakfast. It was equally inevitable that having arisen at three in the morning they should arrive at the office at seven-thirty with distended stomachs and grossly overloaded digestive systems and be virtually useless. By ten o'clock they could talk politely but not communicate, the clerks would have their heads on their arms on the desks and the office orderlies would be scattered around on the floor fast asleep, looking in their dish dashes like bundles of discarded laundry.

If you were lucky and had Christian (usually Indian) office staff you could have a cup of tea or coffee during working hours providing you kept a weather eye open for the occasional Omani who might still be on his feet. If however, your staff were of the faith, then you had to drive back to your room and brew yourself a furtive cup.

The problem with trying to achieve a reasonably productive day however, lay in finding another office or officer who was similarly inclined. It was then that your patience could wear thin and you questioned the practicality of Ramadan in the modern world. If you were fortunate you might find another non-believer capable of dealing with your particular problem or business and, on very rare occasions you might locate a sophisticated Omani who regarded Ramadan in much the same way as most Europeans now look upon Lent. In the great majority of cases however, day to day business wound down as the Fast wore on. A perfect example of this was in the delivery (or rather non-delivery) of mail.

As I mentioned earlier, the mail service was usually bad, with air mail letters arriving from the United Kingdom anything between five days and three weeks after posting. This erratic service became truly appalling however, with the arrival of Ramadan, because after the first few days all incoming mail stopped arriving at the officers' mess. During those first few days a handful of letters would be placed in the pigeon holes in the mess entrance hall but as Ramadan lethargy overtook the post office sorters so the mail dried up. From then on we could write and post letters until we were blue in the face, but no replies would be received for six weeks or so.

The end of Ramadan brought no letters either, for the four days of Eid Al Fitr were a national holiday, but even when the mail started to arrive it only increased out irritation for these letters would have been posted recently and another month would pass before we caught up with all our correspondence. As we learnt, during the Fast any mail bags that arrived from the airport or the docks were just emptied onto the steadily growing piles in the post office. Thus, after Eid Al Fitr, the sorters worked their way down, the most recent arrivals being delivered first.

Heavy jokes prevailed among us unbelievers during this trying time; particularly popular was that oldie from many wars ago: 'You shouldn't have joined if you can't take a joke'. It was a generally held opinion however, that if the Arab nations wanted to move into the twentieth century (and there was some doubt about that) changes would have to be made to some of their religious practices. A good example of how this could be done was shown by one Head of State further up the Gulf.

In Oman (and throughout the Arab world) Ramadan did not end, nor Eid Al Fitr start, until the new moon had been sighted by one of the country's religious leaders. To Western eyes this was a ridiculous situation because it all depended on the vagaries of the weather, including passing dust storms and the eyesight of some ancient priest who could probably only read the Qu'ran with the aid of a magnifying glass. One never knew until literally the last minute when Ramadan finished and Eid Al Fitr started and it was impossible to make any arrangements, professionally or socially, with any certainty. As the shops, which operated on restricted hours during Ramadan, closed down entirely for the holiday period, it was not uncommon for a household to be caught unawares and find themselves low on food and with no means of replenishing stocks until life returned to normal.

This situation was intolerable, but it took a near riot of young mothers who found themselves without food and milk for their children before something was done about it. Apparently the sight of the suddenly closed doors of the well-stocked Ruwi supermarket had been too much for them.

Common sense edged religion a little out of the way and radio and television were used to announce when Eid Al Fitr was to start, which chemists would be open in the major towns and even more important, that the shops were forbidden to close for all of the four days. I did not envy the Sultan his task of moving Oman into the twentieth century and I could well imagine some of the problems he would encounter with the country's religious leaders. Fortunately, I gathered, they were a much more tolerant breed than their counterparts across the water in Iran.

I wondered if, in the time, His Majesty would be allowed to follow the example of another Head of State further up in the Gulf. This ruler had already decided that last minute uncertainty about the start of a national holiday was a ridiculous situation he would not tolerate. He was a well-educated and ingenious man and having ascertained from navigational almanacs when the new moon was due to appear over his country he announced that date as the end of Ramadan well in advance. On the due date he then sent his senior Imams up to thirty thousand feet in his personal Boeing 727 thus ensuring that the new moon was sighted whatever the weather.

In the Sultan's Armed Forces and the Ministry of Defence the end of Ramadan became a somewhat farcical business because each Commander decided in his own good time and for his own good reasons when the Eid Al Fitr holiday would start for his service. The Land Forces whose working week was never a demanding one, managed to expand the four days into at least a week, often more, and as the force comprised well over half of SAF's strength, it could be argued that this showed a somewhat casual approach to defending Oman. CSOAF tended in the opposite direction for 'Biggles' as he was known amongst his flyers was an unmarried man who was not very keen about leave as an institution. The Navy, whose boats were largely officered by deputationists (loanees) from the Pakistani Navy, played a fairly straight bat. I wondered whether Sir Timothy would ever get SAF to follow the UK example and all go on leave over the same period. Not that this would ever entail the departure of the whole force to their homes for nearly half of the Sultan's Armed Forces came from Pakistan, India or the UK and for them, Eid Al Fitr meant no more than a brief relaxation from the daily round.

When I worked in Hassan's office, the end of Ramadan and the beginning of the holiday became an even more exasperating affair. A commander would decide when his chaps could go on leave and send off a signal to his force (copy of MoD) giving them the magic date - say the 28th. In swift order, we would then receive copies of the signals from the other commanders stating that their lot was going to leave on the 26th and the 30th. Confusion was compounded totally however when His Highness and His Excellency, following the advice of the Palace Office, the Imams and the moon sent off their signals. So far as I was concerned, the outcome of all this was usually a constantly ringing telephone and irate enquiries along the lines of 'For Christ's sake Alan! I've got four bloody signals in front of me. When is this f***ing holiday going to start?'

A few of the older and more disenchanted among us managed to achieve one small victory during Ramadan however. Some of the larger messes, such as those at Muaskar al Murtafa'a were fortunate because, although they only served soft drinks in the bar, somewhere amongst the myriad accommodation would be a room, known only to the cognoscenti, which operated on the style of a speakeasy. This sort of deviousness was not possible in a small camp like Bait al Falaj. We could of course have retired to solitary drinking in our own rooms, or multiple drinking in somebody else's, but this was not a very happy arrangement and usually led to over-indulgence. We could equally, of course, have given up the hard stuff for Ramadan, but most of us only wanted a few drinks in sociable company for an hour or two and the usual exchange of light-hearted gossip that went with it. It was here that the hip flask came into its own, for, should an Omani come into the bar (unlikely) a whisky soda looked like a ginger ale and it was impossible to tell whether a tonic water contained gin.

So the dreary twenty-eight days went by and we were all thankful for the arrival of Eid Al Fitr. Not so much for the holiday, but for the fact that in a few days we could all get back to work. Whatever the Qu'ran claims, I saw little evidence of enhanced spirituality during Ramadan (but plenty of enhanced lethargy) and it is certainly not true that the breath of a man who has fasted smells sweetly. Quite the contrary.

Now our lives returned to normality, if such a word could be applied to the daily round at Bait al Falaj; and as I discovered during the next month the Shariya Court also resumed dispensing its own peculiarly practical form of justice. The episode of Sarah and the ancient she had bumped with her car was furthest from my mind when I met Steve.

We were both going on leave and were sitting chatting in the departure lounge at Seeb Airport. The aircraft was late and over our second cup of coffee we talked about what we were doing in Oman. Steve was a New Zealander, a young draughtsman who worked for one of the large UK construction companies. When I asked him where he lived, assuming either in the Capital Area or in one of the many domestic sites, he told me he wasn't quite sure. 'I gave up my room when I moved into Rumais Prison a couple of months ago,' he said. He saw the look on my face, grinned and explained.

He had been driving back from Nezwa very late one night. There was no moon, but only the dark shapes of the jebel on his left. 'I was probably driving too fast' he guessed. 'No,' he shook his head as if remembering a hard earned lesson. 'I was definitely driving too fast. If I hadn't been I could have stopped when the young woman stepped in front of me.

'I tried to explain but the Shariya Court weren't impressed with my argument that you don't expect somebody to walk across a desert road, sixty miles from the capital at one o'clock in the morning.

'I killed her,' he said. There was no smile now. 'And I was stone cold sober.

'Anyhow, the Shariya Court decided that although she was mainly responsible for her own death I was also responsible because I was driving too fast. So they sent me to Rumais. I never did find out how long I was supposed to be in there for, but after the blood money was paid, the ambassador and the company made representations and after a couple of months the court decided that I had been punished enough. And I had been,' he concluded and shivered slightly.

I couldn't help myself. 'What was it like in Rumais?'

He had recovered and grinned slightly. 'Not too bad, funnily enough. Depends what you're used to, I suppose. It was tolerable, once you'd got over the culture shock. There was about twenty of us in this big cage. An open bog and a tap in the corner. Omanis, Indians, Pakis and me.' He grinned once more. 'There was a jebali in our cage. He'd been done for raping a sheep.' He laughed out loud. 'If it had been his own there'd have been no problem, but it belonged to a neighbour and he complained to the police. Anyway, everywhere the poor sod went in prison all the other prisoners kept on bleating at him. Sounded like a bloody farmyard.'

'Did they let you out of the cage much? Did you get much exercise?'

'As much as you liked. All of the locals had to work during the day. There's a helluva big farm there,' he added. 'The white faces didn't have to work though, unless they wanted to. I spent most of my time reading and writing letters. As long as you did as you were told there was no problem.'

I gazed at him in some admiration. Obviously an equable youngster who had accepted his incarceration philosophically. I had been told that the discipline inside was very strict for, in accord with the simple logic of Islamic justice, you were not inside to be remodelled into a better citizen but to be punished for your wrongdoing.

Later, as I drove to Dubhai for the occasional weekend of pseudo civilisation, I got to know Rumais Prison quite well (from the outside only, thank God). Standing back a couple of hundred yards from the main (and only) road to the Emirates it lies about thirty kilometres north of Seeb Palace. It is instantly recognisable for it is a brilliant white fortress with high walls, a watch tower at each corner and the huge doors which only prisons and old castles seem to have. The surrounding trees, vegetable gardens and flower beds went some way to alleviating its forbidding appearance but it could never be mistaken for anything other than a prison.

When I returned from leave it was to find that Bill was flirting with the idea of going to prison and nothing we could say seemed to dissuade him. As I have mentioned earlier, Bill did not suffer fools gladly and this character weakness, if such it was, seemed likely to lead him into one of the cages that Steve had just left.

The Royal Oman Police were an impeccably attired and highly disciplined force whose cars, motorbikes and constables positively gleamed. It was an unfortunate fact however that, at the bottom end of the rank structure, some of them were not bright. Impressive as some of the traffic policemen might appear when they dismounted from their shining machines, when they arrived at the side of your car their English would often be restricted to 'Driving licence' and 'You speeding' as they tried unsuccessfully to copy down the English or Arabic information on your licence. Their other weakness was their cavalier approach to setting speed traps, frequently doing so on the six lanes of Qaboos Street during the rush hour. Thus, driving comfortably along in the middle of a gaggle of cars and lorries you would suddenly find a policeman hurl himself in front of your bonnet and wave you into the side of the road. When your hands had uncurled from the steering wheel and your pulse rate had slowed down you would be accused of speeding. Twice I had been caught like this and on both occasions it was pointless to argue for his English was as minimal as my Arabic. On the first occasion I had paid the fine, on the second I became irate and discovered that one of my Omani officers had a relative in the traffic section.

It seemed that Bill had been caught and although his reaction of indignant fury was understandable we warned him that he couldn't win. 'In the Shariya court it'll be your word against his, we told him. 'Are you going to call him a liar?'

'The dim bastard didn't have any idea what he was bloody well doing,' Bill protested.

'It doesn't really matter,' we said but there was no way that he was going to accept this grave injustice. He was going to plead not guilty and go in front of the Shariya Court. 'If the judge gets pissed off, you could finish up in Rumais' was another threat, but to no avail.

Came the day and, smartly dressed as a civilian, Bill left his MAM office and disappeared towards the Capital Area.

As was so often the case in Oman, it was a simple non-delivery of a message which led to the furore, but when he failed to appear in the bar that evening rumour and alarm was rife. 'Poor old Bill. But we did warn him,' was the trend of the conversation.

I telephoned a friend at Qurum Police Station (where entrants to and prisoners from Rumais usually stopped in transit). 'No,' he said. 'The day's records shows no trace of a Mister Hirst going in. A Mister Hawkins has gone in,' he offered helpfully, 'but he was a drinking man who had an accident.' The mystery remained and it didn't clear until nine o'clock when Bill arrived at the bar, the worse for wear. It had been an ongoing lunchtime party, we gathered. He had transmitted a message to me via his chief clerk who had failed to pass it on. When the hubbub died down I asked him the crucial question and for a few minutes my conversation with Bill sounded like a second rate cross-talk act.

'Well, how did you get on in court?'

'I don't know.'

'What do you mean for God's sake - you don't know?'

'I mean just that. I don't bloody well know.'

I sighed. 'Alright. Tell me exactly what happened. In words of one syllable.'

'Well, the judge listened to me and the copper. Then he said:

'Not guilty. Fined ten rials'.'

The bar fell silent while ten European minds grappled with the concept.

I was brooding about this conversation a couple of days later. There was a sort of off-beat logic in the judge's finding. 'Not guilty,' kept Bill happy while 'Fined ten rials' kept the Royal Oman Police happy.

It was a Friday morning I remember and I was lying on the swimming raft some hundred yards or so offshore from the Aqua Club. It was about eight o'clock and the sun was still low enough for its warmth to be welcome. Another few hours and I would be seeking shelter from it.

Some splashing and puffing and the raft swayed a little as another swimmer clambered on board. I opened my eyes and closed them again quickly, pretending to be asleep. It was Ronnie, a pleasant enough chap who I had first met years ago on one of my overseas trips from MoDUK. Lord knows what RAF station it had been; he could remember no more than I could and we had settled into the relaxed attitude of old but casual friends. The problem with Ronnie now however, was that he was totally deaf and steadfastly refused to wear a hearing aid. Conversation with him became a shouting match and I had no desire to ruin the peace of the morning.

He was an ex-Squadron Leader and during his first few years in the Sultanate had been carrying out the 'trained monkey' job that Big Jim had filled. Now he worked for the Research Department, the country's intelligence organisation. I wondered idly, as I had often done before, what Ronnie did within that secret body. Couldn't be interrogation I decided, and smiled inwardly at the thought of some spy sweatily pouring out his confession and secrets while Ronnie cupped his ear in that familiar gesture and interrupted: 'Sorry, what was that?'

I was at a party some weeks later when I got my opportunity. I was chatting to an acquaintance who I knew worked in the hilltop compound at Qurum and we had both drunk enough to make conversation easy. I broke a minute's companionable silence.

'Tell me old mate,' I said earnestly, 'how in the name of God did your mob take on Ronnie Smyth Cooper? He's as deaf as the proverbial post.'

He glanced over his shoulder in the traditional manner then tapped the side of his nose before sniggering loudly. 'Simple,' he whispered, 'a mistake.'

'A mistake?' I repeated with some astonishment.

Another furtive look over the shoulder. 'Yes. The two guys who were interviewing him thought he was a deep one. Not giving away much. You know. We often meet 'em in our game.'

I looked at him in disbelief. 'I don't believe it.'

'It's true,' he urged me. 'It wasn't until after he started work that they realised he hadn't answered half their questions because he hadn't heard them. Now, everybody's too embarrassed to do anything about him.'

I sat back as my mind whirled into a fantasy land of stone-deaf spies who gave away nothing under interrogation.

Yet Ronnie's recruitment as an office supervisor (as I later learnt) was less strange than some of the jobs various colleagues obtained. Whether the Omanis had a touching faith in the abilities of the British or whether the applicants painted their abilities well beyond reality I do not know. The intrinsic loyalty of the Omanis was certainly a factor though. Take Ted for instance.

Ted was already a serving contract officer in SON when I arrived in Oman. He was engineer officer on board *Shabab* Oman, the sail training ship. *Shabab*'s massive auxiliary engines at that time had a reputation for unreliability and the reason for this was difficult to establish. The Navy put most of the blame on Ted and poor maintenance whereas he blamed SON for their consistent refusal to spend any money on replacing old and worn engine parts. Whatever the truth, he found himself looking for another job, this time on dry land. Not that *Shabab*'s rare sallies from Mina Qaboos at that time could be said to resemble a life on the ocean wave in any way. As the lad's SON contract began to run out so he would join us occasionally in the Bamboo Bar and report on his job hunting. Sometimes his reports were hard to follow because he had visited the SON mess in Muscat before coming onto us and this led to a fairly garbled narrative which left you unsure whether he had just read about a vacancy, had just been interviewed for a post or had actually got a job. I remember in the course of one evening he was going to be responsible for maintaining the lifts in a large new office and shopping complex near the Ruwi roundabout; then he was in charge of all engineering matters in the complex, including sewage, electricity, air-conditioning and so on, and next he was actually going to be the chief engineer for the whole of the Middle East for the company that built the complex. Such rapid promotion before he had even got the job left us all a mite dazed although most of us had already noticed that the importance of the job rose in direct proportion to the number of Fosters that Ted had downed.

He disappeared for a few weeks and when I enquired I learnt that he had gone to run a new yacht chandlers that was opening up in Dubhai. Later, *Shabab* visited Dubhai for an overhaul and his ex-colleagues discovered him working (for a bloody pittance, as he put it) as a storeman in one of the shipyards. Six or seven months later he reappeared in the Bamboo Bar. To my question whether he was on leave he replied: 'No. Got bloody well fed up with that job. I'm looking for another one down here.'

Along the cost to the east of Muscat there is a small bay among the jagged cliffs and peaks and in it is the Capital Area Yacht Club. Its membership is multi-national and its committee mostly Omanis and British. In general, it seemed, the sailing craft (including the Hobie Cats) were owned and sailed by the European members and the high speed motor-boats by the Omanis; the wealthier ones I hasten to add, for to most of the Sultan's people, the concept of leisure was a novelty in itself without hurtling across the water at high speed. It was in this marine rendezvous for the sons of the wealthy Omani families and the expatriates that Ted found his next niche: manager of the CAYC.

Lack of previous experience had clearly been no bar to getting the job and, to be fair, he certainly had the grey matter to learn the ropes quickly. He settled in and within a few weeks appeared again in the Bamboo Bar for the occasional jar. At last it looked as if he had found a job which suited his temperament and called on his maritime knowledge.

For some time life ran smoothly, then he hit a problem that some of us had met already. This was the drunken young Omani who waves his nationalist fervour in front of a white face. I had met it once in the Bait al Falaj mess at a cheese and wine party and was only prevented from panning the extremely obnoxious young Omani guest by the apologies of his brothers who dragged him away. This was a growing problem and one of the many that had worried the Sultan's father - how would his people react to alcohol? Qaboos' solution was to place a financial limit on the amount of alcohol that his Omani officers could buy in their messes. Unfortunately, at the occasional mess party, there always seemed to be one young guest who only needed a glass of wine to unleash his dislike for the infidels who lived and worked in his country. 'We do not need you' was an oft repeated cry of these young lions and of course they were right, providing they were ready to slip back into a simple agricultural and fishing economy without hospitals and education.

In Ted's case however, he was walking a tightrope for his job depended on the goodwill of the Omani members of the yacht club, some of whom were the spoilt offspring of the wealthier families who resented any white face attempting to control their behaviour.

It was late on a Friday evening and the group of youngsters were very drunk and they had not put their speedboats away. Ted asked them to nicely, pointing out that their boats were blocking the ramp for anybody who wanted to launch the following morning.

One of the young sprigs, whose colloquial English was better than his upbringing, told him to 'F*** off.' Ted responded by closing the bar. In high dudgeon they got into their cars and drove away. Ted closed the now empty club, switched off the lights and went off to his caravan to go to bed. Ten minutes later there came a knock at the door and he answered it to be confronted by two policemen. He asked them their business and was told that he had insulted the Sultan and the Omani people. He was arrested, taken to the local copshop and put away for the night.

A day or two passed before the committee, common sense and the Palace Office intervened. I heard that the Omani youths were suitably chastised and Ted was released with apologies and offered another job. Authority had learnt its lesson and insisted that the CAYC should be managed by an Omani in future. The last time I spoke to Ted, he had just been offered the post of manager of a new very up-market restaurant along the Corniche. It had its own small man-made harbour and I could easily envisage him doing his salty, sea dog, dinner-jacketed scene. How long for? Perhaps Allah knows, although he is probably wondering too.

Chapter 7

It was not only Ted who had an uncertain future however, for I was beginning to have some doubts about my own recently acquired position as Inspector of Establishments. Sir Timothy's initial approach had been to impose personnel reductions across all of SAF. This suggested a good healthy start for, if nothing else, it made the commanders examine their own establishments and personnel numbers, and hopefully implanted some sense of economy where little, if any, had existed previously. In the event, I had now learnt that nothing at all had come from it and the commanders had prevailed upon CDS to forget the idea.

Where does this leave me? I asked myself. If I don't have the declared and visible support of the Chief of the Defence Staff any future efforts of mine towards economy will have no effect at all. I had learnt this lesson well in MoDUK on a number of occasions when a lot of effort from our committee had come to naught because Air Marshal This had complained to General That. Wait and see, I said to myself, but those clouds on the horizon were definitely dark ones. For the immediate future I carried on progressing my recommendations regarding the Under Secretary's Department and allowed life to follow its usual dull routine: up at five-thirty, drive to the BAF or MAM office, back anywhere between three and four in the afternoon, siesta or swim, another shower, bar and gossip, letter-writing or reading and bed. Because of the daily temperature and my age any sporting activities were fairly restricted but I managed to go sailing most Fridays and swimming most afternoons.

I had watched Oman Television on a few occasions shortly after my arrival and then turned my back on the set for the next four years. Unlike the mediocrity of the United Arab Emirates in the north the Omani programmers were truly awful. I can still remember with a shudder their version of: 'What's My Line?' and the incredibly badly painted backcloth against which the dishdash-clothed panel sat. I had been told that all of the technical operations of Oman TV were controlled by Dutch engineers and producers and this I could well believe. I know Holland well, have many friends and relatives living there and admire its people tremendously but its television is abysmal; clearly their standards were being well and truly planted in Oman.

To be fair to the Netherlanders though, I doubt if they were responsible for the content of the 'News in English' at ten o'clock for in this programme the world revolved around the Persian Gulf. I watched it a few times seeking enlightenment on the world's happenings but instead it was some twenty five minutes of: 'A spokesman for the Gulf Cooperation Council said...'; 'The holy brotherhood of the Arab nations will ensure...'; 'In audience this afternoon His Majesty stated...'; 'His Highness the Deputy Prime Minister for Defence said...'.

At the end occupying a minute or two came the world news we were waiting for. As always, it was our radios and the BBC Overseas Service that kept us informed about the real world.

Whenever I drove to my office at Muaskar al Murtafa'a it was impossible to ignore evidence of the strides that the Sultanate was making away from the dark age of Said bin Taimur. Blocks of flats, groups of town houses, factories, shopping complexes and ministry buildings were growing out of the featureless sand in all directions. Invariably they were Arabic in concept and graceful in design. Past Qurum however a very unattractive double row of nearly completed town houses climbed up a small rocky incline beside Qaboos Street. So unattractive were they in fact that I pulled off the main highway on one occasion to examine them at my leisure. Closer inspection revealed that they were not only unattractive, they well qualified for the description of downright ugly.

I felt a small sense of pride in my aesthetic standards a few weeks later when I drove past and saw a large crane with a huge metal ball slowly reducing them to rubble. How the builder obtained permission to build so many monstrosities in such a small space I never did find out, although, being Oman, it was very easy to believe the stories about bribery/builders' relatives in the Ministry of Housing. What I did learn however, was that Sultan Qaboos had recently driven past, noticed them for the first time and ordered their immediate destruction. It was a salutary lesson to the builder and a sharp warning to others.

I was beginning to wish that I had similar powers. Under the Head of Resource Management I was supposed to be responsible for the numbers of personnel in SAF, but recent statistical research on my part showed a steady growth in the force. If, as seemed probable, it continued, the long-term implications were alarming and try as I might, I could find no sensible reason for it. SON had new ships on the way and their increase in personnel was understandable; SOAF had plans for two squadrons of Tornados, but they should only bring a small increase in aircrew for the hordes of servicing personnel required would be recruited by Airwork (the aircraft maintenance contractor) and would be British civilians; SOLF had acquired a handful of American tanks but their crews and maintenance staff could be located and did not account for the overall growth that was taking place.

Given the military mind and its firm conviction that more men is the solution to every problem, the picture that was beginning to emerge was an inevitable one. Common sense would go out of the window as the specialists sought to achieve a gold-plated standard. I recalled two perfect examples from my MoDUK days.

If war breaks out in Europe the RAF Harrier squadrons in Germany leave the comfort and security of their base and disperse to forested areas where, in theory, they are hidden from the enemy but can still operate using their vertical take-off and landing capability. This is no secret. However, even in the forests they still require the engine and airframe technicians, the electricians, the armourers, the radio and radar men and all the other ancillary support staff. As soon as the Harriers take off for their dispersed sites therefore, so these support personnel follow them by road in their four-tonners, coaches, radio vans in convoy. The station catering officer wanted an extra thirty men and six four ton lorries converted into mobile fish and chip vans for the journey. He was an earnest young man with a good degree in catering and I listened, almost open-mouthed, as he quoted the old saws about: 'marching on its stomach,'and: 'hot food is good for morale'.

'I have this picture,' I told him, 'of this long convoy drawn up on the autobahn while the airmen queue up for their fish and chips. Is this what you have in mind?'

He nodded enthusiastically. I was as kind as I could be. 'I'm sorry,' I told him, 'you'd better forget it. The enemy is not going to wait for your chaps to have a good hot meal. If Russian or East German aircraft saw that convoy they wouldn't believe their luck. Give the lads compo rations. They can eat them on the move.'

The other case of professional tunnel vision involved an accountant in Germany. 'The contingency plan,' he said earnestly 'states that all the wives and children of the servicemen are placed in coaches and lorries and driven straight to the Channel ports for evacuation to England.'

'Yes?' I said encouragingly.

'Well, the wives have got to have sufficient funds when they get to England to enable them to travel onto their destination.'

'So?'

'I intend to open up a cash pay out office when the emergency starts so that I can provide all of the wives with money. I need another twenty accounts trained chaps to man it.'

'What will you do with these twenty when there's no emergency?'

'Oh, I'll find something for them to do,' was the vague reply.

'Why not give the wives travel warrants for the journey on from Dover? You could do that now - to be used only in the emergency.'

'They still need to buy food.'

'Give them emergency rations when they board the coaches.'

The accountant officer looked at me for a minute. 'Are your refusing my bid? It's written into the contingency plan you know.'

I thought for a minute and decided to be brutal.

'Look. The essence of the contingency plan is to get the wives and kids away quickly. Isn't that true?'

'Yes.'

'And you're suggesting a queue of hundreds of wives and children outside the accounts office with the distinct possibility of Russian aircraft coming in at zero feet at any minute.'

He thought for a minute. It began to dawn on him that other transactions too place in war, apart from monetary ones. I saved him any further embarrassment. 'Make other arrangements,' I told him. 'Travel warrants: make 'em out now. Food parcels: go and see the caterers and the suppliers. Tell the married men to make sure that they keep some English money available for such an emergency.'

But those two episodes were in the past and I was becoming very unhappy with the present. I told Fred, but it seemed to make little impression. Over fifty percent of your military costs go on personnel I told him, but his MoDUK background had not involved him closely in establishment matters and he did not fully appreciate the seriousness of the trend. Also, he had a lot of other problems on his mind. Sir Timothy Creasey was a soldier's soldier with a massive contempt for civilians and Fred was beginning to find his position as Head of Resource

Management a difficult one, trying to balance his budget against the arrogance and overbearing insistence of his master.

I did not envy him and having made my point as strongly as I could I shrugged my shoulders and left his office.

The future was beginning to look a little depressing and, increasingly bored with my surroundings, I decided that a few days away would be good for me. Another religious holiday was approaching and this, linked to a Juma, would enable me to take a short holiday. But where? I had been to Tanuf (strafed out of existence during the fifties rebellion) many times. Overshadowed by rocky bluffs and with an ice-cold open falaj system the ruins had a certain quiet charm; the Wahiba Sands, a thousand square miles of sand and gravel, didn't beckon me any more and Quryat (a small fishing village south of Muscat) had no charm except that it was at the end of an interesting drive. There were many beautiful and remote parts of the Sultanate still to be seen (the Jebel Akhdar and the Dhofar were good examples) but did I really want to visit even more isolated parts of the country? No, I decided. I was not looking for a Lawrence of Arabia lifestyle and the officers' mess at Bait al Falaj was primitive enough. A touch of the Hiltons or the Interchontinentals was what I was seeking and there was only one place where I could get that easily - the United Arab Emirates, some five hundred kilometres to the north - probably Dubhai. By local standards that had been a sophisticated city when I first knew it in the sixties, so it should be quite a place by now.

In the north of Oman, squatting across the border with the UAE, is a town known, if you lived in the Sultanate, as Buraimi; in the Emirates it is called Al Ain. Some years ago this township was the cause of a scuffle between Oman and Abu Dhabi (the emirate which controlled Al Ain) and the scuffle escalated as far as the United Nations. This was during the pre-Qaboos period and when a plebiscite was held to seek the residents' views they understandably opted for rule by Abu Dhabi. The story goes that the Omani Royal Family have never forgiven this slight and this is why Buraimi has developed so little compared to the rest of the Sultanate. It is easy to believe when you visit the town for the border is clearly delineated, without notices and signs, by the contrast between the mud hut grime of Buraimi and the clean modern buildings and wide tree-lined roads of Al Ain. Sordid as it was however, there were two distinct advantages about Buraimi. One was that there was a fort outside the town manned by a company of SOLF soldiers (and this provided me, a MoD official, with a reason to visit the town); the other was that out of Al Ain, a good road ran north to Dubhai.

Although this method of entering UAE smacked of subterfuge there was every reason for using it, for the alternative was wearisome. This involved presenting a fee and an application form to the Royal Oman Police for a pass which allowed you to drive into the UAE via the Wadi Hatta, many miles to the north of Buraimi. This involved waiting at a police station for a check to travel across the border and, if for any reason you could not make the journey on the specified date, then the whole business had to be gone through again. My method called for a typed note which stated that I was visiting Buraimi and its presentation at the border post in the Wadi Jissi, near Sohar.

I made this, the first trip, with some trepidation for I was not entirely sure that such a simple method would work, but it did, and I found the drive extraordinarily pleasant. North out of Muscat, past Seeb Airfield, past Seeb Palace, then Rumais Prison and two hundred kilometres of the coast road running through the Batinah (the coastal plain). On many stretches the old tarmac road had become one side of a fast growing dual carriageway and this added spice to the journey for where these existed the locals used both sides to travel in both directions. Bill was with me and voiced my thoughts. 'It'll be a bloody massacre when they complete this UAE motorway and start trying to use it properly. Can you imagine it?' I could and resolved not to travel on it for three months or so after it was opened. It was a delightful journey however, more so because it was new to us. On our right the deep midday blue of the Gulf of Oman and on our left the slowly receding Hajar mountain range. Villages with small children and equally small donkeys, groves of lime tress, the occasional supercilious camel and, less pleasant, the occasional camel corpse, bloated and stiff legged at the roadside.

After the police post in the Wadi Jissi the mountains were soon behind us and beyond a low range of drab brown hills Buraimi Fort appeared. A distant scene from Beau Geste. A few more kilometres and we entered a typical grubby, rubbish-strewn Arab town. This was Buraimi. Across a roundabout, down a small alley and there it was: tree-lined wide roads, gardens, tall spotless buildings - Al Ain. The difference was truly staggering.

We hired a car in Al Ain because I had considerable doubts about the wisdom of using my MoD Oman vehicle in the UAE, then drove on for another hour across undulating multicolored desert. I had heard about this stretch of road so was not unduly surprised at the many wrecks and camel corpses which lined its length. Many underpasses had been built so that the creatures could wander from one grazing area to another without crossing the road, but I suspected that they were unaware of the real reason for the tunnels under the road. I was musing on this as the distant white towers of Dubhai came into view. How do you train a camel to use a tunnel? They were bloody-minded at their best.

We stayed at the Ramada Hotel and the long weekend was everything we had hoped it would be. Comfort, luxurious rooms, delicious food, new bars to drink in and new people to talk to. Dubhai had changed enormously since I last visited in the mid-sixties, much more so than I had imagined it would and it was now a truly modern city with attractive wide streets lined with flower beds and parks, magnificent shopping complexes, high rise hotels and apartment blocks. I was almost relieved to see that a trace of the old Dubhai still existed at the creek side, lined as it was with dhows, boums, cargoes and passengers from all over the Gulf. The vessels' high sterns were still marvellously decorated and the thunder boxes still hung over them. Do they still use them alongside in Dubhai I wondered? Or do they walk across the wide promenade to the public conveniences. Looking around me I imagined there was probably now some city ordnance which prohibited defecating in the muddy waters of Dubhai Creek.

We had hired our car from Avis in Al Ain and had decided that we would return it to Avis in Dubhai and return by taxi to Al Ain. There would be no problem about this, the charming lady in the Al Ain office had assured us. She was wrong. The equally charming lady in the Dubhai Avis was not interested.

'I am extremely sorry Sir,' she explained. 'This car belongs to Avis at Al Ain and that is in Abu Dhabi. This Avis is in Dubhai. We cannot take your car from you for this car does not belong to us.'

I contained my impatience. 'But you're both Avis,' I pointed out very reasonably, 'and Abu Dhabi and Dubhai are both in the United Arab Emirates.'

Anyway,' I concluded 'Al Ain is only an hour's drive away.'

'That is very true, Sir,' she agreed, 'but we cannot take your car.'

I was about to continue the argument but stopped. If I couldn't return the car because the Dubhai Avis would not accept it, I could keep the car and return it to Al Ain myself, and there was no way that they could charge me for the extra day's use. Indeed, they would be lucky to have the car returned for them for I was quite entitled to leave the damned thing outside their Dubhai office. I raised my hand to halt any further apologies.

'OK, OK,' I sighed, 'I'll drive it back for you. But I wonder what you would have done if I'd been travelling on to England.'

We left the lass pondering that one. Two years earlier, shortly after I had arrived in the Middle East, I would undoubtedly have been infuriated by that idiot scenario where Avis Abu Dhabi refused to co-operate with Avis Dubhai. Now, I hardly raised an eyebrow. That meant something, but I wasn't sure what.

I had heard much about the suq in Sharjah and decided to use one of our extra car days to drive along the coast and see it. It was an interesting, yet depressing journey for the road connecting the two cities no longer ran across flat desert sand as I remembered it. Now, garish bill boards and hundreds of car wrecks lined the road. This appalling vista was made more revolting by a number of scrap-yards filled with rusting vehicles, cranes and other machinery. In certain areas, oil from the wrecks had soaked into the already saline sand producing large black pools of what had been brackish water. It was a conservationist's nightmare and the reason for this hideous sight was a simple one that I should have been able to guess. Neither Dubhai nor Sharjah could agree on their border and their areas of responsibility along that awful road. Every local knew it and used it as a vast rubbish tip.

Inevitably, Sharjah had changed beyond recognition from my recall and, although not as large and as well-designed as Dubhai it was a growing conurbation and no trace remained of the mud hut village near RAF Sharjah that I remembered. At that point gold smuggling from India and Pakistan was a major activity and visitors like myself made straight for the one or two shops dealing in the precious metal. Particularly well-known and well-used was the tiny kiosk operated by Sheik Robin. A charming old crook with a ready grin, he would proudly point to the wall when your business was completed. There, where he indicated, was a framed cheque. Written and signed by a British major in the old Trucial Oman Scouts some years ago it said: 'Pay Sheik

Robin Bastard.' The old lad always gave an appreciative chuckle when his customers read the cheque and enjoyed the joke.

Now, the suq in Sharjah was a group of four vast two storeyed buildings housing hundreds of shops, all located in groups according to their speciality: jewellery, carpets, radios, cameras and so on. I eyed the seemingly endless row of goldsmiths and decided not to try and find Sheik Robin. We were sorry to have to start out on the drive back to Muscat the following day.

In the Bamboo Bar that evening there were many questions to be answered about the trip and how successful (or otherwise) our entry into the UAE had been and I began to feel more like a returning explorer than somebody who had been away for a long weekend. 'Did you get to the hospital?' asked one and there was a hush for a moment, followed by a roar of disbelief as I answered: 'No. Didn't even look at it. Hired a car at Al Ain and drove straight onto Dubhai.'

In the monastic existence of our life in the officers' mess at Bait al Falaj, the Al Ain Hospital had become a sort of Shangri La of beautiful and desirable femininity. Wild stories regularly circulated and many of them were true. In that isolated Arab city in the desert, an hour's drive from Dubhai, there was a large modern hospital and, so the story went, it was staffed by over a hundred nurses, most of them British and all of them panting with unsatisfied lust. There was some truth in the story because I knew a number of officers in the north of Oman who enjoyed a happy, regular sex life with girlfriends at the hospital. And, as we used to say, good luck to them both.

As the news about my trip and how easy it had been spread around so one or two other contract officers at Bait al Falaj began making the journey north; not to Dubhai so much, but to sample the treasure trove at Al Ain Hospital. Phil was one of them and it could be argued that he really did let his enthusiasm run away with him.

By profession and appearance Phil certainly did not give the impression of being a bit of a 'goer'. Short, balding and plump he was an auditor in his mid-thirties. He was one of a breed not exactly known for living licentiously, but he made a successful foray and met a young and attractive nurse called Ruth. Their affair went swimmingly. Rumour had it that she earned extra money as a belly dancer in one of the Al Ain night spots and those who knew her well reckoned that it was highly likely for she was pretty enough and had a lithe body. How long Phil's happiness would have lasted if he had been more circumspect I had no idea, but one weekend Ruth told him she would like to see Muscat and where he lived, so he brought her down to the mess at Bait al Falaj for the weekend. Finding that bringing her down and taking her out through the Wadi Jissi was no problem he started to make a regular thing of it and Ruth became a very welcome addition to the mess social life. Like most nurses she had an earthy sense of humour and we loved her.

In this life however, there is always some miserable bastard who hates to see somebody else enjoying himself; particularly if there is a touch of illegality about the scene and conditions are such that the miscreant has absolutely no right to be enjoying himself. Inevitably, Phil's happiness was brought to the notice of Roger, his boss, the Chief Auditor. Roger was the archetype auditor, unpopular with nearly everybody, thin-lipped and humourless and cordially detested even by his own staff. He pointed out to Phil the error of his ways and, with true auditorial precision, recounted in detail all of the immigration laws that had been broken, all of the mess rules that had been broken and how the auditors' image had been badly dented. This rather sordid business had got to stop.

Phil had been becoming increasingly discontented with the boring routine of his job and increasingly unhappy with the even more boring routine of life in the mess at Bait al Falaj. He thought of the many months ahead of him without Ruth and it was too much. He told Roger in even more detail how he regarded him, the job, and the officers' mess in Bait al Falaj and then departed in a huff and flew to South Africa.

The opposite sex also brought another change to our lives but this time it was more lasting than the transient charms of Ruth had been. I had first noticed the phenomenon some weeks ago but it wasn't until after my Dubhai trip that it attracted my attention properly. Ever since I had been in Oman you could stroll into the ante-room on any afternoon to check on the age of the English newspapers and occasionally you would meet one or two other contract officers doing the same; often it would be empty. Very rarely would you see an Omani officer there unless a local football match was being televised, in which case you abandoned any idea of reading a paper and returned to your room, their viewing support being very vocal.

Now however, I began to find two or three Omanis there reading the local Arab newspapers. At first I thought little of it for there was always a small transient population drifting in and out of the mess, then Harvey complained to me one day that he was having difficulty in providing accommodation. It seemed that during the past few months a number of Omani officers, young and old, senior and junior, had asked to be provided with a room in the mess.

I was curious about this and spoke to Saif, a young civilian officer whose English was impeccable. He burst out laughing. 'If you ask them Alan you will find that they all have two wives, some of them three.'

I played the innocent. 'So?'

His grin widened. 'Two wives are twice as much trouble and three are even worse. Sometimes their complaints and their other demands,' and his left eye drooped, 'becomes too much for the poor husband and he must have a rest and get some peace and quiet. Now they tell their wives that they have to stay at work or they are acting as duty officer.'

There was much ribald discussion in the Bamboo Bar that evening when I passed on the results of my investigation. Comments ranged from: 'I'll take over from Khalifa if he can't manage his latest, she's a lovely girl,' to: 'Dear God! We're becoming a bloody rest home for shagged-out Arabs.'

A couple of days later the internal mail brought me a letter from Fred. It contained some manpower information that he had asked for and I had supplied. It bore a note in HRM's usual scrawl. 'I of E. I'm not sure how to handle this now that we have abandoned establishments as a means of controlling manpower. Can we discuss, please?'

I sat and stared at 'abandoned establishments' for quite a while. What did he mean? Did he really appreciate the significance of what he had written? Did he not think it a slightly unusual, if not eccentric method of telling the Inspector of Establishments that his *raison d'etre* had disappeared? How was he going to control manpower (and manpower costs) without establishments? It was like a bank deciding to abandon financial records. What on earth was going on? Yes, I certainly did want to discuss this.

At our meeting I soon realised that Fred had no real conception of establishments and their role in the structure of the armed forces. He was a money man but a money man without the full understanding of how it was that men took most of the defence money. It was not just their pay but their myriad allowances, their accommodation (and electricity, water and sewage), their food, their transport, their gratuities, their pensions, their hospitals, their schools and other training establishments, their doctors, dentists, nurses and so on. If you control manpower, you control all of these massive support costs; If you fail to do so, you will find less and less cash to spend on weapons.

I asked the obvious question. 'How are you going to control manpower without establishments?'

'With money,' came the reply and my heart sank.

'It won't work Fred. It's been tried before. It's too clumsy.'

I had his interest now. 'What do you mean?'

'Using establishments they have to calculate their personnel costs for the coming year on a capitation rate basis. You know, cost per head times number of officers and men. Then the total cost is amended for various factors, manning or recruiting shortfall, inflation and so on. The advantage of this system is that the calculations can be checked step by step and you can easily see if their bid is a reasonable one. Under your system it all becomes a question of guesswork. This year they have a thousand million and they ask for thirteen hundred million for next year. 'No,' you say, 'too much. You can only have twelve hundred million.' They complain like hell but they go away highly delighted because they've got a hundred million more than they really need. It's like trying to weed a garden with a bloody scythe. What on earth made you go for this?'

His answer confirmed what I had heard already. His finance officer, a young man who may have been an excellent accountant but had no military experience, had sold him the idea. I thought about both of us as I listened. Fred was a pretty typical civil service administrator and I guessed I was a standard civil service executive. Theoretically he was the thinker and I was the one who put his thoughts into effect. Within the constraints of the government service in the UK we would have had a good working relationship; out here he had no requirement to and had failed to ask my advice on the practical problems involved. He had been attracted by the apparent simplicity of an inexperienced staff officer's proposal. I made one last effort.

'Fred. You know what a profligate bunch the commanders are. Now you're giving them the right to ask for hundreds of millions a year without requiring them to justify the extra expense. You're encouraging more waste.'

He was a courteous and a kind man and I disliked my role for I could see that I was beginning to irritate him. 'Anyway,' came his final rejoinder, 'it's too late now. I've already told Sir Timothy that we're abandoning establishments and going over to finance control.'

I couldn't help the expletive. 'Jesus!' I said as I gathered up my papers, 'thanks for your time Fred.' I knew that nothing would send him back to CDS to tell him that he had changed his mind. He wouldn't be allowed to anyway; the commanders would see to that.

I thought furiously during the drive back to Bait al Falaj. My job title was a sham now. Inspector of Establishments? What establishments? But how could the services operate without establishments? Answer: they can't. Somehow they would have to keep maintaining personnel records of some sort or another, whatever they might call them. It was about a week before I discovered the true situation that existed. Fred might have abandoned establishments as a means of assessing manpower money requirements, but SOLF, SOAF and SON had not. Now, with HRM no longer interested in establishments they felt free to place an arbitary increase on their personnel requirements knowing that they would not be examined. To quote: They've never had it so good. It became a ridiculous scene so far as I was concerned. My title suggested that I had some sort of control over manpower numbers but in truth, I had none at all. Before this recent decision of HRM's there might have been some slight chance of involving him or Sir Timothy against the more blatant examples of waste or stupidity. Not now. SAF had been given the nod to keep all establishments information away from our office. The only data I would have access to now would be the monthly manpower returns made to the Central Records Office. Not that there was a lot I could do with that information for it would only tell me what had happened but, at least I would be able to see if my fears were justified.

Should I resign? With the three months notice that I had to give there was little point. By the time I left I would be well into the second half of my current contract year. Should I apply for another years extension to my contract? Unlikely, given the present scenario. No, I decided. During the next few months I'll be able to see how the manpower scene changes and whether there is any hope of getting it back under control again. If it turns out as I expect it will I'll just complete my present contract year then go.

Oliver was a recent arrival at the Bait al Falaj mess and within a few weeks had achieved the distinction of being its most unpopular member. He loudly and frequently proclaimed his erstwhile membership of a famous British regiment, how disgusting and primitive were the living conditions in the mess and how he was used to much, much better. The last was probably the one statement that nobody could fault, for everybody had been used to much, much better. He was an appalling snob and often spoke about his last position as secretary of a well-known London club, although he was not so forthcoming as to tell us why he left such a superior position. Nobody asked of course, for to do such a thing was to break the golden rule among the contract officers. Why any of us were there was our own business. He also had a most unpleasant habit of speaking to his inferiors tersely and with barely concealed contempt and this grated badly for most of the staff were pleasant and willing Indians and Pakistanis who dared not make a rejoinder.

The words 'British' and 'English' featured prominently in his conversation and on the fairly regular occasions when he became unpleasantly and gloweringly drunk he would almost spew bitter diatribes against his numerous enemies who, I suspected, were mostly imaginary. He had a deep olive complexion and this, coupled with a massive inferiority made me suspect that he had what, a few generations ago, would have been termed a 'touch of the tarbrush'. He was a poorly covert homosexual and a pitiable figure, particularly after his horribly public downfall.

There were about a dozen of us in the Bamboo Bar that evening and, in between sips of my whisky soda, I was trying to read the *Oman Observer* . I was finding this difficult for Oliver was holding forth in that frightful plumy voice of his. I gathered that some ignorant Pakistani corporal clerk had had the temerity to be rude to Oliver that morning and had been put firmly in his place.

The door opened and an Omani dressed in open neck shirt and slacks entered. He was slim, of medium height and something about his young face topped by greying hair was familiar. It took a moment and as recognition came I slid off my bar stool and greeted him. Ali Majid, the oldest and closest friend of Sultan Qaboos; a brigadier who held the position of First ADC to His Majesty and President of the Palace Office. He was also an old comrade and friend of Hassan Ehsan and it was in his office that I had met Ali Majid a couple of times. I offered him a drink and recognising somebody vaguely familiar he accepted. I asked the barman and glanced hastily around. It was clear that nobody else knew Ali Majid and I hoped to God that they all behaved themselves. Unfortunately, Oliver was still holding forth about his victory over the clerk and as I handed the drink to Ali I could see that the booming voice was already irritating him. He thanked me, put down his glass and there was a moments silence.

'You,' he addressed Oliver.

Whatever Oliver's thoughts were about being spoken to in such a manner, he was not stupid. This casually dressed man was clearly an Omani (and they paid our wages) and equally clearly, he spoke with authority in his voice.

'Yes?' Oliver replied.

'What do you do out here?' asked Ali.

'I'm in the Land Forces Headquarters.' Oliver teetered on the edge of adding 'Sir'.

'What's your name?'

Oliver told him.

'You're not British then.'

Oliver bridled and his complexion darkened. By now, everybody was listening.

'Of course I'm British. I've got a British passport.'

'That's as maybe,' Ali replied placidly, 'they're ten a penny nowadays.' He downed his drink and turned to me. 'Thanks very much. I must go now. I have to see His Majesty in twenty minutes.'

As he walked towards the door his progress was followed by the eyes of everybody there and as he reached for the handle he half turned and delivered a parting shot. 'Nobody with that name is British. There is Arab in the name. You must come from Malta.'

A minute or two passed before the conversation started up again. 'Who the hell was that?'

I told them and the silence descended again.

A week later Oliver moved out of the Bait al Falaj mess and into the garrison mess at Muaskar al Murtafa'a.

The next few months saw a number of changes taking place, none of which I found encouraging. Personnel numbers increased steadily as I had expected, but it was still too early to identify a positive trend. One of the regular recruiting visits to Baluchistan could easily add a few hundred to the SOLF figures and this would be nothing to get excited about. Six months should be enough to show something which could be commented upon with justification so, for the present, I put that problem on ice.

More disturbing in its implications however was a meeting of the Commanders which I attended. It was chaired by Sir Timothy and I began to suspect that the Supremo concept was being replaced by a quadripartite assembly. 'F***ing civilians' entered the conversation a few times and this was greeted by dutiful titters from all except the four 'f***ing civilians' present at the meeting. This only served to confirm my long-held opinion that our Chief of the Defence Staff had all the tact and courtesy of a wounded buffalo. It was clear that he had well earned his nickname of 'Bull'. More important however was that the air was thick with: 'What do you think, Erik?' and: 'How does that strike you, John?' and: 'Looks alright to me, Boss' and various other chummy remarks. The meeting began to sound more like a darts club get-together than a collection of the senior military. Perhaps, I decided, Sir Timothy has wearied of trying to exercise his authority and rank and is content to act as some sort of an umpire. It had been plain for some time that the original concept of him assuming overall command of the Royal Guard and the police and the security service in wartime had been abandoned. This, I was sure, was due to Arab ambivalence, but it was now beginning to look as if SAF was going to be run on a committee basis. Good grief! I thought. Back to the six forces, each doing its own thing. If the balloon does go up I hope to God the Americans get here quickly.

A few weeks later, (mainly because I had told Fred my view of the changing style in command and he had disagreed) I made a bet with him.

In any large organisation it is occasionally worthwhile to find out exactly how many hours are worked in a week by employees. The figure that results from carrying out such an exercise is called the Effective Working Week. It is calculated by taking the net working days achieved during the year (365 minus weekends, leave, public holidays, etc.) and the net bench/desk hours achieved every day (say 8 less meal breaks, toilet time and other diversions). Multiplying actual working days by actual bench/desk hours and dividing by 52 gives the 'effective' hours achieved by an employee every week.

A number of factors affect the final figure but the major one is undoubtedly diversions. In the civilian world these can be chatting around the tea trolley, a ten-minute smoke in the loo or a half-hour wait in a technical store for a tool or spare part to be produced. In addition to these, the military world also suffers from such disgressions as pay parades, clothing parades, medical checks and so on. Because of this, it is hardly surprising that the armed forces usually achieve a comparatively low figure, somewhere about 28 'effective' hours per week. It is when the 'effective' working week turns out to be too low however, that you start to look for the reason and the remedy.

The Commanding Officer of the EME workshops was responsible for this latest brouhaha. Anxious to achieve more productivity in repairing lorries, tanks and guns he produced a range of alternative solutions and supported them with effective working week figures. From the comments that were made to me it was pretty clear that when he presented his paper he was the only person present who knew what an effective working week was. The figures he quoted were in the mid-twenties and taking the standard of employee and local conditions into account they were not too bad at all. His only mistake of course, was in not appreciating that nobody really understood what he was talking about. Sir Timothy became irate and, rumbling such comments as: 'Only twenty seven hours a week!' and: 'What the hell's going on?' threw the submission at HRM. The latter, also unsure about effective working weeks, passed it to me with the comment that it seemed very disturbing and would I find out why the figure was so low. It was too good an opportunity to miss. I could have just explained that EME's figures were reasonable and why but, better than that, I would explain and substantiate their reasonableness by comparison with other sections of SAF, like the Land Forces Headquarters. God knows, it was time that attention was drawn to their working week.

They started their working week on a Saturday as we all did, but from then on their efforts could hardly be described as Herculean. At about seven-thirty they would lurch into action and at nine o'clock, exhausted, they would retire to their messes for breakfast. An hour or so later they would return to their offices and hang on until one o'clock when they finished for the day. If this less than arduous duty was carried out six days a week as the other headquarters did, then perhaps the breakfast break could be forgiven. As it was they closed down early on Wednesday and did not re-open until Saturday.

I had made enquires about this early closing and found the reason to be ingenious, even if totally irrelevant. Some sixty percent of SAF were Omanis and a number of them had to travel some distance to spend their weekends at home in their villages. So that they could achieve this it was decided that they could leave early on Wednesday. Not surprisingly, this practice became very popular and spread throughout the Land Forces, even to their headquarters. As the overwhelming majority of the headquarters staff were either British, Pakistani or Baluchi it was difficult to accept that they had to finish work early on Wednesday to make journeys of less than a kilometre to their respective messes. Assessed at its kindest, there seemed to be some lack of motivation.

I carried out the exercise and the highest and the lowest figures were very interesting. The civilian artisans in the civil engineering workshops achieved 32 effective hours per week and the military staff in the Headquarters Sultan of Oman's Land Forces attained 17 hours per week. I hesitate to use the word 'effective'.

I won my bet that nothing would come of my exercise. The information went to CDS and Sir Timothy passed it onto General John Watts. He, CSOLF, became irate at the suggestion that his headquarters staff worked far less hours than everybody else and the matter was dropped. I didn't have the heart to say: 'I told you so' to Fred, nor to collect my five rials. It was clear that he was becoming pretty depressed as well and he had a lot more on his mind than I did.

Fortunately, or unfortunately (for Fred), the MoD Engineering Division started crying for help with their manpower planning problems and HRM (probably gladly) volunteered my assistance.

MoDED was responsible for the maintenance of buildings, roads, sewage, electricity and water supplies and some of the smaller construction tasks. Any major project such as a new barrack or housing complex or the new naval base at Wudam would be carried out under contract by one of the major construction companies such as J & P (Oman) or Cementation. Competition for such contracts was of course, fierce, for annual expenditure ran into hundreds of millions of rials and at that time the Omani rial was worth nearly two pounds. It is not too much of an exaggeration to say that the number of these building tasks was equalled only by the number of rumours about bribery and corruption. Whether there was truth in any of them I do not know but some of the senior officials in MoDED were in the very vulnerable position of having to recommend selection of companies to carry out very large and very profitable projects.

Hitherto, my contacts with the organisation had been at the working level at Bait al Falaj and, although great socialisers and outstanding in their drinking prowess, the pair of them were very much your local plumber and electrician. I had a passing acquaintance with the Chief Engineer and his directors but this was only because they were responsible to Hassan Ehsan as the Under Secretary and had passed through the office when I was there. MoDED was an odd organisation and quite unlike the civil engineering support of the military that I had known in my MoDUK days. Whereas the Department of the Environment/Property Services Agency (DOE/PSA) was organised and motivated to support the armed forces, MoDED appeared to be a rather large and languid building company who would give assistance if required. At a personal level there seemed to be no regular servicing of air-conditioners and other domestic equipment and life consisted of breakdown after breakdown with the machinery only receiving attention when it had given up the ghost. With an outside temperature of 125°F it was not amusing to realise that if your air-conditioner failed after lunch it stayed that way until the following morning.

I suspected that there was one major reason for this rather detached attitude which permeated MoDED and that was a total lack of military experience in the upper echelons. With one or two exceptions among senior officers of my vintage most of the directors and the chief engineer were men in their forties whose only experience had been in the civilian world. I doubted this theory momentarily however and began to suspect sheer thick-headedness when I learnt that they had a most embarrassing problem, having just recruited a naval architect to design the new naval base.

Whatever the reason, there was no doubt that there existed an almost total lack of motivation towards the military world and this was exemplified when I asked our local engineer what he would do if Oman became embroiled in another war. He would, he said, grab a case of Fosters, leap into his car and piss off to the Emirates en route to the UK. A colleague of his was to make a similar remark at a later date which would lead to a massive shake up of MoDED.

It was when I paid a few visits to the CDS residence however, that I discovered the areas in which MoDED did excel.

Sir Timothy Creasey was now installed with Lady Annette in their seashore mansion on the outskirts of Seeb Village and I found myself making a number of visits there. He liked sailing and having commandeered a Bosun dinghy from the SAF Aqua Club he, or rather his staff, were having problems in getting it seaworthy. It was a magnificent house and I could well believe the rumoured rent of ten thousand rials a month. Civilian cooks, stewards and gardeners were in abundance as were military guards and drivers and I found the occasional hour working on the boat's rigging a pleasant diversion from the nugatory activities in the office.

The swimming pool was huge and possessed a poolside bar and changing rooms and, courtesy of MoDED, an enormous canopy on steel pylons which protected the swimmers from the sun and the pool from falling leaves. The tennis courts were impeccably maintained and the house, the guest annexe and the servants' quarters in the grounds, provided clear evidence that MoDED staff spent a lot of time there. Bill came with me on a number of occasions and he told me that the place had been deserted and almost derelict when CDS decided he wanted to live there and MoDED had pulled out all the stops and achieved the transformation within a few months. I could not resist the passing thought that the chief engineer was clearly a man who, if nothing else, knew how to award priorities and allocate resources. It was because of this that I thought CDS rather ungrateful when I heard that he was seeking to replace CE. Inevitably rumour abounded but in spite of the more unkind and highly coloured stories I suspected that the true reason was MoDED's laid-back approach to the military scene. Put bluntly and crudely, there were too many 'f***ing' civilians and too much civilian thinking for the Boss's liking.

The chief engineer's departure and his replacement with an ex-brigadier sapper was inevitable and the MoDED turmoil that followed his arrival equally inevitable.

Bob was forceful and blunt in speech and possessed considerable energy, devoting a large portion of his first few months to visiting the fifty odd SAF installations scattered throughout Oman. These visits were to be responsible for a number of quite dramatic personnel movements later on. At the end of three months however, Bob had a very clear idea what MoDED needed in the way of reorganisation and increased staffing to make it an effective adjunct to the Sultan's Armed Forces.

Edicts, directives, orders, demands and proclamations began to drift down over MoDED like snow. All were notable because of the new CE's penchant for two line paragraphs, but all made it clear that things were going to change. Bob was a firm believer in the responsibility of the senior officer and when he discovered, on his travels, that various misdemeanours were taking place, he became very angry, especially when he also learnt that some of his directors had never even visited the sites where crimes were being committed. Some senior staff suddenly found themselves looking for a new job and some junior staff suddenly found themselves looking out through the bars of a Rumais Prison cage whilst awaiting Tin Budgie.

Then he visited his staff on the Musandam Peninsular.

This neck of mountainous land protrudes into the Straits of Hormuz across from Iran and the site is strategically vital. Inhabited by a fairly primitive tribe, efforts were being made to open up the area and two white foremen controlled a gang of Pakistani labourers engaged in blasting roads through the rocky slopes. Neither of the bosses were young and they enjoyed themselves immensely living on cheap cigarettes and beer brought in illicitly from the Emirates and collecting the weekly cash contributions made by the gang. These donations went into their pockets and they, in turn, allowed the labourers to earn regular weekly overtime. It was a common enough scene on the Indian Subcontinent and the gang knew better than to complain. This unpleasant manner of extracting money from the already poor might have escaped notice if the two sahibs had not been stupid enough to give Bob an honest answer when he asked them what they would do if war broke out. Their reply was even more succinct than the one I received at BAF. 'F*** off to Dubhai. It's only a couple of hours away.' Bob returned most unhappy with the pair of them and ordered an investigation into their neck of the woods. The result: Rumais.

It was at about this point that I became embroiled in the MoDED scene. 'I want you to draw up an organisation and the required manpower for me,' he said at our first meeting. 'I'll let you have the basic parameters. We should be here to support the Sultan's Armed Forces in peace and in war. I'm having a bit of trouble about the last bit at the moment but I'll be able to sort it out. Most of the staff seem to think that they can all go home if things get unpleasant. Nobody does anything without getting permission from this headquarters and half of the buggers here have never left MAM and gone out to see what conditions are like for their staff in the field. I'm going to change this. Split the country into areas. Put an Area Engineer in charge of each area and make him totally responsible to me for everything that happens in his area.'

'How many areas?' I asked and as he told me and I listened to him expand on the detail of the organisation my heart sank. He was talking about thousands of extra staff, British, Omani and from the Subcontinent. 'Sounds lavish and very expensive in manpower,' I ventured and I saw the ex-senior military officer come to the fore.

I know that,' he snapped irritably. 'I've spoken to Sir Timothy and told him that if he wanted a truly militarily-orientated engineering division to support them it would entail a lot more men. He said it was OK and to go ahead.'

He would, I thought. He doesn't have to worry about where the money's going to come from - that's poor old Fred's problem. Oh well, I thought, a meeting of two military minds. There's no way I'm going to be able to prune this to a reasonable level. CDS has given CE the go-ahead and he will not accept anything likely to detract from his super gold-plated organisation. I wonder if Hassan Ehsan knows about this? As the senior Omani officer he's the one that the Ministry of Finance and the Palace Office will challenge. Should I warn him? In the event I suggested to Bob that whatever the views of Sir Timothy, his chain of command went through the Under Secretary. He took the hint.

I started drawing up the new organisation and detailed it down through each area with its Area Engineer, its Finance Officer, Office Manager, clerks, plumbers, carpenters, fitters, electricians, plant operators and labourers - skilled and unskilled. It attained a very impressive total, some two thousand more bodies than MoDED already had.

Fred was wildly plaintive but got little sympathy from me. 'I'm sorry,' I told him, 'there has been a meeting of military minds between CDS and CE and Sir Tim has agreed with whatever Bob wants.' I lapsed into sarcasm. 'I've already learnt that it's a waste of time trying to contain the manpower explosion out here. You reckon that it can be done with finance. You go ahead and try.'

Protestations that we couldn't afford it were very short-lived. Indeed, if there was a battle between HRM and CDS it was over so quickly that it was arguable whether it ever started. With the blindfold well-adjusted Sir Timothy rumbled: 'The man wants to do a good job. For God's sake help him and stop nagging about money.'

While this was going on I enjoyed setting up the new organisation and reading some of the MoDED correspondence that passed through my hands. One submission from his plant operators Bob passed along to me, knowing that I would enjoy its poetry. Seeking a higher grading they had written:

> Sir,
>
> A plant operator's job is comparatively so much tough and dangerous that no other trade in M.O.D.E.D. matches it. Plant operators do construct the road on such dangerous heights where a hill goat seldom dares to climb as well as in so deep vallies which hardly where a human foot printed in years. We operate the most costly machines with artistic accuracies and sacred cares.
>
> A plant operator while discharging his duties is bound to add more dust to his food than to the normal human diet. And no machine does ever moves unless an operator makes himself steel hard both bodily and morally to match the machine he is operating and when he retires after a days work he is not better than a dead log. And in old age what is left of a operator once a competent and

strong man is a skeleton with rheumatic, swollen and gritting joints shaken by the steel giants he has had been wrestling with in his youth.

In view of this, the plant operators are highly paid tradesmen in all the construction establishments except in M.O.D.E.D. where we are not considered equal to the painter even who could be trained to 1st Class in a week.

It is requested that the plant operators may kindly be promoted to grade 10 as 1st Class and in grade 9 as 2nd grade. We hope that our case may please be considered sympathetically for a generous and favourable action.

Thanking you in anticipation.

The splendid isolation in which some of Oman's ministries operated never ceased to amaze me. It could be argued that it was a measure of their inexperience that they failed to consult other departments but their British advisers were supposed to be there to prevent such blunders. Sometimes decisions were taken and everybody else remained in ignorance until some occurrence brought the edict of light. One of the most infuriating and fatuous examples of this emanated from the Royal Oman Police.

I never did find out which potential recruit triggered off the great uproar, but, as with all staff about to be employed in MoD or SAF his details were sent to the immigration department of the ROP so that they could issue an entry visa. As sometimes happened, the application was refused; thus the following telephone conversation:

MoD - Why have you refused to issue a visa to Major Smith?

ROP - Because he is over fifty-five years of age.

MoD - What's that got to do with it?

ROP - It has been decided that nobody over fifty-five may be employed in Oman anymore.

MoD - What?

When the battle started it was learnt that the ROP had also unilaterally decreed that nobody under the age of 25 could be employed in Oman as well as nobody over 55.

The under 25 rule created few problems because it was doubtful if any man of that age would have the skills and experience that the Sultanate needed. The over 55 bar was very different however because this group included the men who had just retired from a lifetime of employment. At senior officer and staff officer level it included exactly the people MoD was looking for; recent retirees from the British forces looking for a lucrative four or five years stint where their vast experience could be usefully employed.

The over 55 battle continued with no clear victory on either side and occasional sniping was still going on when I left with the ROP invoking the over 55 rule on occasions and senior officers being dragged in to resolve each skirmish.

Another example of muscle flexing concerned our two local Christian churches. To the north of the Al Falaj roundabout they were small structures built on rocky wasteground near a steep escarpment. It was an enlightening and humbling experience on a Friday morning to watch the hundreds of Protestant and Catholic Indians arrive by bus, car and on foot. Unfortunately, the demolition of half of a small mountain for the new road to the north showed how easily rock could be removed and the rapid construction of new flyovers began to make the road from Ruwi to Muttrah an attractive commercial proposition. Covetous eyes began to be cast on the land occupied by the churches and before long they were told that they had to vacate with six months. As an act of reparation they were given some land at Bawshar. The only problem was that Bawshar was about twenty kilometres outside the Capital Area. It was hardly a reasonable exchange and I could not help recalling the magnificent mosque recently built in Regents Park near central London. Appeals were being made to various ministers when I eventually left the Sultanate and I never learnt whether avarice gave way to charity. I suspected that His Majesty would have to be petitioned before the churches could hope for success.

Geoff was portly, bald and an ex-senior officer in the British forces. He was recruited as an administrative officer in the Under Secretary's Department at Grade 19 (equivalent major) and within a few weeks realised that only one step up the civilian ladder to Grade 21 and he would attain accompanied status. This became his primary target and I soon learnt that any recommendation of mine to Hassan Ehsan concerning a Grade 21 post always received Geoff's enthusiastic support - so much so that I thought he had over-reached himself when he described a little too floridly the rare privilege and honour he would receive if he were allowed to serve His Excellency in one post that was becoming vacant.

Some months passed and his wife came out to Oman on holiday. Her presence engendered quite a few unkind remarks, for she was short, dumpy, had little or no conversation and her dress sense was unappealing. Typically, Hazel referred to her as: 'The oh-so-exciting Cynthia' and after meeting her, few of us males could understand Geoff's burning ambition to achieve accompanied status. Truly, love is blind.

Almost inevitably, there came a day when it was decided that Geoff should take on more responsibility and as a reward he was promoted to Grade 21. I knew how much it meant to him and made a point of telephoning my congratulations. He was over the moon.

It was a few months before our paths crossed again and in the meantime I knew that Cynthia had arrived and, at the insistence of the senior Omani officer who owned the property, Geoff and his beloved had been installed in a pleasant house on the road to Seeb Village. I assumed that he was a happy man now and after a cheery greeting said 'How's life?' I expected a beaming smile and agreement, instead, I received a worried and furtive look. 'Not too good,' he answered gloomily.

I adjusted my facial expression. 'What's the problem Geoff?'

'It's the house.'

'What's wrong with it? I heard it was quite a nice place.'

'Oh, it is, it is.'

'Well?'

'It's Cynth. She doesn't like it.'

I tried to reassure him. 'She'll get used to it Geoff. She's been around. She'll settle down.'

'Oh, it's not that,' he said hastily.

I sat back, completely at a loss. 'What is it then?'

Geoff looked over his shoulder as if to reassure himself that nobody was listening, then he leant forward and muttered. 'It's the bedroom. The ceiling. It's a bloody great mirror. You know. You lie in bed and look at yourself all the time.'

I reeled mentally at the picture it conjured up and my response was pretty feeble. 'Oh, I see.'

With occasional episodes like this to brighten my day I pressed on producing the detail of the new MoDED organisation. There were over a hundred engineering and clerical trades and with gradings the variety ran into hundreds. It was a tedious business and occasionally bogged down I would leave my office and go and talk to somebody just to clear my mind. I was a firm believer in the maxim that: 'When you're up to your arse in alligators, it's difficult to remember that your original intention was to drain the swamp.' I did not want to lose sight of my original intention among the minutae of welders, fitters, painters, clerks, costing and so on.

In spite of my total ineffectiveness as Inspector of Establishments my advice was occasionally sought and gladly given.

One young major telephoned me. He had a responsibility for the personnel numbers in the Land Forces and was greatly concerned at an establishment bid he had just received. It was a request for another 100 soldiers for the Signals Regiment to provide batmen for the officers. He had already discussed it with the lieutenant colonel who nearly started the Third World War and, inevitably, that individual had told him that it was alright. In spite of this, or perhaps because of it, he wanted reassuring. 'There's something wrong somewhere,' he said.

'You're absolutely right,' I told him. 'It's rubbish. Batmen and stewards appear on the establishment of the mess that employs them, not on the regiment of the officers. Anyway, do you think that some seventy odd officers in the Signal Regiment have managed without batmen uncomplainingly for the past ten years.'

'That's it,' he said. 'That's what was at the back of my mind.'

'Good for you,' I told him, perhaps a trifle sarcastically, but the compliment was well meant.

As I mentioned earlier, Tim's swift repartee was only equalled by his speedy action with a glass and it was soon after Geoff and Cynthia's face to face encounter with erotica that Tim produced a fine example of his wit that was reported and repeated throughout the BAF mess.

Tim was terrified of flying. Not just afraid, he existed in a state of sweaty panic from the moment that contact was lost with the runaway until that reassuring rumble took place so many hours later. Inevitably, his leave journeys to and from the UK were appalling nightmares which he could only endure after hours of concentrated injections of Dutch courage. By booking in time he was well anaesthetised and usually there was somebody else going on leave who would escort him to his seat and maintain a watching brief until Heathrow, where his daughter took over.

It was not surprising that once he was in his seat his head slumped forward and he slept deeply through the terror of take off. On this occasion however the sedative had not been strong enough and he awoke while the aircraft was taxiing out to take off. He pressed the bell and the stewardess hurried forward. 'Yes Sir?'

He focused on her pretty young face. 'A very large whisky and soda please, my dear.'

She noted the gentle dew on Tim's forehead and smiled sympathetically. 'I'm sorry, Sir. We haven't taken off yet.'

He focused again, drew himself up in his seat and spoke with dignity. 'You may not have taken off yet, me dear, but I can assure you that I have.'

His escort recorded to the girl's and Gulf Air's credit that she hurried away grinning and returned with a nerve steadier.

Finally I completed the seemingly never-ending task of producing the new organisation for the Engineering Division. It was hardly surprising that it turned out to be a giant volume with hundreds of pages devoted to the thousands of professional men and tradesmen who would be required to maintain the SAF bases. Some of these, like Muaskar al Murtafa'a, housed innumerable headquarters and the thousands of troops and civilians necessary to man them. MAM was a very large town by any standard and the engineering support was an amalgam of the Electricity Authority, the Water Board, the Sewage Board, the Highways Department and included all of the local council activities associated with such a place.

Unfortunately, it was necessary to produce a dozen or so copies of the magnum opus for various senior officers including HE and HRM and I dared not use any of the MoDED clerks to carry out the copying for me. One sight of it and it would be common knowledge in the Pakistani Mafia and hundreds of clerks would have written to thousands of relatives in the Subcontinent who would, in turn, have written to MoDED. I appropriated a large photocopier for a few hours and locked the door.

Bob was delighted with the end result and particularly pleased to see his planning published in such a format that it could form the basis for recruiting action. Other recipients were not so enthusiastic and the reaction from His Excellency the Under Secretary and the Head of Resource Management could best be described as one of stunned silence.

Bob's enthusiasm went so far however, that he offered me a new post he now wanted to create, that of Director of Recruiting and Establishment. It would have meant a small promotion and the achievement of accompanied status but my wife was very happy with her home, her job and the family nearby in Australia. It would have been no improvement in her life to exchange that for the social aridity of Oman. As for me, working directly for Bob, life would consist of endless arguments as I tried, unsuccessfully, to act as some sort of restraining influence on the expanding MoDED. I liked Bob on a personal level but I thought his ideas lavish and I knew that, given the go-ahead by Sir Timothy he would not be thwarted in anyway. Millions and millions of rials were going to be spent in recruiting, paying and housing the additional staff and I was sick of the waste.

Bob's approach to the responsibilities of his department were absolutely right. Power supplies must have back-ups in operational areas. It was ridiculous to have to wait for the Oman Electricity Authority to turn up and do something when the lights went out. MoDED should have an instant reaction system for 24 hours a day. Equipment should be regularly serviced. Staff should be made to understand and accept their responsibilities in peace and in war. Bomb holes in runways had to be filled in immediately. Of course all this required more men. That I accepted. What I did not accept was what I called the gold-plated approach. Staff the organisation with enough people to cover every possible contingency short of the Black Death. Every additional post should be examined and substantiated, instead hundreds where scores would suffice, scores where tens would have done. I had had enough of it.

I had a few months left before my contract ran out. I would go back to my MAM office and have a final look at the SAF numbers game. If my worst fears were coming true then I would say so - loud and clear, verbally and on paper. Then I would leave Oman on the due date, fairly unhappy at what I was leaving behind but fairly happy that I had done all I could.

A few of those one saw in the evening in the Bamboo Bar had known Bait al Falaj during the Dhofar War. Such a one was Peter, the Camp Commandant, who could remember clearly how you walked out of the front gate of the camp onto the end of the runway. Parked there would be a Viscount or Dakota and after a white knuckle take off through the nearby jebel peaks you would turn south for the war. That runway was now part of the road from Muttrah to Al Bustan. It was not Peter though, who recounted the story of the Mummy Wadi. This account, a very human one, would certainly not have met with the approval of the MoD (UK or Oman).

My views on courage are not firmly held. Some argue that it is either something that you have or do not have, while others say that it is a bottle of wine that may be emptied in dribbles until there is nothing left. These theorists also say that it is a bottle that takes a long time to refill. I favour this latter opinion and I would like to think that this was the sort of failure that led to the naming of the 'Mummy Wadi'.

Julian was a romantic and joined the British Army to seek adventure. He thrived during Sandhurst and thrilled to the battle honours on the flags and the battle stories that he heard and read about. When he graduated, he went to one of the better line regiments. Two years in Germany and he yearned for action and, when the company noticeboard announced the opportunity, he volunteered for service in the Sultanate of Oman.

High on the Dhofar plateau, with the monsoon cloud swirling around the sangar it was easy to see shapes appearing and disappearing in the mist. He was finding it very difficult to master Baluch and, because he couldn't always follow the conversation of his soldiers, he sometimes suspected that their laughter was aimed at him. His brother officers were contract men; most of them ex-soldiers from the British Army who had gained their commissions in the Sultan's Land Force because of battle experience in Malaya, Kenya, Aden or Northern Ireland. He felt very young and inexperienced in their company and was convinced that they regarded him with condescension or contempt. All in all, he was very unhappy, very unsure of himself and found the dark, grey gloom, nothing like the sunlit battlefields he had imagined in Germany.

It was about ten o'clock one morning when the pale sun generated enough heat to partially disperse the mist and it was shortly after this happened that the first mortar shells began to arrive. You did not need glasses to see the scurried activity on the far side of the wadi, nor did you need to be a soldier to calculate where the mortars were sited. Sooner or later there was going to be a lucky (or unlucky) hit and the carnage inside the sangar would be appalling.

Crouched low behind the rocks and earth James outlined his plan. He would lead a couple of groups to encircle and come up behind the ado. 'When you see my green, open up with everything, including the mortars. When you see my red, stop. OK?'

Julian flinched at a nearby explosion and nodded. 'Couldn't we just use our mortars now? That'll stop 'em.'

James looked at him hard and long. 'We're here to kill the bastard not just drive them away,' he said. He made Julian repeat his instructions, set watches and took off. Half an hour later he was frustrated and furious. He and his men were pinned in the wadi bed, crouched behind boulders and unable to move because of the heavy fire coming down on them from the slopes ahead. He had already fired two flares but there had been no response from behind. 'What the hell's going on,' he raged at his Baluchi sergeant who grinned sympathetically and ducked even lower. A few minutes later James shouted: 'Cover me,' and crouching low he ran an erratic path back up his side of the wadi. He fell over the wall into the sangar where he had left Julian and looked around at the Corporal and the soldiers. 'Where is your officer?' he panted and the Areef pointed towards a narrow rough path which curved away around a small cliff to the south of the sangar. James nearly exploded with 'What the hell's he doing there?' but stopped himself in time. After a hasty glance over the sangar wall to where his men were still crouched a few hundred feet below he took off and raced along the track.

Around the corner he come to the first of the caves below the overhang. Nothing. To the next. Nothing. It was at the fifth cave that he heard the moaning and sobbing and, it was so appallingly sad he said afterwards, that it made the hair on his neck prickle. There was Julian, on his side and curled into a tight foetal ball sobbing 'Mummy, Oh Mummy.'

'Christ!' thought James. 'Have to sort this our later,' and he raced back to Julian's sangar to start extricating his men.

Chapter 8

According to Sir Timothy Creasey, the Morale Guidance Branch had become a problem. Before this pronouncement it was, to my mind, no more and no less efficient than any of the other offices or branches run entirely by Omanis with Pakistani support. They were not overly active nor enterprising but MGB seemed to satisfy the senior Omani officer, including Hassan Eshan.

Essentially the Morale Guidance Branch was the public relations organisation for SAF. Inevitably, its motivation possessed strong Islamic overtones. They covered all the major military functions (eg, exercises and passing out parades) for television, radio and the newspapers. They also produced various publications for distribution throughout SAF and the civilian world extolling the delight and virtues of serving His Majesty in one of the fighting services. An Islamic priest was on the staff to ensure that Allah featured somewhere in all of their releases. It was not my cup of tea and very clearly it wasn't Sir Timothy's either. The publications were garish (as are most Arab magazines) and aimed at a fairly low level of intelligence and none of the films or video clips would have won any prizes at Montreux but they seemed to be aimed at the right target. I discussed MGB with a number of senior Omani officers and they all expressed satisfaction with its performance.

So far as I could make out, Sir Timothy's main criticism was that MGB releases rarely appeared in the *Oman Observer* or any other Gulf publications in English. I failed to see the point of this complaint. The branch existed to enlighten SAF soldiers, sailors and airmen (all Muslims) and the local population (also Muslims). Anything that appeared in an English publication was a bonus but certainly not something that MGB should be working towards. This viewpoint was not accepted and 'something' had to be done about it. This 'something' seemed to go on for ever.

I had already examined the branch and interviewed its officers during my review of His Excellency's department. I came away with the impression that they were all on a learning curve, possessed considerable enthusiasm and were progressing well under the guidance of an Egyptian lieutenant colonel, a professional PR man on loan.

Circumstances called for another and more detailed investigation of the organisation.

Inevitably, nobody had told them that CDS regarded them with disfavour and I had to invent a spurious and acceptable reason for the new exercise. They may have been concerned or bewildered but, as always, they concealed it well and welcomed me happily, particularly when I told them that this new examination might lead to some improvement in their lot. This time I also used an English speaking Omani civilian from outside the branch as an interpreter, so that I could interview the few Omani soldiers and NCO's in MGB as well as the officers, all of whom spoke English well.

There were 19 officers and men involved and I spent a couple of weeks with them. At the end of the period I had much the same impression that I had received previously. Masses of enthusiasm and hard work. Maybe their approach lacked a little sophistication but, by God (or Allah), you had to give them top marks for application. Young Nabil was a captain and titular head of the branch and he showed me his diary for the past few months. A typical sort of day would start at seven-thirty in the morning and at nine-thirty at night he would be recording a radio programme. It was enough to give a British trade union official a heart attack.

At the end of the fortnight I debriefed Nabil and the Egyptian adviser. I told them their standards could be improved (which they knew) and more high quality professional training was required (which they also knew). To this end I would be recommending an increase in staff to 28 during the next year and, so far as was practicable, courses in TV Production, Film-making and Publishing in New York and London, as well as in Cairo, should be made available to the officers and SNCO's. As qualifications and experience increased, so should promotions. I produced what I regarded as a practical programme for improving the expertise of MGB and increasing its staff to remove some of the present over-long working hours they suffered from. I submitted my findings to CDS.

In my submission I was stupid enough to say that the branch was doing a good job by Islamic standards, the staff undoubtedly required more professional training but senior Omani officers approved of what they were doing and, indeed, Sultan Qaboos had recently complimented them on a particular task they had just carried out. An unconscious pun, but it was the proverbial red rag to ...

'Rubbish!' came rumbling down. Followed shortly by: 'I totally reject your findings. I am going to ask a committee of senior Omani officers to examine the Morale Guidance Branch and give me their recommendations.'

I had no answer to the last suggestion except one which would have earnt me the justifiable accusation of being impudent and facetious. I beloved the Omanis dearly but, usually, they had enough problems coping with their own jobs. To ask them to pronounce on an exotic field like public relations was like asking a Roman Catholic priest for advice on the best way to run a brothel.

The findings of the senior officers' committee were not unexpected. The Morale Guidance Branch should be headed by a full colonel, not a captain and the staff should be increased from 19 to 52. To be fair to them they did admit that they weren't too sure about the sort of talents required to operate well in the public relations field. They were also equally uncertain about the chances of finding 33 extra officers and men who knew anything about PR work. This last comment earnt my award for being the understatement of the year.

As fatuous and impractical as the recommendations were it came as no surprise to me to learn that they had been endorsed by CDS. The massive increase in numbers guaranteed it. I made my apologies to the bewildered young captain and the Egyptian adviser in Morale Guidance. In place of the targeted expansion in numbers and training that we had worked out together they were now saddled with an utterly useless paper exercise.

I felt bitter about the situation I had been placed in and the complete lack of judgement constantly being displayed in the establishments field. My comment to Fred was fairly terse: 'The fatuity of replacing a carefully considered training and expansion programme for MGB with the muilt-page ramblings of an Omani officers' committee is beyond description.' There was no reply, nor did I expect one.

It was shortly after that when an incident occurred which took my mind off the SAF manpower scene for 24 hours.

The Gulf of Oman teams with life: crayfish, sea snakes, barracuda, sharks and rays, to name a few. When I was at MoDUK the mess at RAF Masirah made a small fortune out of selling the surplus catch of the station fishing club. I often returned from there with a frozen barracuda, sliced and filleted, minus head and tail and still measuring over four feet in length. It was delicious meat.

Of all the sea-life though, I loathed sea snakes the most. There was a large variety of them but the ones I knew best, from my sailing dinghy I hasten to add, had translucent bodies with dark brown spots along the length. They were all poisonous but the local ones were lethal I was told. As they moved through the water with that peculiar sideways undulation I could easily believe it.

Then came the box jellyfish and the danger of bumping into a sea snake whilst swimming became a distant worry about an unlikely event. The box jellyfish is a weird and wonderfully unpleasant creature. Its body can best be described as like a large bishop's mitre with a square base. From each corner of the base a long thin tentacle extends. It is quite transparent and the only colour present is a small dark blob at the end of each tentacle. This is the sting. Its biggest danger is that it is impossible to see in the water and like all of the breed, they travel in large groups.

Its arrival at the SAF Aqua Club was announced by screams from the water and people limping or running to the club manager's office for some soothing lotion or, in some cases, the administering of a sedative. There could be considerable shock resulting from the sting of these unpleasant creatures and in a few cases, particularly where children were involved, transportation to hospital was necessary because of the danger of a serious allergy.

I was told that the sting of a box jellyfish could be fatal and those around Muscat had tentacles four to five feet long and they could produce unpleasant enough effects. When I came to live in Australia I learnt that the box jellyfish off the North Queensland coast will attain tentacles over ten feet long and have a body size to match. It needed little imagination to accept that this variety could kill.

At the Aqua Club the annual migration had come and gone, so everybody, including me, believed. I was swimming some thirty feet off the shore and towards the boat ramp when my arm met a rubbery resistance in the water and a remarkably fierce burning sensation started at the base of my neck. By the time I reached the shore my armpit was swollen and sore and as I quickly dried off and climbed into my car I could feel a certain loss of feeling in my right arm. My journey back to Bait al Falaj took me past the al Khoulah Hospital and as I drove I monitored my reactions. If it gets worse I'll drive into the casualty department I promised myself. It didn't and I continued my journey. It was a good twenty-four hours later however, before all the after-effects had disappeared.

Roger was the Chief Auditor, the one who told Phil that it was letting the side down to bring your belly dancing girlfriend into the BAF Officers' Mess for a dirty weekend. He was regarded by most, if not all of his staff as a pain in the bum, but I knew from the occasional beer with him that, though he might be a humourless auditor, he was good at his job and his heart was in the right place.

If I was becoming increasingly disenchanted with the absence of man-power control in SAF, Roger had even more reason to feel unhappy about his situation. I cannot go into details because he only hinted at what he had found beneath the stones he had turned over but, where I was becoming frustrated at the asinine decisions being taken in my field, Roger was becoming infuriated by the lack of interest shown in the findings of some of his auditors. It was always possible that CDS was after bigger fish (and there were plenty swimming around) but Roger was convinced that some of the grubbier activities he had come across should be examined by the police and his pleas for further action were being ignored. Of course, it was always possible that he was apply-ing Christian moral standards and wasting his time, but he was a big boy and should have known his way around, as I'm sure he did.

But, he was becoming disenchanted to the point where he was now losing interest and he decided that it was high time that he moved onto fresh fields. Let somebody else worry about the problem, preferably an Omani. I will find an experienced local with the right professional back-ground and train him to become my successor. It took a lot of time and a lot of interviews, but eventually he found the right man. Ishmael.

Ishmael was a professionally-qualified and senior official in an Omani bank and he was looking for ways to improve himself, not so much financially as professionally. The world of figures was a fascinating one to him and he saw Roger's advertisement in the newspaper as a chance to widen his knowledge. At the interview he began to have doubts about the military scene but Roger won him over and, promising him a large car, rent allowance and an increased salary, he eventually got Ishmael to take the job.

After a few months, the Chief Auditor designate had settled in well. He was a quiet and dignified man in his forties and he was much like by his Omani and British colleagues. Roger had great hopes for him and was beginning to take the first practical steps towards vacating his chair. All was looking good when the bombshell burst.

During the past year the hierarchy had become increasingly concerned about the performance of the Chief of Finance (he who built a house with an official loan, etc). It was not that he was into anything more blatantly outrageous than his brother officers but that he was so bloody erratic. He was either overseas on leave, at his farm on sick leave, visit-ing somebody in another ministry or overseas on a long visit which had a thin miasma of duty surrounding it. As an example he would be the Omani Representative in Rio de Janeiro attending the Pan Arab World Conference of Racing Camel Breeding, if such a conference took place and such an organisation existed. I never really found it in my heart to blame him for, let's be honest, there are more exciting places than the Sultanate of Oman but, without his presence and his signature, a lot of activities came to a halt. Work bored him, he took off whenever the chance presented itself and 'Rashid in today?' became an often asked question. Clearly something had to be done.

The trouble was that he was rumoured to be a powerful man with many influential friends and from a tribe that had no love for the Sultan, or the Sultan's tribe. In other words, if you gave him the sack, God knows what he'd get up to. It looked as if the well-known military and civil service manoeuvre was called for - a sideways posting. Whether it was Fred or Sir Timothy I don't know but the decision was taken to make Rashid the new Chief Auditor to replace Roger.

There was no doubt that expediency was the name of the game and it was certain that Rashid would be less disruptive in his new post; somehow, they had even convinced him that it was a bit of a promotion. He was delighted anyway, promotion or not. His new staff would literally do all of the work and occasionally he would have to put his signature to an auditor's report. Nobody would give a toss where he was, or what went on in his office and the less that CDS or HRM saw or heard about him or his chaps the better. He already knew from past conversations with auditors that nobody loved them and if they uncovered a multi-million dollar fraud nobody thanked them for such a find only led to scandal and ruined reputations. He thought about the endless possibilities of his new post and almost rubbed his hands.

Whilst Rashid may have found it all most amusing and encouraging, Roger did not. He was furious and justifiably so. He knew Rashid and posting him in as a replacement was an insult to him and to the post of Chief Auditor. All of his years of unavailing effort to impose some sort of standards and morality onto the Omani Defence scene and his reward was to see himself replaced by somebody who he had always regarded with the deepest of suspicion. This was bad enough, God knows, but what was he going to tell Ishmael? The man had trusted him. He had talked him into giving up an excellent senior post at a well-established Omani bank in order to become the Chief Auditor to the MoD. Now he was about to be shouldered aside from that post by somebody who was not only lazy and incompetent but totally uninterested in audit, accounts, finance and, let's face it, work itself. The more he thought about it the more angry he became. He picked up his phone and when his call was answered he forgot the hierarchical niceties. 'I'm coming to see you, Fred,' he barked and slammed down the receiver.

He received no more from HRM than I did with my complaints and that was courteous interest, patience and immobility. He asked to see Sir Timothy and this request was granted. When I last saw Roger he had just left the office of CDS and he was on his way to pack. He ignored my greeting and I realised that he was beyond speech and white with fury. I can only imagine what was said for although softly spoken,

Roger spoke his mind as well as Sir Timothy and he justifiably considered that expediency had been allowed to triumph over moral obligation and rectitude.

When I left, poor Ishmael had been found some spurious financial post in Fred's organisation and he was still wondering what had happened to all those promises that Roger had made. I believe that he had his rent paid and he had a car, but it was not as big a car as he had been led to expect and he had no idea what the future held for him. He wore an almost permanently bewildered expression and once said to me, in sorrow: 'I thought that Mister Roger was a man who kept his word.' When I assured him this was so, he looked even more bewildered.

Thinking of Roger and his departure reminded me that there were not too many months left for me. I also occasionally wondered who would be the next contract office to leave in a hurry. It was a fairly regular occurrence and I knew from friends in the personnel branch that there was a standing short-list of uniformed contenders for seats on the Tin Budgie. It was beginning to look now as if there were a couple in the mess at BAF also jostling for the honour, for I was not the only one to wonder how it was that Tim and Robin had managed to last so long. Both were heavy drinkers, even by Bamboo Bar standards and at a certain point in their drinking they both suffered a rapid decline in behaviour. Tim normally had a delightful sense of humour which became razor-sharp after a few glasses; a few glasses more however and his conversation would become a stream of contempt and vilification against the Omanis. None of us ever knew why. We all thought them the most pleasant and friendliest of the Arab races and when sober, Tim treated them with all of the good humour and courtesy in the world. His loud and drunken shouts of 'F***ing coons' embarrassed us all and there was no doubt that somebody would take strong exception to his behaviour sooner or later. It was a pity that it had to happen only a couple of weeks before his contract ran out and he had to leave on the Tin Budgie instead of the flight he had booked.

Whereas Tim was regarded as old enough to keep his own nose clean, Robin, some years younger than nearly all of us, was an object of pity. We all knew he had a heart condition (and wondered how he ever got to Oman) and that he was divorced and had three children at expensive private schools in England. There was an air of desperation about his giant drinking bouts however and because of this most of us either ignored his behaviour or told him to shut up and go to bed. Occasionally he became a public nuisance and I still recall with embarrassment one of our rare semi-formal mess functions when he lurched from table to table, sampling and spilling the wines and enquiring loudly and drunkenly if the guests were enjoying themselves.

We all did our best to protect both of them although we knew that all of our talk and proffered excuses would come to nothing if the wrong person saw them at the wrong time. An Omani friend had already told me that two of his brother officers had been deeply offended and were out to 'get' both Tim and Robin. I passed on the warning but it was almost a waste of time for neither of them could control themselves after the fatal one too many.

Other things began to occupy my mind however. I had started to look at the manpower strength returns and the first glance suggested that they were going to be even worse than I had imagined. My position as Inspector of Establishments for the Sultan's Armed Forces was an obvious nonsense and I made a written submission to Fred in which I detailed how establishment control had been emasculated by him and CDS and I concluded by recommending that my post be done away with, in fact, disestablished. The presence of the post on the staff in the office of CDS and HRM suggested that there was some sort of interest in establishment control and this was blatantly untrue.

HRM asked me to come and discuss my letter and after a lengthy chat I went away to consider a possible change of title and employment for myself. I did so, felt no inclination to start in another field and, because I felt strongly about the way manpower costs were escalating decided to put my views on paper. I summarised:

'Having no useful work to do is unpleasant enough, but working on successive projects which always come to naught is even more frustrating. Two examples of such wasted efforts is that CDS did nothing about the appallingly low effective working week achieved by the staff of Land Force Headquarters (HQ SOLF), then, my carefully researched investigation of the Morale Guidance Branch which led to a planned expansion from 19 to 28 (with the appropriate training) was replaced by a recommendation that MGB should all be uniformed and increased from 19 to 52. At least, the Omani officers who produced this last gem had the sense to confess that 'there was a lack of manpower caused by a shortage of (suitable) Omanis?.'

I concluded by saying that: 'It is now abundantly clear to me that no recommendation (no matter how justified or economically sensible) will have a chance of acceptance if it is likely to be unpalatable to those in uniform. Nor are those in uniform ever to be subject to examination to see if they earn their money.'

HRM's rejoinder to this was to call me in for another meeting during which he tasked me with examining the long-standing and very thorny problem of purchasing. Most of our buys took place in the UK and Western Europe but I suspected that because of vested interests my research and recommendations would prove no more successful than the many previous efforts. But it was a different field and my MoDUK experience in contracts, audit and costings gave me some insight.

Examining this area, talking to the MoD purchasing officers and reading their many papers was one long record of criticism, complaints, innuendos and downright suggestions that 'old so and so' is doing very nicely out of this company, or that contract.

'The MoD Purchasing Branch is manned by a bunch of useless old has-beens from the British Army,' said the supply officers of SOLF, SOAF and SON. 'They never bloody well get us what we want when we want it. They're always late on delivery.'

'SAF supply officers are just bloody incompetent,' was the blunt rejoinder from the Purchasing Directorate. 'They've got useless stock records and they're always demanding priority and delivery in two months on articles that they know take at least four months to manufacture. Or they suddenly realise that they're running out of something and panic around us as if we can produce five thousand combat suits next week.'

There was some justification in both lots of complaints and it helped neither side that they operated from an antiquated stock record system maintained by uniformed Pakistani and Omani clerks. Replacing the records systems was already underway with the decision to go for a computer immediately, but optimistic estimates by the installation experts put that at least two years hence. There was nothing I could do about that. Equally, there was nothing I could do about the clerical support. They operated on a different time track and their initiative was not strong. I remembered my Chief Clerk from the unhurried Joint Staff days. We would run out of pencils regularly and this continued for months, until I made it plain that his job depended on the famine ceasing. The conversation was a fairly short one:

'For God's sake, George! When did you last go to the stationery cupboard?'

'Yesterday, Sir.'

'How many pencils were there?'

'There was one, Sir.'

'Perhaps you should have gone to the stationery store yesterday George. There are ten of us in this office and one pencil is not going to last very long.'

I saw the light appear in his eyes. Perhaps there was some sense in what this old man was saying. 'Next time I will go, Sir.'

'George.'

'Yes, Sir.'

'Don't wait until there is only one pencil left. Go to the stationery store when there is only one packet of pencils left. Then if we have a meeting or everybody in the office wants a new pencil at the same time, you can give them one.'

George's grin widened. This was definitely forward thinking. As I say, I couldn't see myself achieving much in the area of clerical support.

Accordingly, there was only one activity in which I might obtain some improvement and that was in professional buying and commercial expertise, preferably away from the tangled web of gossip and rumour in Oman. According to the latter:

a)   Very important dignitaries in the Sultanate were very interested in seeing that certain companies received contracts to supply the Sultan's Armed Forces. This covered everything from aircraft, through 155mm artillery to clothing.

b)   Some senior British officers were dedicated to seeing that the really big money contracts (aircraft, tanks, etc,) went to British manufacturers for good patriotic reasons (and preferably those in whom they had shares or a hope of a future directorship).

c)   Some not so senior British and Omani officials in the Purchasing Directorate were receiving a regular income from ensuring that certain contractors retained certain contracts.

d)   Some not so senior British officers in the Supply Branches of SOLF, SOAF, and SON were receiving a regular income from ensuring that certain contractors retained certain contracts.

e)   Charles Kendall and Partners in London and Airwork at Hurn Airport and other agents in the UK had long-standing agreements with the Sultanate to provide a wide range of supplies and services, many on a percentage commission basis. This had been going on for many years and the argument went, that as they received a percentage commission on the amounts involved there was no incentive for them to seek out the cheapest and the best supplier.

It was clear that probably self-interest, lack of expertise and strict financial control and scrutiny were the major weaknesses in the present system. It also evoked memories of old establishment battles to read that, in 1978, referring to a report prepared by a visiting team of financial experts a senior official from the UK Ministry of Defence had this to say:

'Paras 423 and 424 of the Report refer to shortcomings in the methods of justifying expenditure before commitments are authorised. Its recommendations in this respect are sound, but from my own discussions I gained the impression that Service HQs might be disinclined to accept that financial staff, particularly in MoD, have sufficient technical expertise in, say, the equipment field to challenge the soundness of justifications. Any such attitude should be firmly countered. Justifying the need for equipment is not just a matter of exercising technical expertise. It is also a matter of exercising powers of reason and logic and of reaching judgements about orders of priority. These are intellectual processes whose validity can quite properly be tested by non-technical experts such as finance staff. In fact, a more effective critique can probably be applied by an observer detached from responsibility for the original formulation of the requirement.'

I thought about this for a moment, then of the proposal for a fish and chip van on the autobahn and of the families queuing outside the accountant's office when war broke out. I decided that the comment was as appropriate to establishments as it was to equipment.
From my observations of the purchasing field so far, it seemed that nobody had been able to call upon the military in SAF to justify their expenditure on equipment. This was in spite of the sound advice given in the report. If anybody had, they had been singularly unsuccessful. It grieved and irritated me. Oman was a country struggling out of the dark ages and yet just under 40% of the annual budget was being spent on military personnel and equipment. One could almost live with that appallingly high expenditure if one knew that the money was being spent wisely after careful examination by 'observers detached from responsibility for the original formulation of the requirement'. It was not so for the British commanders before and since Creasey's arrival had refused to accept firm outside professional control of their expenditure.

Now, as before, the only limit was how many they could extract from the Oman Ministry of Finance and some of those officials were not exactly disinterested.

And what were these hundreds of millions of rials being spent on? Rapidly escalating numbers of personnel (because I was not allowed to examine and exercise any control) and equipment?

It seemed to me that we were spending millions on men we didn't need and equipment that was inappropriate to our location and any potential enemy. Situated on one side of the Straits of Hormuz we were the key to defending Western access to the Gulf and its oil. If anything threatened that, current treaties brought the USA and NATO to Oman within hours. The Dhofar war had proved that supersonic multiweapon aircraft were useless against ground troops out here for they dispersed into wadis and caves at the first sign of air attack. And the Chieftains we had spent millions in buying? A glance at the map suggested that only about five per cent of Oman was suitable for them to operate in. Would any enemy be so obliging as to deploy in that area? Who were the Jaguars, the Tornados, the Chieftains and the Exocets to be used against?

Basically, there was only one sophisticated potential enemy and it was ludicrous to imagine the Sultanate taking on Soviet Russia and its satellite to our south. If that happened, our allies' ships and aircraft were literally only minutes away and much heavier support only hours away. There was only one reason for such waste and extravagance to my way of thinking and that was virtually uncontrolled spending by the military. It was an expensive lesson that the British Parliament and government had learnt long ago.

In the light of this I was not optimistic about being allowed to introduce any improvement in the purchasing field.

As any suggestion of mine would have potential for economy and possibly some element of control in spending, my proposal would have to be carefully thought out and carefully presented. If not, there would be automatic rejection from the military. I gave the matter considerable thought, then put up my ideas to HRM and CDS.

I had been told that the aim of my study was to seek a method which would 'enable us to control our capability to purchase and ship stores more efficiently and economically' and one solution advanced was 'to establish our own purchasing and procurement cell in Europe'. Later on in the paperwork it was suggested that such a cell 'could either replace the present direct machinery, supplement it or be grafted onto it'. It was plain that it would not be easy to propose a system which would be acceptable to CDS and the commanders. But it can be done, I decided, if they move one inch away from their inbuilt rejection to anything that they regard as interference in their affairs.

It was an unusual occurrence, but I did agree with them that to contemplate replacing our present system was a nonsense. It would involve setting up a large complex and expensive organisation that would take years to amass the contacts and enjoy the close working relationships that our present agents enjoyed with the manufacturers and suppliers and if it failed it would be a disaster for our supply system.

My eventual solution was a small cell of men, young civilian professionals in finance, freight and market intelligence established in the UK. They could take over most of our bill paying (which was costing us over half a million in agents' fees). They could co-ordinate and oversee our present rather shaky methods of freight delivery - particularly urgent cargoes and finally, they would provide something we desperately needed and that was up-to-date information about suppliers and prices. This lack of market intelligence was probably our biggest and most expensive weakness.

The advantages of this proposed small office was that it should be acceptable to the military, would not upset our present contractors and operate at comparatively little cost (estimated at RO15,000 per annum) compared to the hundreds of millions we spent. Moreover, it could provide a base for possible expansion into direct purchasing and, if it failed to provide the savings and increased efficiency that we expected its closure would not affect our present system. I finished my submission by pointing out that more detailed research would be necessary if we wished to proceed. Firmer information was needed about location, availability of accommodation and employees, wages and other costs.

The reactions of the three services were tepid with the Land Forces inevitably suggesting that expansion of the present Purchasing Directorate (ie, more men) was the answer. I forbore to ask them if they wanted to expand the present inefficiency as well. HE's Department clearly misunderstood the proposal and their comment was irrelevant. CDS and HRM were warm to the idea however and I was sent off to the UK.

From my point of view the visit was a highly successful one. Once I had assured the staff of our various procurement and freight agencies that I was not there to seek an alternative to them they were hospitable and very helpful. Plainly, London would be no location for our Forward Procurement Agency (as I now called it) because the rents and the wages were too high, but Bournemouth and its environs was eminently suitable because of its cheapness and its juxtaposition to Airwork at Hurn Airport, the freight organisations, and Southampton and the docks. The Department of Employment in Southampton were enthusiastic and assured me that they could provide all of the staff I required at less cost than I envisaged. Indeed, I was a little depressed at the low wages our positions offered, but the D of E officer was adamant that no more should be given.

I returned to Oman and after a few days submitted a detailed plan for setting up the FPA. I suggested that it should be managed by a retired high-ranking officer from the supply field who would possess the military knowledge and the contacts in MoDUK and among the manufacturers, but that the specialist staff should be young civilians dedicated to their expertise in the finance, purchasing and freight worlds. Given the go-ahead, I added, it could be operating within two or three months, for I even had a choice of office suites ready for occupation.

CDS and HRM thought it had merit but the three services rejected it. Oh well, I thought, probably too many people interested in keeping the present system. I had no illusions about Sir Timothy imposing his views and I also knew that Fred would do exactly what CDS wanted him to.

I was now well into the stage where I expected nothing in the way of success or improvement in the present, largely grossly inefficient status quo. I was a little sad about that wasted journey and all that wasted effort. At least I could now return to the equally depressing manpower scene and start to think about packing.

The various research exercises into SAF manpower took a few weeks and each one produced a more depressing picture. I again asked HRM to present the figures to Sir Timothy but he prevaricated endlessly and gave me more and more research to do. This was a totally self-defeating exercise for every study I completed showed a blacker and blacker picture. Personally I thought that the facts now challenged the credibility of Sir Timothy Creasey as Chief of the Defence Staff and Fred was afraid to present them to him. Since Sir Timothy had arrived three years earlier:

a)   His initial demand for a reduction of 10% in the strength of SAF had resulted in a massive increase of 40%.

b)   During that period, the number of senior officers had increased by a ludicrous 75%.

c)   His demand for an increase in Omanisation had resulted in a decrease in the proportion of Omanis in the Sultan's Armed Forces.

Only SON (whose strength was a mere 7% of SAF) had a programme to account for their increase and in a comment to HRM about the strength explosion I wrote:

'This is exactly what I would expect when military commanders are given virtual autonomy in manpower matters.

'It is also appropriate to comment on the truly appalling increase in the ranks of lieutenant colonels/wing commanders/commanders and above. It seems that the gravy train has not only collected many more passengers but that most of the first class seats are occupied by British officers...

'This senior officer phenomenon is well-known in the establishments game and it is called the 'Indian Chief Syndrome'. If it continues unchecked, the theory goes that eventually all of the tribe sit in their wigwams discussing tribal policy towards buffalo hunting but nobody actually goes out and hunts buffalo. Another, less subtle title given to it is: 'Empire Building'.'

It would be nice to record that HRM's reaction was to take the information straight to Sir Timothy. Instead, he mused that CDS 'will probably be very angry'; a statement I could not disagree with. 'I think I want an appropriate moment to tell him' was his next remark. 'There never will be one Fred' was my final comment as I walked out of his office.

CDS had welcomed the abandonment of establishment control when HRM had suggested it and, so far as I was concerned, they were both reaping the appropriate harvest. I doubted whether CDS understood what it meant, but Fred certainly should have realised that every one of those extra bodies had to be trained, fed and cared for medically. Now the appropriate support arms would soon be crying out for their extra men to enable them to cope with all the other extra men.

As I drove back gloomily to Bait al Falaj I thought of my recent letter to a friend who knew Oman well. 'Clearly, HRM is not about to put these figures to good use for fear of incurring Sir Timothy's wrath. CDS is equally to blame however, for his total failure to exercise firm control over the Service Commanders who, unfortunately, are now in a stronger position than they were before his arrival.'

It was early evening by the time I went through the BAF gate and waved a reply to the guard's greeting and it was almost dark as I walked from my room across to the mess. Ramadan again and the usual depressing silence hung over the camp; indeed, over the whole of the Capital Area. Another hour before the feasting could start, although I had been told that after the first week of fasting not much food was consumed at the end of the day, for stomachs had shrunk and sleep was more important.

I climbed the stairs and glanced into the ante-room. There was nobody there; there was probably nobody in the Bamboo Bar but I would have a look in case there was somebody to exchange the latest gossip with. At least it would provide some sort of light relief in what, so far, had been an absolute sod of a day. I almost sighed with relief as I opened the door and saw a shape huddled on a bar stool. It was difficult to see who it was in the gloom - somebody on the mess committee had recently decreed that bright lighting was suggestive of gaiety and pleasure and was inappropriate to Ramadan - but when I got closer I saw that it was Peter, the camp commandant. From his wide grin of greeting it was plain that he welcomed company as much as I did. We had been friends too long for him to waste time on formalities and he summoned the one barman on duty and ordered my soda water. As it was placed in front of me I reflected that there had been none of this furtive drinking during Ramadan when I first arrived. Then we just had to keep it discreet and away from the sight of Omanis. This was not difficult in the mess. The return to fundamentalism seemed to be gaining ground everywhere in the Gulf States and it was taking many forms. The denial of the presence of British advisers was another one. I had got used to never seeing white faces in newspaper pictures of the armed forces but, at a recent military exercise with the United Arab Emirates, the Omani Land Force convoys had been stopped at the frontier and all of the British officers and SNCOs had been refused entry and participation in the exercise.

I topped up my soda water from my hip flask and raised the glass in silent greeting to Peter. He was not a whisky man and I didn't go to the trouble of offering him the use of the flask.

'Heard about Robin?' he asked.

'No?'

'I got a phone call from Creasey's office this morning. Ordered to collect Robin and escort him into Rumais Prison.'

I looked at Peter and almost guessed the answer to my question.

'What the hell for?'

'Sticky fingers,' he answered cryptically. 'Took about three thousand rials out of the tender board account.'

I thought about the past four years and nodded. I could believe it. Robin had mentioned his bar bills to me one or twice, always with an embarrassed laugh. The amounts had been truly appalling. Knowing his background, his salary and his commitments in England I had occasionally wondered how the hell he managed. Now I knew. His pilfering would have been yet another worry to add to the many he already had. No wonder his drinking had been such a desperate business. Massive sessions followed by vitamin injections to get him through the after-effects. Poor bugger.

'What was it like in Rumais?'

'Spotless,' said Peter. 'Beautifully maintained. Mind you, they don't stand any nonsense.'

I looked enquiringly at him.

'I drove Robin down in the Land Rover and he had a few toilet things in a grip. We went into the reception office and it was air-conditioned and I was bloody glad. Jeez! it was hot. Robin came in with me and they immediately ordered him outside - there was no air-conditioning for him. He had to stand at attention outside while I handed him over, so to speak. Then they marched him off.'

I thought of the temperature, 122°F (50°C) and shivered in the draught from the bar air-conditioner. What was it young Steve had told me about the prison? Twenty in a big cage, an open bog and a tap in the corner. Except that, being Ramadan, the tap would be turned off during daylight hours. And from his drinking habits, Robin's dehydration would be much worse than that of a normal person.

'Christ!' I muttered to Peter. 'I hope the poor sod lasts out.'

He understood exactly what I meant. 'I hope so too Matey. This is no time of the year to be going into Rumais.'

It was two days later I remember, the Friday having intervened, when I returned to my officer at Muaskar al Murtafa'a. I was running down and beginning to clear my desk of bits and pieces. Mike was always an early starter and it was no surprise when he wandered in shortly after I arrived. He conveyed his news in a typical blunt Yorkshire manner, although, knowing him, I could see that he was upset by what he had to tell me. He was carrying a cup of coffee and balanced it carefully as he sat down in the armchair.

'Might as well tell you straight out. Robin's dead.'

I could not, in all honesty, express too much surprise or shock. I had suspected that Robin's going into Rumais during Ramadan was tantamount to a death sentence.

'How?' I started to ask but Mike had finished sipping his coffee and moved to the door. 'I'll tell you when I know more,' he added as he left. Mike was a very old friend and a very good staff officer and I knew that he would tell me no more than was considered suitable for general consumption.

It was a few days before I discovered what had happened and, as was often the case in Oman, it was the result of a casual conversation. He was a young Englishman, a friend of somebody in the mess and had turned up for a beer before going back to his flat. I was chatting to him and the conversation moved round to the Omani police, crime and punishment. An Omani colleague of his had just finished a few days in Rumais for some driving offence and he had gone to Qurum Police Station to collect him. He found him waiting in one of the corridors standing rigidly at attention. He made some facetious comment but his friend was not amused, and it was not until a police sergeant told him that he could go and they were outside that his friend relaxed.

'You think I was silly standing to attention in the police station?' he asked.

'Well, it's unusual behaviour for you,' the Englishman replied, 'you're a fairly lighthearted guy usually.'

The Omani turned in his seat and looked at him. 'I was told to stand to attention and I did so. If I did not, any policeman who came past me poked me in the stomach with his stick. And anyway,' he concluded, 'the police station was air-conditioned.'

'What's that got to do with it?'

'In Rumais, there was no air-conditioning and an Englishman died there. Yesterday he tried to drink some water from a tap and the guards dragged him away and put him into one of the punishment cells. When they opened it up this morning he was dead.'

'It took a minute or two for the news to sink in,' the young Englishman at the bar told me. 'After I recovered I asked what these punishment cells are like, and he told me that there is a big room with one small window and there are eight small cells in the room. You can't lie down or sit down in them.'

I absorbed this and tried not to imagine Robin's last hours. Poor bastard. I hoped that he hadn't lasted too long in his punishment cell.

Slowly, the information dribbled out.

The body was taken to the Royal Oman Police Hospital at Qurum for a post mortem. As the ROP were responsible for Rumais Prison the result of the post mortem would probably not be too enlightening and it wasn't. Heart failure it said. Probably true and quite acceptable if you ignore the reason for the heart failure.

Even the British Ambassador in Muscat, anxious to hush up the business, could not accept 'heart failure'. With the case of Nurse Smith's death in Saudi Arabia still erupting regularly in the British newspapers he could well imagine what they would make of 'heart failure' as an officially accepted cause of the death of Robin. He rejected the findings. I never did learn what medical jargon was finally used to account for Robin's early transition to the next world. There were probably some good Latin words available for excessive dehydration but none for the stupid unthinking treatment of the punishment cell.

There were many questions and some answers materialised, but many were left unanswered. In the meantime, Tim, as a close friend of Robin's was asked if he would escort the body back to England. He agreed and knowing his fear of flying I thought it courageous of him. He had however, been almost in a state of shock since Robin's death. One morning he arrived in the office looking quite dreadful and when I spoke to him he told me that he hadn't slept for thinking about Robin.

'All of my chums come to a sticky end,' he remarked plaintively. 'PG was Tin Budgied, so was Bill and now Robin's dead. I reckon I bring 'em bad luck.'

'That's rubbish,' I replied. Tim was not stupid and didn't need me to tell him the common bond that had led them all to a hasty exit.

Before Tim left on his doleful journey there was general agreement that the affair would be treated very low key because of Robin's children. This reasonable intention was soon shattered when the British newspapers and TV got hold of the story, but Tim managed to fend off the media and return to Oman without disclosing too many lurid details. After his return, Granada wrote to him and asked for his cooperation in exposing the 'scandal' but he ignored the letter. This was to no avail, for the Budget Controller who was disestablished after my review of HE's Department took the opportunity to get his revenge on television, painting a far too highly coloured picture of the corrupt and licentious individuals and the lifestyle of the British in MoD and SAF in Oman.

Back in the Sultanate however, other facts came to light. Whatever I thought of Fred as a firm decisive administrator he was a kind man and an old colleague of Robin's. Understanding his problems and the reason for his petty thieving he had pleaded with Creasey to 'Tin Budgie' Robin when the case came to their notice. Others had been for similar or worse offences. CDS seemed determined to make an example of him however and on Robin repaying his 'loot' committed him to Rumais with a promise of early release onto the Tin Budgie.

Three thousand rials stolen against the millions being wasted or lifted elsewhere? I still had some questions.

What if very senior British officer insisted that his office should pay for the stamps on all of his private mail? And all his telephone calls? And what if he spent ten thousand pounds of the Sultan's money on a white gold buckle for his dress uniform? And made MoD (Oman) pay for the hired chauffeur-driven Rolls Royce used to take him and his wife to London whenever he was on leave at his country estate in the UK? And when asked about these expenses replied: 'If they want me they can bloody well pay for me'?

Why had there not been a medical examination of Robin before he went to prison? Standard procedure overseas. Such an examination would have disclosed his heart condition and prevented his death.

When the news of Robin's death made the headlines back in England all sorts of brouhaha erupted in Oman and the British Ambassador came under fire from the Foreign and Commonwealth Office, with all of the missiles he received being rapidly redirected to the office of CDS.

From personal experience I would have credited Sir Timothy with about as much sensitivity as a wounded Cape Buffalo, but I thought he reached a new high (or low) when he tasked Fred with defending all of his actions which led Robin into Rumais and death.

By now I was completely disenchanted with the British military (particularly their commanders) in the Sultanate of Oman. If I had had any doubts remaining about leaving at the end of my contract, Robin's death and the decisions which caused it, removed the last of them. I was sad, for there were many colleagues and friends I would miss.

When it was time to leave Bait al Falaj I found that in some small way I was sorry. Some periods during the four years I had lived in that rather tatty room had been bad ones, particularly those appalling first few days after leave. On the other hand my various posts and tasks had been interesting and, even if totally frustrating, my attempts to introduce some sort of manpower control had contained a remote possibility of success - sufficient to keep me hoping. I had learnt also that even those contract officers with the most routine jobs managed to obtain some element of surprise and interest from their daily round, for the accountant always had a very good chance of uncovering another scandal (even if it was swept hurriedly under the carpet) and the purchaser always had his endless gossip (some of it true) about fiddled supplies and dubious contracts (or vice versa). And finally I had made a number of good friends, even if some of us had been drawn together by a mutual feeling of comradeship, similar to that enjoyed by the medium-term occupants of a prison.

But the new officers' mess, which had been awaited ever since I arrived in Oman, had finally opened at Muaskar al Murtafa'a and nearly all of the BAF mess members had moved there. I had made it clear that I was leaving at the end of my contract, although so many people said this and then stayed on that it was rarely accepted as a genuine statement of intent and I had a bit of a skirmish with those responsible for the move. Finally they believed me and left me in peace in BAF. Practically speaking, it would have been a nonsense for me to move into the Jebel Mess (as it was called) for only a few weeks, but when I visited it I enviously compared the luxury of the new accommodation with what I had lived in for the past four years. A suite no less, comprising sitting room, kitchen, bedroom, bathroom and balcony. The shine was tarnished a little however, by the site of the place. At the edge of the vastness of MAM camp it was remote from everywhere, with only the bare dusty plains and the nearby jebel to look at. It was ten minutes by car to the headquarters and forty five minutes to the SAF Aqua Club and the Capital Area. I was glad I was leaving. A move into the Jebel Mess would have meant exchanging sordid but interesting surroundings for luxury and boredom.

BAF camp and the officers' mess was virtually denuded of its residents and the Bamboo Bar was more morgue-like than it was during Ramadan. Peter and I were there in the evening together with the occasional naval officer who come along to suss out the mess. Rumour had it that SON was going to take over Bait al Falaj to provide desperately needed accommodation for the personnel of their expanding fleet. Many of the SON officers however, were already accommodated in rented flats in the Capital Area and the prospect of moving into our rooms justifiably filled them with gloom. Peter and I used to buy them a drink and try and tell them about the (dubious) advantages of living in BAF - nearest to the shops and so on - but it was rather like a tenant in a block of Stepney council flats trying to convince a Mayfair resident.

The mess was almost empty when somebody had the idea that those of us who used the Bamboo Bar in bygone days should have a final reunion. There were few of us left and it was a happy but nostalgic evening. To honour the occasion a membership scroll was produced, headed by BAF Bamboo Bar Association in English and Arabic and completed by an intoxicated camel recumbent between two date palms. Tim became President and I became Secretary of our short-lived club and the scrolls were issued.

It was late evening and time for me to leave and I could not resist a last minute drive around the camp. Along beside the wadi to the classic fort structure of His Highness' new offices. Was it three years ago when that horrific storm had destroyed a number of his cars and various Joint Staff offices? Past the old fort, now to be guided into its future as a military museum, by a recently recruited British Arabist and historian; the medical centre, the usual sprawl of grubby one storey buildings and, there it was: the old naval gun. Shades of Maurice O'Brien. It was still pointing dolefully towards the ground, with the great slab of stone lying beside it. I denied myself the luxury of getting out of the car and raising the barrel to a more aggressive stance. It seemed more fitting somehow that I should leave the gun as I had found it.

* * * * * * * * *

Within a month of my return to Australia, the British media discovered the 'Robin Walsh Affair' and seized upon it with all of the enthusiasm one would expect. A wide range of opinions were expressed, from *The Times* to *Private Eye* , and I was surprised to read that I had recently enjoyed four years of a lifestyle 'in the sun which centred on drink, sex and fraud'.

Drink certainly did play a large part in the social life of many of us and, if there was any excuse, it was boredom. Sex? As the saying goes 'We should be so lucky'. Fraud? Hardly. Certainly not as a successful and ongoing business. Robin's performance was par for the average contract officers skill in that direction. A few examples of more recent attempts follow, but these are isolated incidents covering a couple of years.

Jack's job, for instance, involved him in a lot of overseas travelling from Oman and he was pretty active in fiddling his expenses. He was also involved with a pilot's wife in the Sultanate. During a trip to the UK however, he found the stress of his hectic lifestyle too much and he confessed to his real wife about her Omani rival. She shot him, but only slightly and while recovering he received a message that if he returned to the Sultanate he would be escorted straight into Rumais.

Another British Warrant Officer hit on the brilliant idea of forging the Chief Accountant's signature and awarding himself an end of contract gratuity of RO 9,000. When he discovered that it would take two days to clear through the bank he panicked and leapt onto the Gulf Air night flight to London.

The last episode had more panache and involved a British contract captain. He collected RO 43,000 for a pay parade, feigned illness and delayed the parade for 24 hours. After dinner in the mess he also caught the night flight to London with RO 37,000 in his suitcase. Even more however, I wondered how successful he was in disposing of the loot. The Rial Omani is not exactly a widely accepted currency and he would find it difficult to offer sixty thousand pounds worth of exotic banknotes to a British bank without a fairly plausible explanation. I would find it very hard to think of one.

No. If there is fraud on a big scale it is not at the level of the average contract officer. But as I pointed out earlier in the book, what may appear distinctly dishonest to the Englishman reading his Sunday newspaper expose in Chipping Sodbury may well be regarded as a very smart bit of business by an Omani in Muscat.

To be fair to the newspapers, only one went as far to call us 'Soldiers of Disgrace' and that rag was so careless of the truth that they described Robin as a British businessman in one paragraph and as 'one of 300 men serving the Arab ruler' in the next; both statements being equally untrue.

One final comment. It took an oil producers' calamity in the form of a sharp fall in prices to remove at one stroke what I had spent a couple of years trying to prevent. The oil crisis occurred in 1986, caused a massive decrease in Omani income, devaluation of the Rial Omani and substantial reductions in Government spending, including a 40% reduction in the Sultan's Armed Forces. So many men unnecessarily recruited and then so many sacked.

Postscript

Over three years have passed since I last set eyes on the sad, old naval gun outside the fort at Bait al Falaj and, during that period, there have been many changes in the higher echelons of the Sultan's Armed Forces. The overall number of British contract officers has been falling, while the number of senior Omani officers has increased.

Directly responsible to His Majesty, His Highness Said Faher is still the Deputy Prime Minister for Defence and Security, but, beneath him, instead of a British Chief of Defence Staff and a British Commander for each of the three forces, there is now an Omani Lieutenant General as his Chief of Staff in charge of the three force commanders. Of these, the Commander Sultan of Oman's Land Forces (CSOLF) is an Omani but SOAF and SON are still commanded by British loan officers. It has been commented upon that the larger US aircraft carriers, which have much the same complement of aircraft and men as SOAF, are commanded by captains in the US Navy whereas SOAF now has a three star air marshal in command.

The post of His Excellency the Under Secretary has disappeared and with it Major General Hassan Ehsan Naseeb into a well-earned and longed-for retirement.

There has been much pressure to remove the ex-patriates, both from within and around the country. Although it is arguable whether the Omanis, in the comparatively short but enlightened reign of Sultan Quaboos, have gained sufficient knowledge and experience to effectively replace all of the British contract officers, it is understandable that they should wish to do so; there is the uniform, the status, the salary, and, above all, the opportunity to help their tribal brothers. It is equally understandable that among the less well-educated Omanis, there is not the same degree of enthusiasm to replace the Pakistani and Indians in the menial jobs, although His Majesty has urged his people not to regard such labouring or semi-skilled tasks as demeaning.

Whether the Omanis learnt the art of 'empire building' from their British tutors or they just possess a natural flair I am not sure, but senior officers are proliferating now even more than they did during my latter years and any colonel worth his salt has, as a number one priority, the task of increasing his satellite lieutenant colonels, majors, captains, lieutenants and their supporting staff. This trend has already started to cause alarm and I learnt from recent correspondence that there is now a growing demand for the creation of an Inspector of Establishments! - a perfect example of: *plus ça change, plus c'est la meme chose* . As I learnt in Oman however, the creation of such a post will acheive nothing unless the incumbent is given executive power and supported at the highest level.

Selected Bibliography

For those who wish to learn more about the Sultanate of Oman I would recommend the following books as containing much factual detail in an enjoyably readable form.

Fiennes, Ranulph. *Where Soldiers Fear To Tread* , Hodder & Stoughton (1975)
Graz, Liesl. *The Omanis - Sentinels of the Gulf* , Longmans (1982)
Hawley, Donald. *Oman and its Renaissance* , Stacey International (1977)
Jeapes, Tony. *SAS Operation Oman* , William Kimber (1980)
Philips, Wendell. *Unknown Oman* , Longman (1966)
St Albans,The Duchess of. *Where Time Stood Still* , Quartet Books Ltd (1980)
Townsend, John. *Oman, The Making of a Modern State* , Croom Helm (1977)